POSTCARD HISTORY SERIES

Ojai

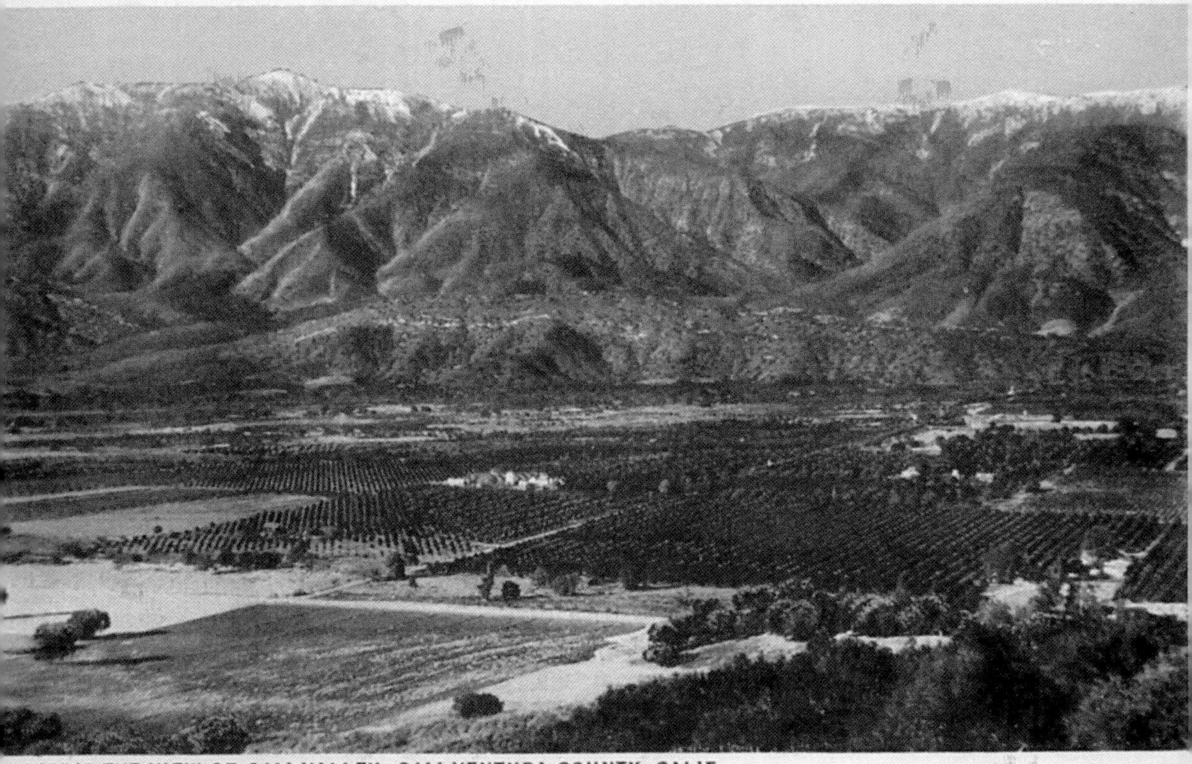

SNOW-COVERED NORDHOFF RIDGE. The Ojai Valley is nestled in the Transverse Range on California's central coast, about 14 miles inland from the sea and from the county seat of Ventura. In contrast to the great California valleys of Sacramento, San Joaquin, and San Fernando, the Ojai Valley is only about 3 miles wide and 10 miles long. (Brian and Connie Aikens collection.)

ON THE FRONT COVER: HANGING ROCK AT MATILIJA HOT SPRINGS. One of the earliest tourist attractions in the valley was the hot springs found in Matilija Canyon. Not only might visitors "take the cure" at one of the resorts, but they were also able to enjoy delightful mountain scenery, as evidenced in this photograph of the famous Hanging Rock. (Jack Davis collection.)

ON THE BACK COVER: THE PERGOLA AND POST OFFICE TOWER. This pergola and the attractive post office tower beyond were constructed in 1917 at the direction of Edward Drummond Libbey, the glass manufacturer. Civic Center Park was renamed Libbey Park in 1971 in honor of the valley's great benefactor. The park is today the home of the Ojai Music Festival and the Ojai Valley Tennis Tournament. (George Finn collection.)

POSTCARD HISTORY SERIES

Ojai

Richard Hoye, Tom Moore, Craig Walker,
and the Ojai Valley Museum

ARCADIA
PUBLISHING

ISBN 978-0-7385-8108-8

Published by Arcadia Publishing
Charleston, South Carolina

Printed in the United States of America

Library of Congress Control Number: 2010922215

For all general information contact Arcadia Publishing at:
Telephone 843-853-2070
Fax 843-853-0044
E-mail sales@arcadiapublishing.com
For customer service and orders:
Toll-Free 1-888-313-2665

Visit us on the Internet at www.arcadiapublishing.com

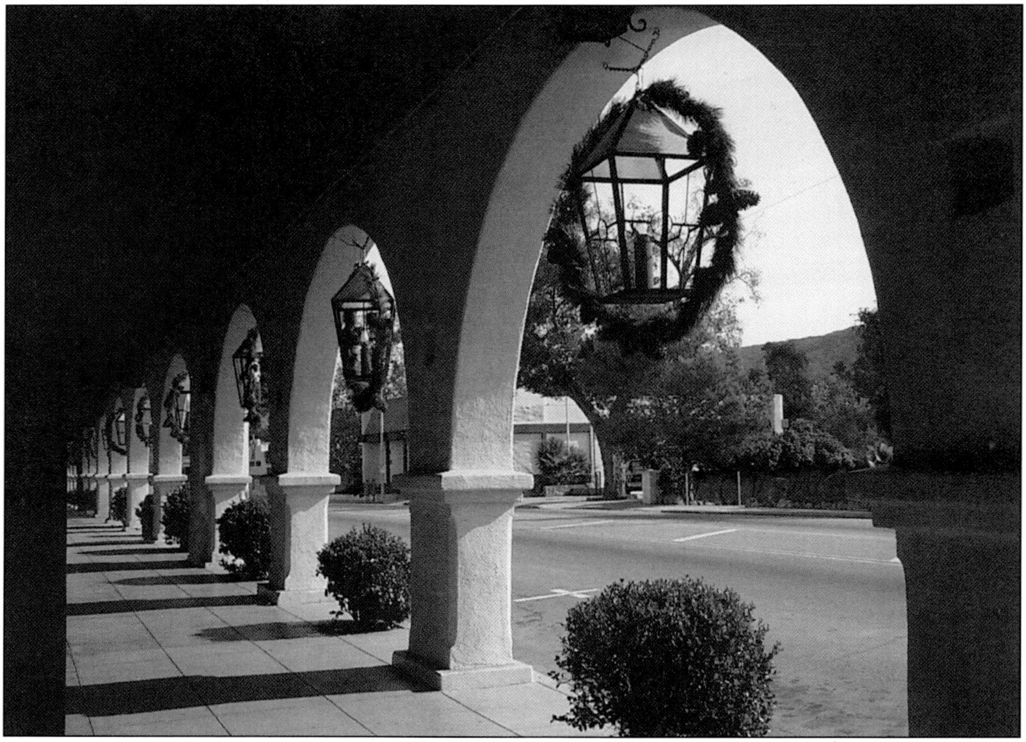

Christmas Lanterns at the Arcade. The business district of central Ojai is only about a block long, and until recently it had only one traffic light. Architecturally, however, it sparks interest because of the prevailing Mission Revival, Spanish Colonial Revival, and Mediterranean design of its buildings. Here Christmas lanterns hang in the archways of the arcade in the 1970s. The lanterns were designed by Rodney Walker and constructed by Bert Combs. (Ojai Valley Museum Collection.)

Contents

Acknowledgments

The authors wish to extend a special word of appreciation to David Mason, a leader among Ojai Valley local historians, for his assistance and advice.

The presentation of images in this book was greatly enhanced by the generosity of the following local residents who presented postcards for inclusion from their personal collections: Brian and Connie Aikens, Richard Barnett, Carol Cohen, Ruth Ann Conklin, Jack Davis, Mary Lee Eaton, George Finn, John Fritsche, Terry Hill, Patty Lunetta, David Mason, Kay Renuis, Joseph Ross, Kenneth Williams, the Krishnamurti Foundation of America, and the Ojai Valley School. There was much duplication in the cards that were brought to our attention. The credit shown following each caption refers only to the individual card that was actually used in the final selection.

Images drawn from the collection of the Ojai Valley Museum are marked with the initials OVM in the text. The authors and the museum also wish to extend thanks to all the people over the years who have thoughtfully and generously given postcard collections to the museum. Their foresight has enabled the museum to more effectively present the story of the Ojai Valley.

This book is dedicated
in memory of Ojai Valley Museum
volunteer extraordinaire and coauthor
Richard Hoye
who passed away on April 30, 2010, in Ojai, California.

His untiring service and dedication to the Ojai Valley Museum
inspired deep appreciation and respect.

He will be keenly missed.

Introduction

Fr. Junipero Serra founded Mission San Buenaventura on Easter Sunday, March 31, 1782. The Ojai Valley was then understood to lie within the reaches of the mission's lands and under administration of the Franciscan missionaries. Native people in the valley (now known as the Chumash) converted to Christianity and became mission neophytes. Spanish names were given to principal waterways in the valley, including Rio San Buenaventura (now the Ventura River) and San Antonio Creek (which runs through the valley).

The land was teeming with bears, coyotes, and mountain lions; consequently, mission cattle were not set to graze in the valley but were kept on the Oxnard plain. Flocks of sheep were maintained along the banks of the Ventura River, and it seems probable that they were brought to graze in the valley. The most important physical resource of the valley, however, was water.

An aqueduct was constructed to control the flow of water for irrigation and to direct water to the mission. It extended about 6 miles from the mouth of the San Antonio Creek along the eastern side of the river to the mission. The great flooding of 1861 largely destroyed the aqueduct, but remnants can still be seen today.

During the Mexican Period, after the mission was secularized, Gov. Juan Alvarado granted Rancho Ojai to Fernando Tico on April 6, 1837. The name of the ranch was derived from the name of a Chumash village in the Upper Ojai Valley. The Native American informant, Candelaria Valenzuela, said that *Ojai* means the moon. As was required by Mexican law for all persons receiving land grants, Tico introduced the grazing of cattle in the valley. Governor Alvarado also granted Rancho Santa Ana on the west side of the Ventura River to Crisogono Ayala and Cosme Vanegas on April 14, 1837. The histories of the two adjacent ranches are closely related.

The era of the great Mexican ranches in California came to an end less than 10 years later, when the United States took control of the land in 1846. Fernando Tico sold Rancho Ojai in 1853, and the ranch passed through a succession of owners. The California Petroleum Company, under direction of the great railroad baron Tom Scott, secured control of the property.

Scott dispatched Thomas Bard from the east coast to California to look after his interests, one of which turned out to be a search for oil deposits on Rancho Ojai. Bard oversaw the work of some 30 men as they drilled one well after another from the west end to the east end of the ranch. Only the last well was successful, yielding a steady flow of crude oil beginning in November 1866. It gushed in May 1867, the earliest known instance of an oil well gushing in California.

An economic downturn, the relatively poor quality of the crude oil, and the excessive cost of transporting it led Scott to conclude that the effort to locate and extract oil should be abandoned. This led to a decision to subdivide the ranch. The first parcel of subdivided Rancho Ojai land was sold in July 1870. There then followed numerous land purchases by incoming settlers, especially during the boom of the 1880s.

The community now known as Ojai was founded in 1874. The first residents immediately petitioned for a post office, and postal service began at Lafayette Herbert's merchandise store on

March 21. The name assigned to the post office was Nordhoff, in honor of Charles Nordhoff, one of the nation's foremost journalists and author of *California for Health, Pleasure, and Residence*, published a couple of years earlier. The community would continue to be known as Nordhoff until 1917.

The post office occupied a central place in the life of the community, providing a link to the outside world and a means for publicizing the great pleasure residents took in the beauty of their mountain valley. At the very time that the community was founded, camps were also established at hot springs in Matilija Canyon, in the mountains northwest of town. Before long, health-seekers and tourists would visit a cluster of these camps, generating many postcard messages.

The principal occupation of the early residents was agriculture. First came the growing of grains, followed by the planting of apricot, olive, and orange groves. Transportation of these products to distant markets was a matter of concern, and the challenge was met when a spur of the Southern Pacific Railroad was extended into the valley. Jubilation welcomed the opening of the rail line on March 12, 1898. The town's postal service improved greatly, as mail could then be carried by railroad rather than horse and stagecoach.

Notable changes began to occur in the valley with Sherman Thacher's opening of a boys preparatory school in 1889. The Thacher School was the first of what would eventually develop into a substantial concentration of private, secondary, residential schools.

Sherman's brother, William, led the founding of the Ojai Valley Tennis Club in 1895 and subsequently the Ojai Valley Tennis Tournament, one of the oldest in the nation.

The tournaments began to draw great numbers of visitors to the valley, but hotel accommodations were limited, so an Ojai Improvement Company, largely comprised of members associated with the tennis tournament, was founded in 1900 to remedy the matter. The company commissioned construction of the luxurious Foothills Hotel, which opened on January 19, 1904. The valley then began to attract people of position and wealth, and the presence of a luxury hotel gave local promoters further impetus to publicize the appealing features of the valley.

The pace of change accelerated with the arrival of Edward Drummond Libbey, who had been drawn to the valley by the Foothills Hotel. The founder of the Libbey Glass Company of Toledo, Ohio, established a winter home in the valley in 1909. He soon began to take an interest in various local development projects. The one that still catches the eye of visitors today was the complete transformation of the central business district's architecture.

Edward Libbey announced his vision for valley development at the founding meeting of the Ojai Valley Men's League (predecessor to the chamber of commerce) on April 24, 1914. Local businessmen responded readily to Libbey's proposals, and a series of major changes followed.

A Mission Revival arcaded walkway was constructed along the front of the central business block. A pergola was constructed across the street from the arcade. The original Nordhoff hotel was razed to open up the area in back of the pergola to form a park. Libbey also commissioned construction of El Roblar Hotel (later known as the Oaks Hotel and still later as The Oaks at Ojai). A Spanish-style tower was constructed, emphasizing the central place of the post office in the life of the community.

Edward Libbey commissioned construction of a country club, now known as the Ojai Valley Inn and Spa, which today is the largest employer in the valley. He also purchased land for a residential development to the northwest of the center of town, called the Arbolada. He envisioned the construction of a major hotel, comparable to the largest in California, but he died before he was able to complete this final project.

Agitation to change the name of Nordhoff to Ojai began early in the valley's history. Editors of the valley newspaper, *The Ojai*, complained that its mail was being erroneously directed to Norwalk, California. The management of the Foothills Hotel complained that persons wishing to make reservations at the hotel were addressing their communications to Ojai instead of to Nordhoff, leading to embarrassing reservation omissions and errors. Finally, the change was made at the time of World War I, and the name *Ojai* was assigned to the post office in March 1917. The City of Ojai was incorporated on August 5, 1921. Ojai today is the smallest incorporated city in Ventura County, half as small as the next largest city, Fillmore. It has reason to think of itself as a village, as it often does.

The community was devastated in June 1917, when a blazing firestorm rushed down upon the village from the northwest. A major portion of the town's residential section was destroyed, along with churches and school buildings. A second fire occurred in the same year, when in November 1917, the western half of the arcade business block was destroyed by fire. Determined residents immediately applied themselves to the task of reviving the town.

A new phase of the valley's history began with the arrival of Krishnamurti. The Indian philosopher established his home in the valley in 1922. He was closely associated with the Theosophical Society at the time, and the society purchased land in 1924 to move its Krotona Institute from Hollywood to Ojai. These were the first developments that led in time to a concentration of metaphysical and self-realization organizations in the valley.

The hard times of the 1930s were followed by the war years of the 1940s, and the Ojai Valley Country Club was occupied by the military during the war. Troops of the 134th Infantry arrived from Nebraska for combat training in March 1942. Firing ranges were set up in the valley, and the local mountains and the riverbed served as locations for training. Anti-aircraft guns were placed on hilltops. After the Nebraska troops left, the 17th Infantry arrived in May 1943 from Fort Dix, New Jersey. They were replaced by Seabees in May 1945.

After the war, the Libbey Foundation sold the country club, and it was reopened in 1947 as the Ojai Valley Inn. This inaugurated yet another phase of the valley's history, since the new owners promoted the inn as a gathering place for Hollywood stars. Norma Shearer, Claudette Colbert, Robert Young, Francis Langford, Bing Crosby, Esther Williams, Jimmy Dorsey, Fred MacMurray, and many others visited the inn. Over the years, a good number of persons connected with the entertainment and motion picture industries have made the valley their home.

Yet again, a new direction for the life of the valley was taken in 1947 with the first performances of the Ojai Music Festival. Over the years, the world-renowned venue has hosted such famous personalities as Igor Stravinksy, Henry Temianka, Ingolf Dahl, Marilyn Horne, Aaron Copland, André Previn, Pierre Boulez, Ravi Shankar, and Michael Tilson Thomas.

The post office is still at the center of the community, easily visible as the highest structure in town. Familiar places in the Ojai Valley are still featured on its postcards—the unique architecture of its business district, its schools, and its cultural buildings, as well as its mountain scenery. The postcards reflect the enthusiasm of a visitor-friendly town.

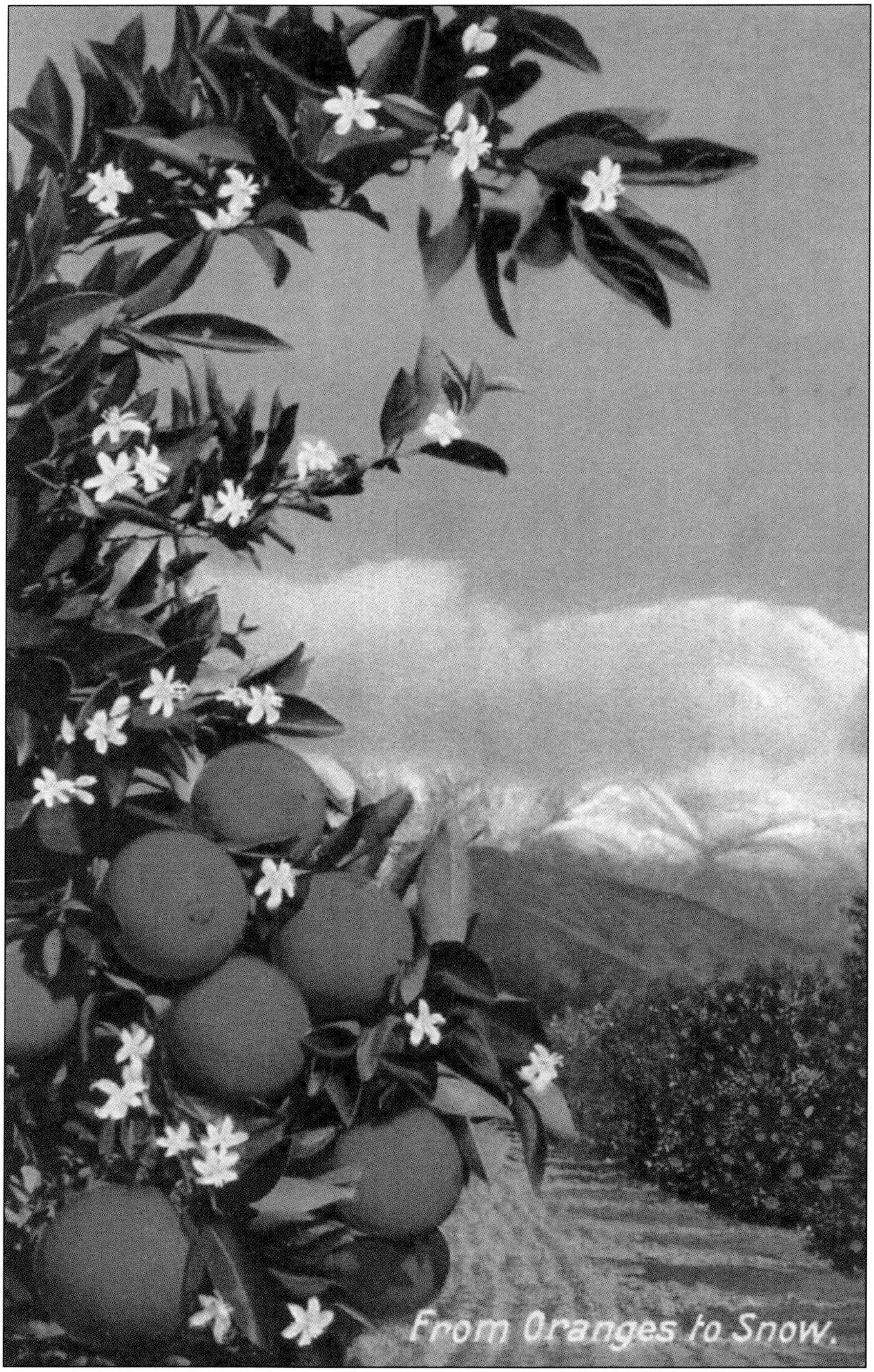

ORANGE GROVE AND MOUNTAIN VISTA. While this postcard depicts a scene typical of many locations in Southern California, it is a winter view familiar to all Ojai Valley residents and one of the valley's enchanting attractions. The mountains that form the valley are close at hand, and the looming presence of the snow-capped Topa Topa Bluffs becomes strikingly beautiful in the winter air. (David Mason collection.)

One

Valley of the Moon

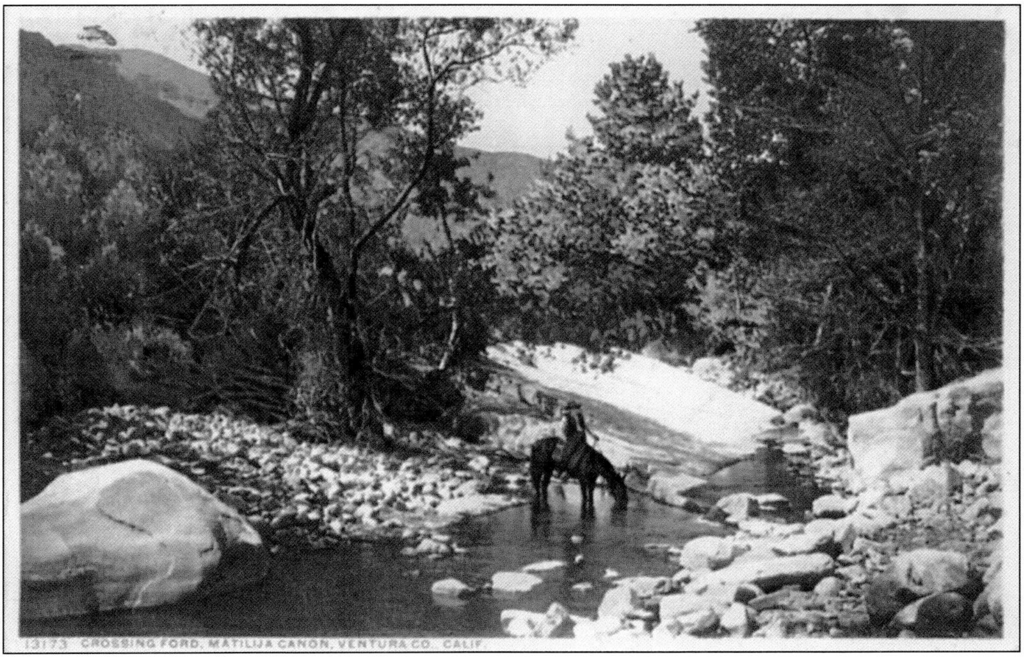

Idyllic Scene in Matilija Canyon. The Ojai backcountry with its canyons and mountain streams is a natural treasure much enjoyed by valley residents and visitors. Some streams flow year-round. Horseback riding is a favorite backcountry pastime today; in earlier years, horses were the only way other than walking to reach the canyon depths and mountain ridges. (David Mason collection.)

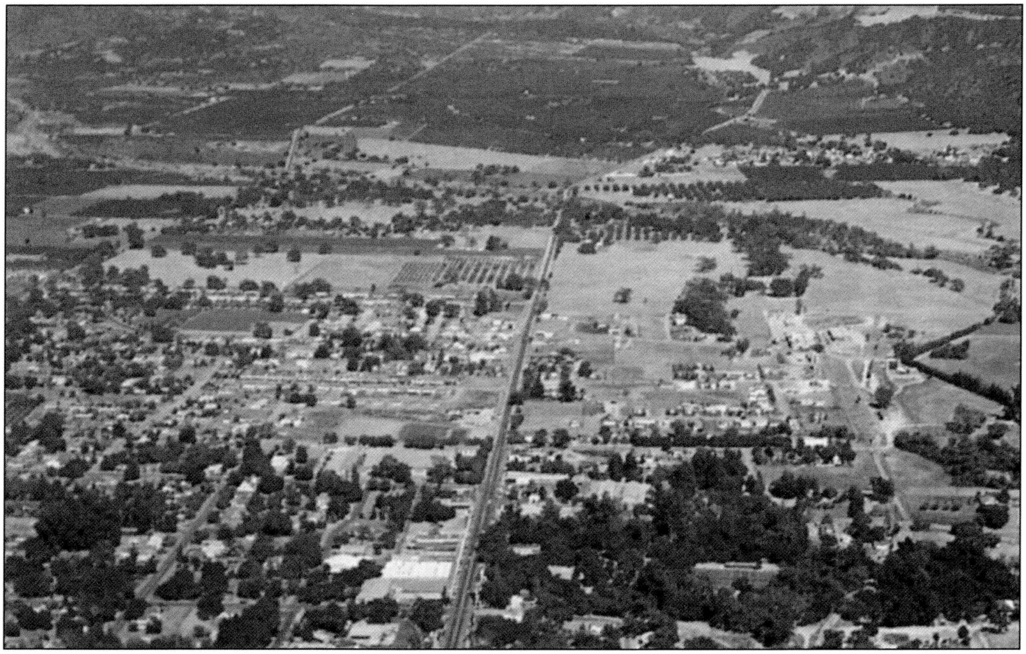

Aerial View of the East Valley. The central part of Ojai is visible in the lower part of this photograph. At center right is the large Soule Ranch, later turned into a county golf course. Beyond the open fields are the orange groves in the upper portion of the photograph. Soule Golf Course opened in 1962, so this photograph was probably taken during the 1950s. (OVM Collection.)

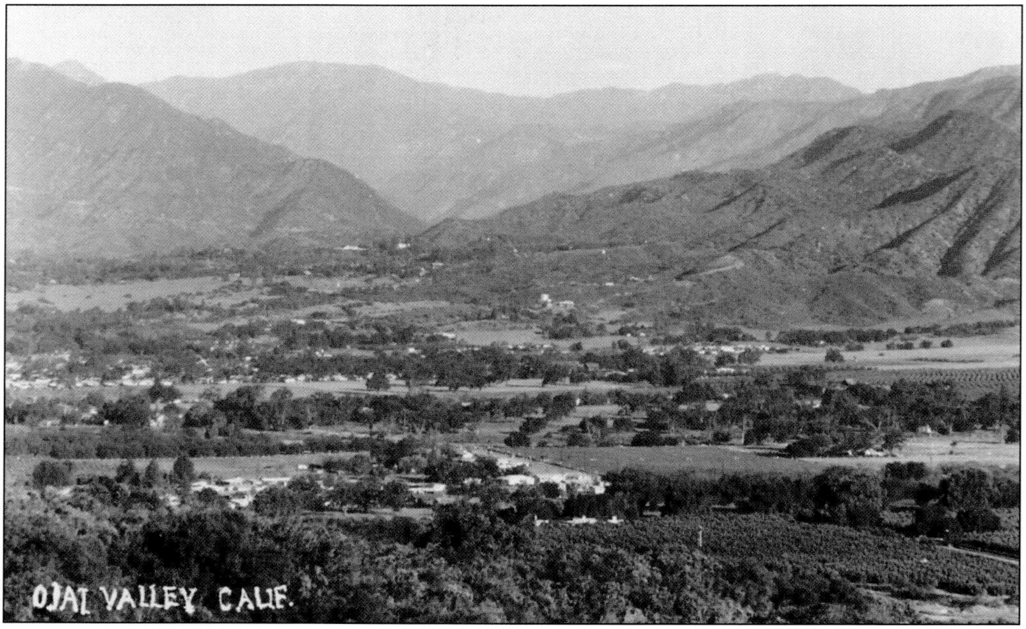

View toward Matilija Canyon. This photograph was taken from Krotona Hill, west of central Ojai. The residences and businesses on the valley floor at this location are within the unincorporated community of Meiners Oaks. Waters flowing from Matilija Canyon are the principal source for the Ventura River, which flows to the sea toward the left of this view. (OVM Collection.)

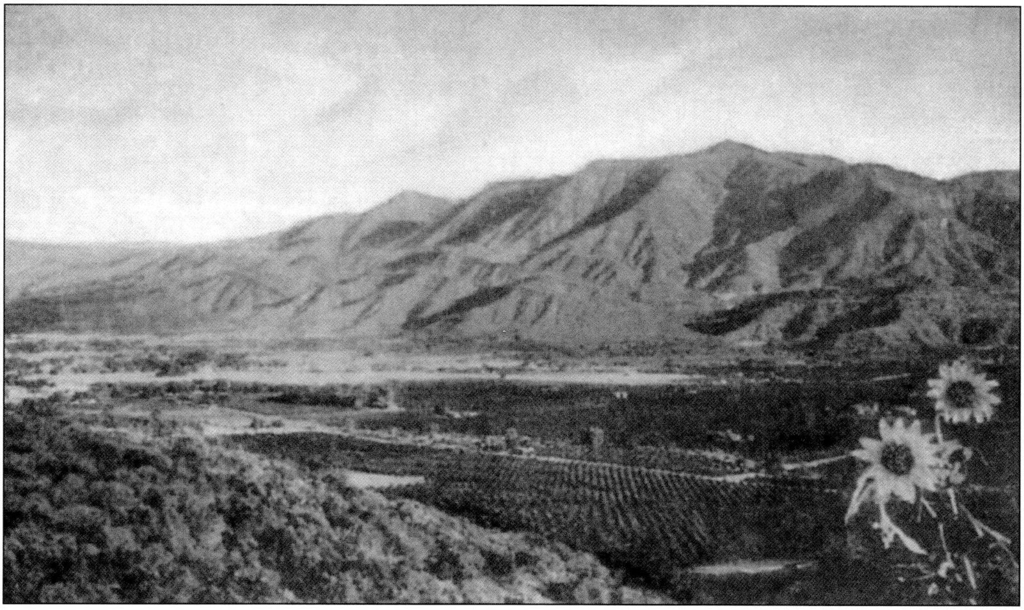

Distant View across the Valley. Most of the Ojai Valley can be seen in this photograph. Nordhoff Peak in the distance boasts an elevation of 4,485 feet. The city of Ojai, on the valley floor, rests at 746 feet. The elevations are not high, but the steep-sided mountains give unmistakable definition to the mountain valley. (George Finn collection.)

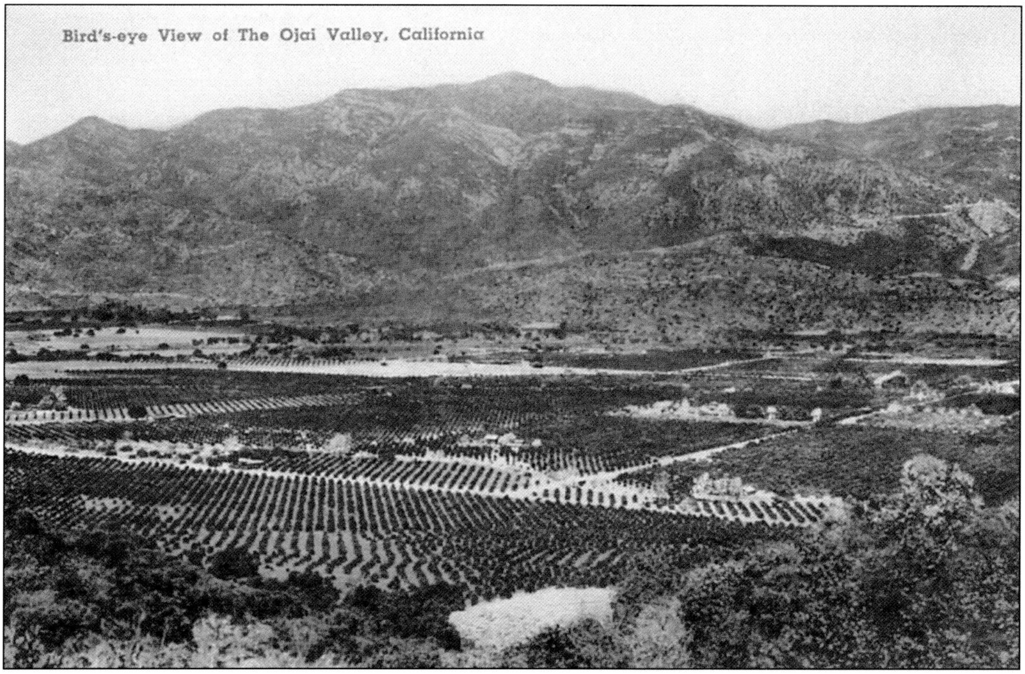

Orange Groves on the Valley Floor. Here are the extensive orange groves on the valley floor. The *Ventura Signal* reported on November 3, 1877, that F. S. S. Buckman "has in an amazingly short space of time covered what was a mass of chaparral with oranges, lemons, limes, etc." Thus the growing of citrus produce, principally oranges, has been underway in the valley for over 130 years. (Patty Lunetta collection.)

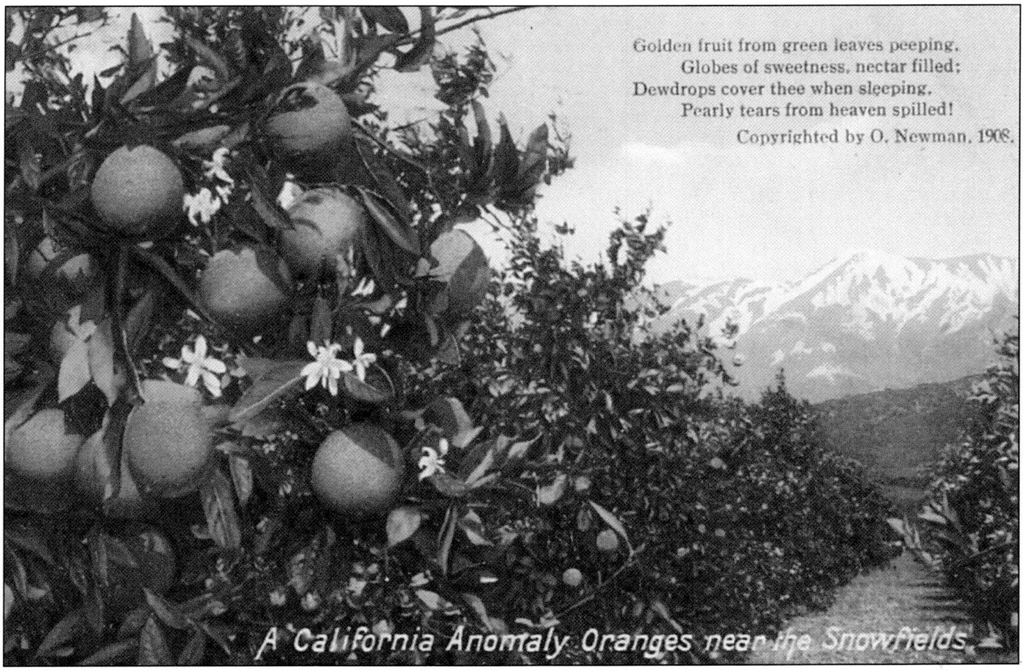

A California Anomaly. The Ojai Citrus Growers Association was formed in 1894 and became the Ojai Orange Association in 1908. The association constructed a packinghouse near the center of town that went into operation in 1909. It continued in service for 60 years, until it was sold to the Southern Pacific Railroad in 1969 and razed in 1970. (David Mason collection.)

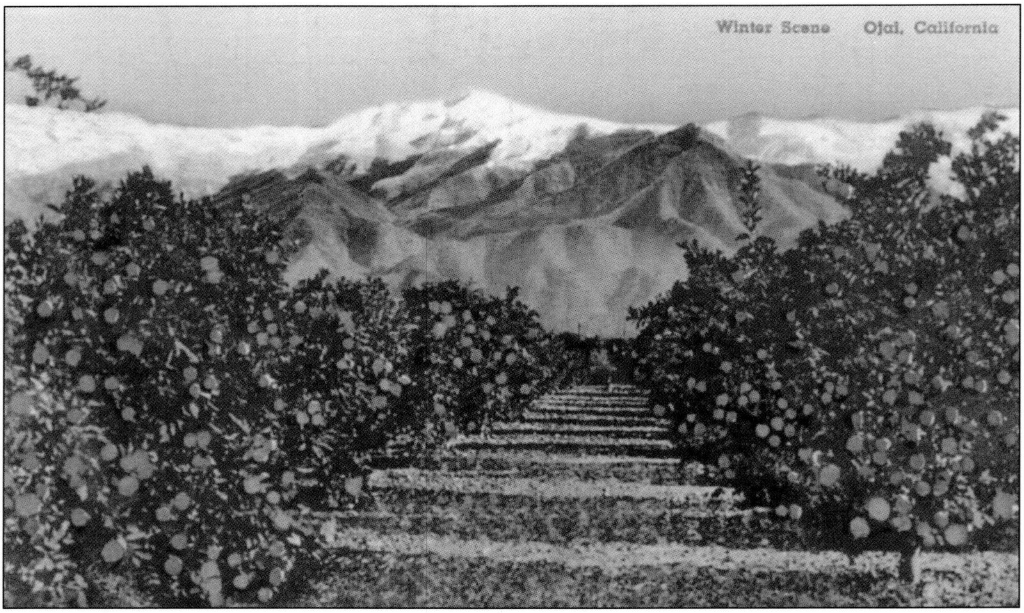

Winter in the Ojai Valley. This photograph shows Chief Peak covered with snow at the rear center of the picture. The scene is beautiful, but winter brought the threat of frost damage to the groves. *The Ojai* newspaper reported on January 14, 1949, the "Heaviest Snow in History: White Blanket Engulfs Ojai Valley in First Snowfall Since January 1932." Boys at Nordhoff High School were called out to help crews smudge the orange trees. (Patty Lunetta collection.)

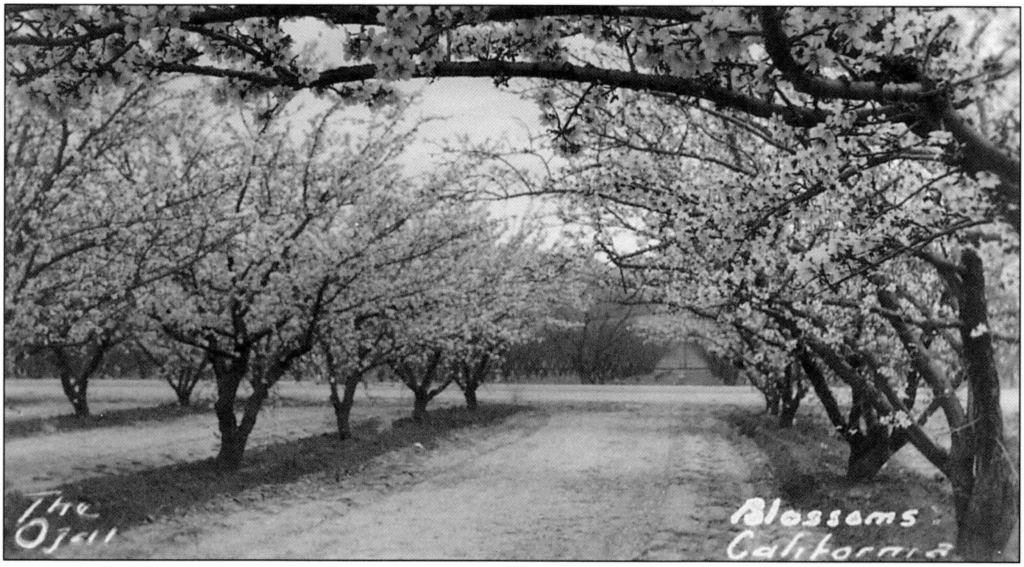

Springtime in a Valley Grove. Until World War II, apricots were the largest agricultural crop produced in the valley. Thomas Bard, the valley's earliest real estate agent, planted the first apricot trees in the valley in 1867 as a demonstration for prospective ranchers of the type of products that could be produced locally. The apricot groves were largely pulled out and replaced with orange trees in the 1950s. (OVM Collection.)

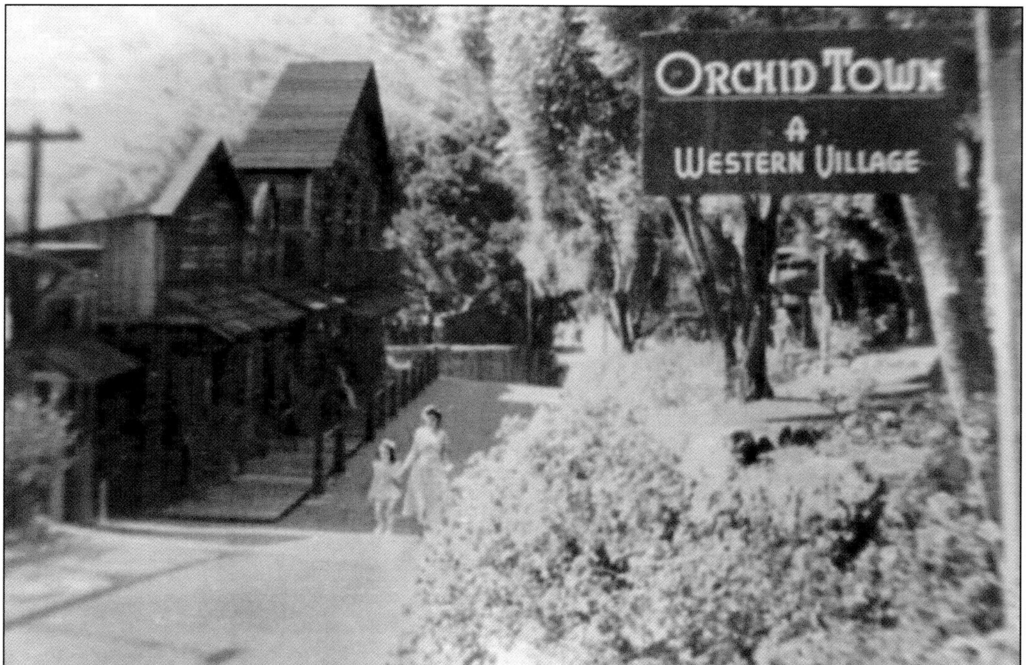

El Rancho Rinconada. Louis M. Boyle established El Rancho Rinconada in 1939 a short distance northwest of the center of the city of Ojai. He developed it into a major orchid-raising ranch and promoted his business with a simulated Western village called Orchid Town. In this picture, Clara Robinson and her daughter Sandy stroll the street at the village. Boyle became one of the nation's major orchid producers. (David Mason collection.)

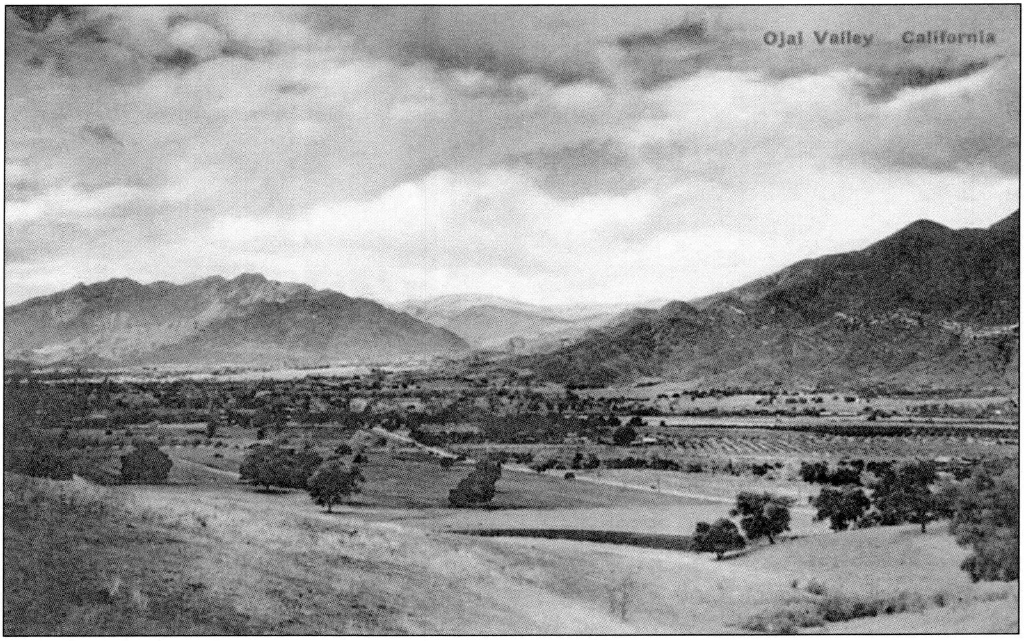

View Westward from the Valley Floor. Two Mexican land grants were made at this location in 1837. First Rancho Ojai was granted to Fernando Tico on the east side of Ventura River, and then Rancho Santa Ana was granted to Crisogono Ayala and Cosme Vanegas on the west side. The valley floor in the picture is within Rancho Ojai. (David Mason collection.)

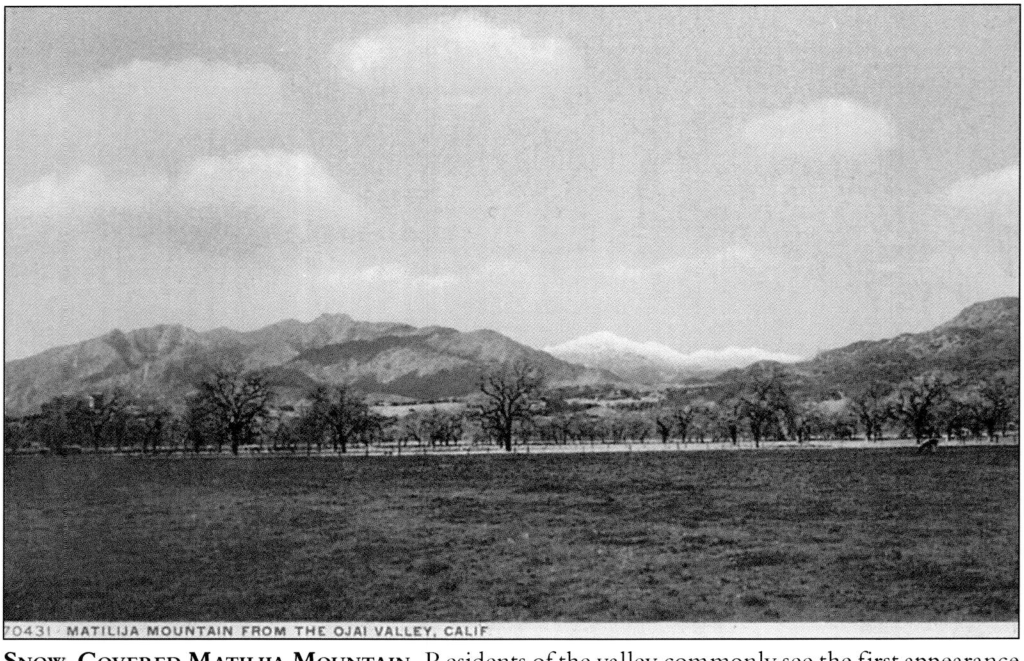

Snow-Covered Matilija Mountain. Residents of the valley commonly see the first appearance of snow during winter months on top of the ridges seen through the mouth of Matilija Canyon. A series of ridges rises to the heights of 8,832-foot Pine Mountain (Mount Pinos), some 26 miles north of the valley as the bird flies. The snowpack is a principal water source for the Ventura River. (OVM Collection.)

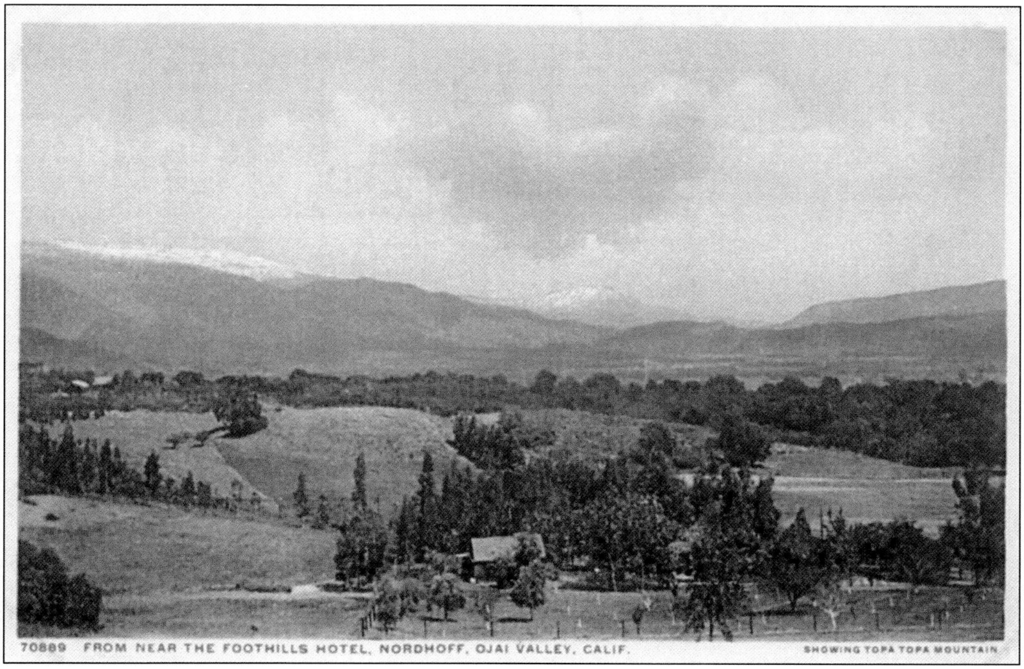

VIEW TOWARD SANTA PAULA PEAK. This photograph differs from the rest of similar photographs in this book, since it is a view eastward toward Santa Paula Peak (at the rear center). The photograph also gives a suggestion of the appearance of the Topa Topa Bluffs, seen at left center. This idyllic country view was one sought by visitors to the Foothills Hotel. (David Mason collection.)

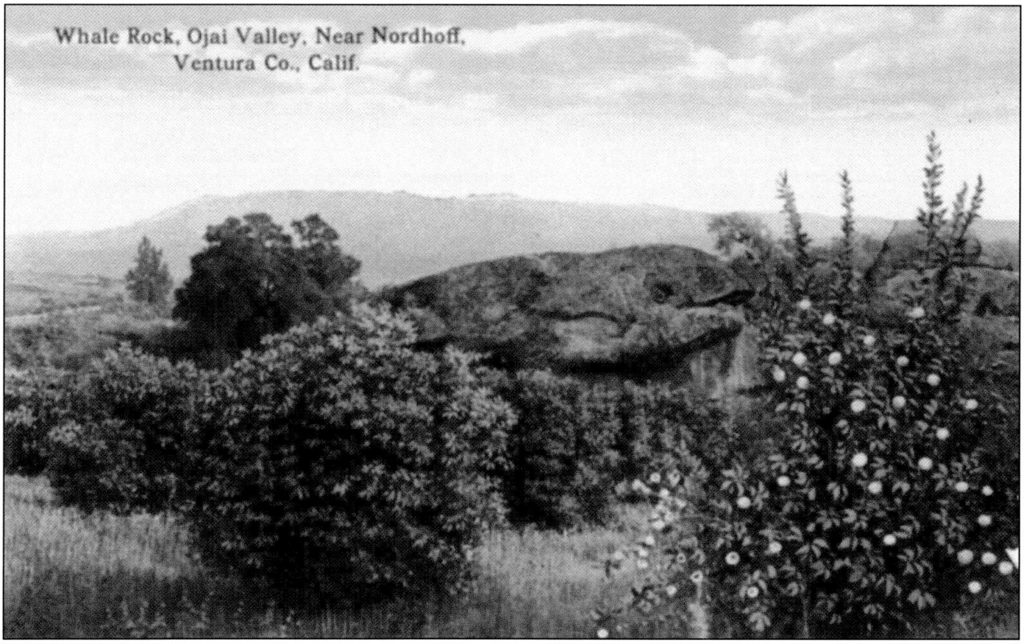

MYSTERIOUS WHALE ROCK. Whale Rock is a natural formation, located on a ranch in the east valley. Its appearance suggests the form of a whale. Its mystery lies in the probable use of the site as a place for spiritual contemplation and rites for unknown years in the past. (David Mason collection.)

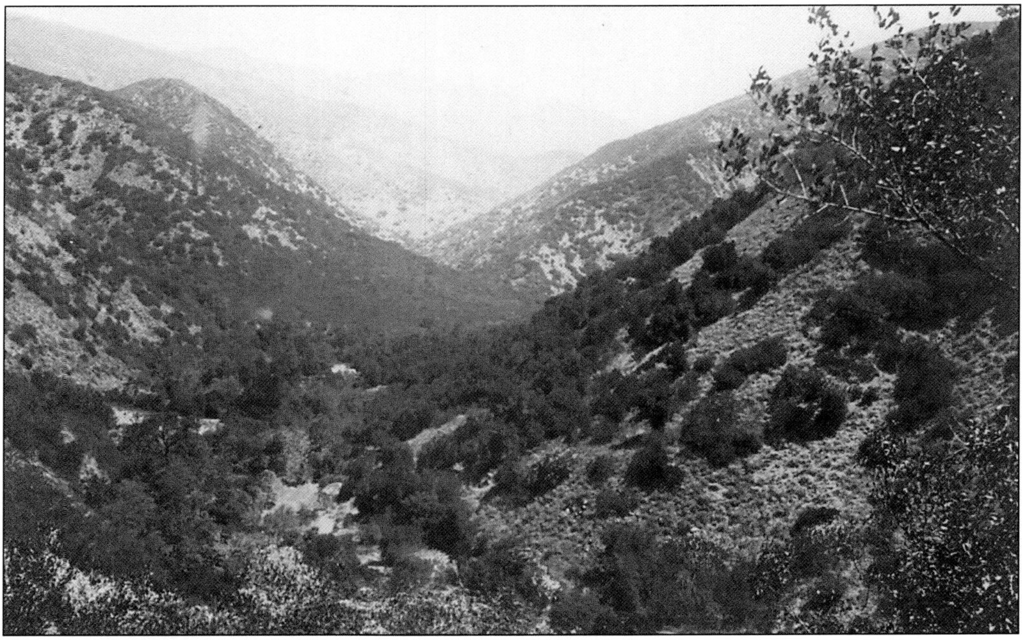

Typical Valley Canyon. This scene is typical of the canyons that penetrate into the mountains around the Ojai Valley. Heavy chaparral creates sometimes impenetrable barriers—impenetrable, that is, until burned away by wildfires. The canyons remain to this day the home of coyotes, brown bears, mountain lions, turkey vultures and, to the delight of many, reintroduced California condors. (Terry Hill collection.)

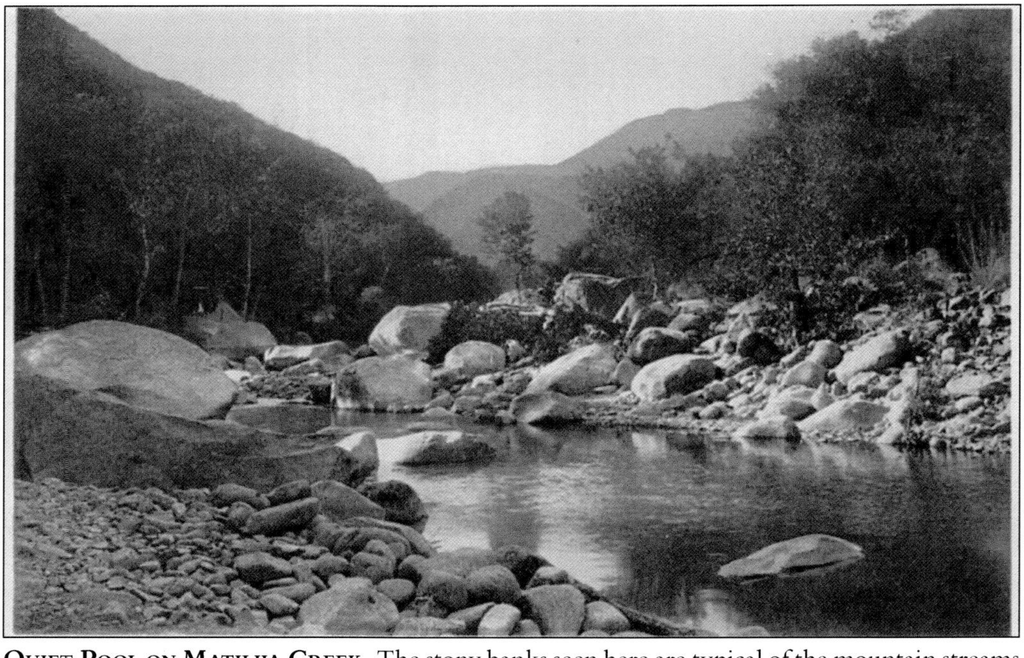

Quiet Pool on Matilija Creek. The stony banks seen here are typical of the mountain streams around the valley. In some instances, the size of the boulders rolled loose during winter flooding is astonishing. Much of the east end of the valley floor is filled with stones carried down over millennia from the mountain streams. (Brian and Connie Aikens collection.)

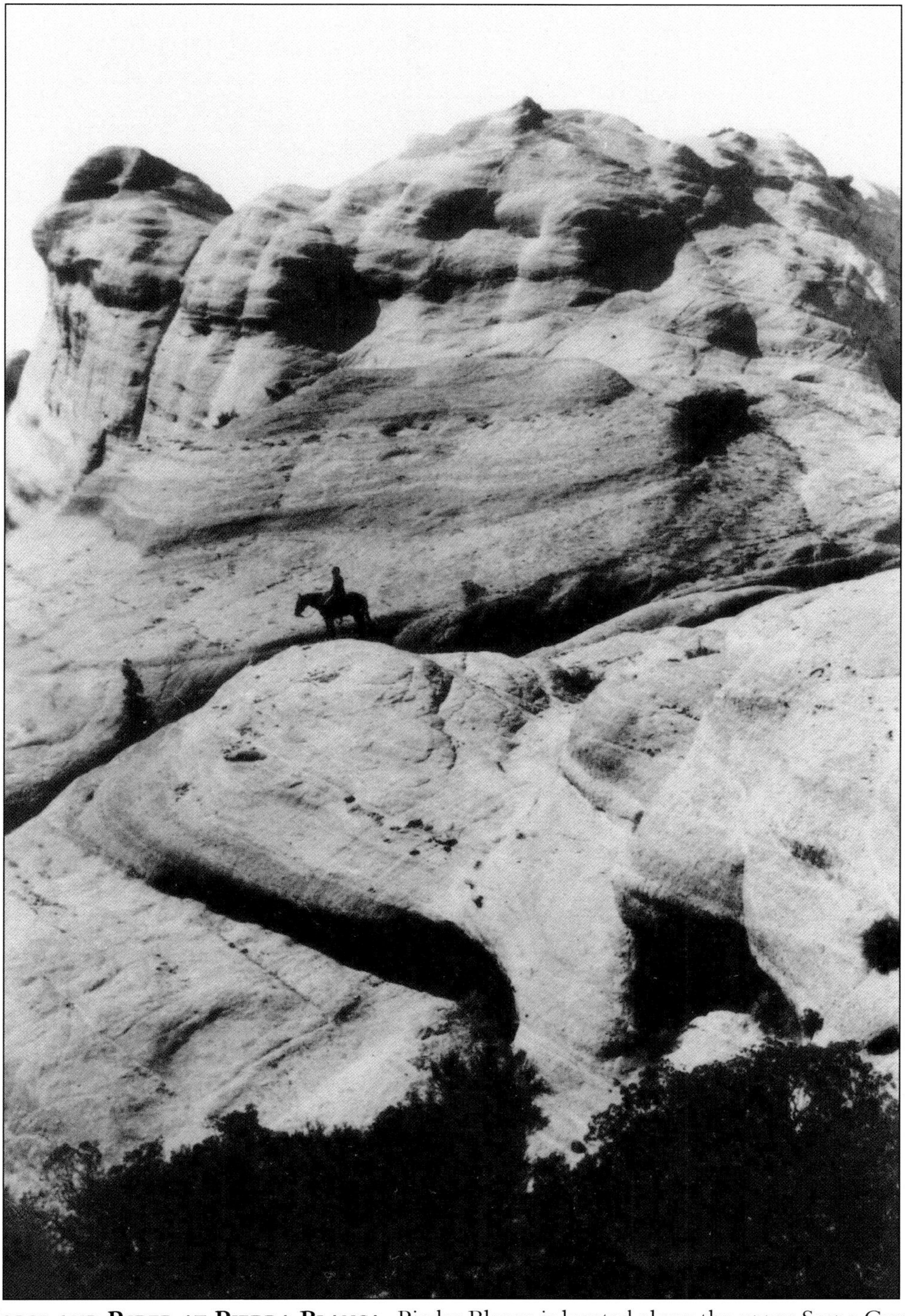

Horse and Rider at Piedra Blanca. Piedra Blanca is located along the upper Sespe Creek in Los Padres National Forest, well to the north of the Ojai Valley. The wondrously convoluted appearance of the exposed sedimentary rocks easily shows why it was a favored destination for valley residents. The site remains a favorite hiking and camping spot for those enjoying the wilderness of the national forest. (OVM Collection.)

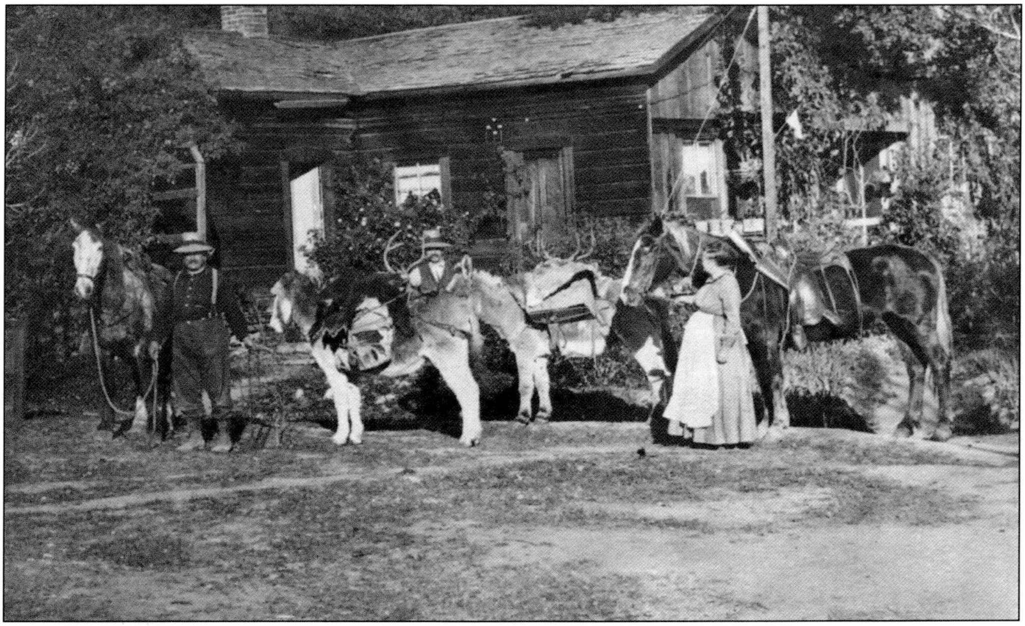

Hunter's Pack at Robinson's Ranch. Robinson's Ranch was located in the Upper Ojai Valley, and here is a hunter with his pack train. The man at the head of the train is Jim "Stubby" Fordyce. He addressed the postcard to Mrs. W. H. Robinson on January 6, 1911, with the note, "Had picture taken the other day, and this is what the camera saw." (OVM Collection.)

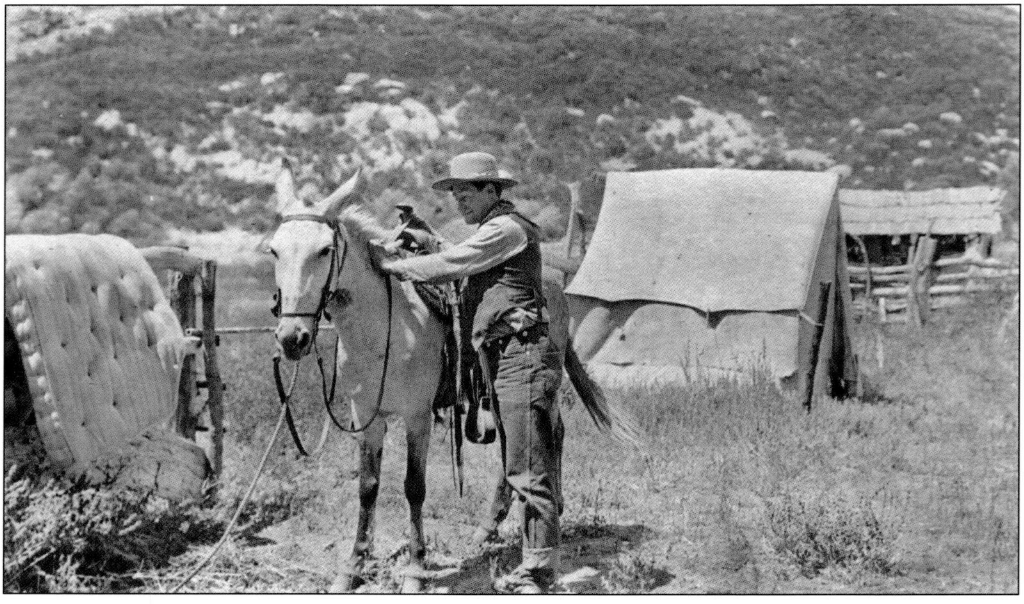

Howard Bald at Backcountry Camp. Howard Bald led camping trips into the mountains north of the valley for visitors at the Foothills Hotel. Both he and his father, George, were U.S. Forest Service rangers. On occasions, Howard would go on hunting trips with the famous Ventura mystery author Erle Stanley Gardner. Bald was a resident of the valley for about 80 years. (OVM Collection.)

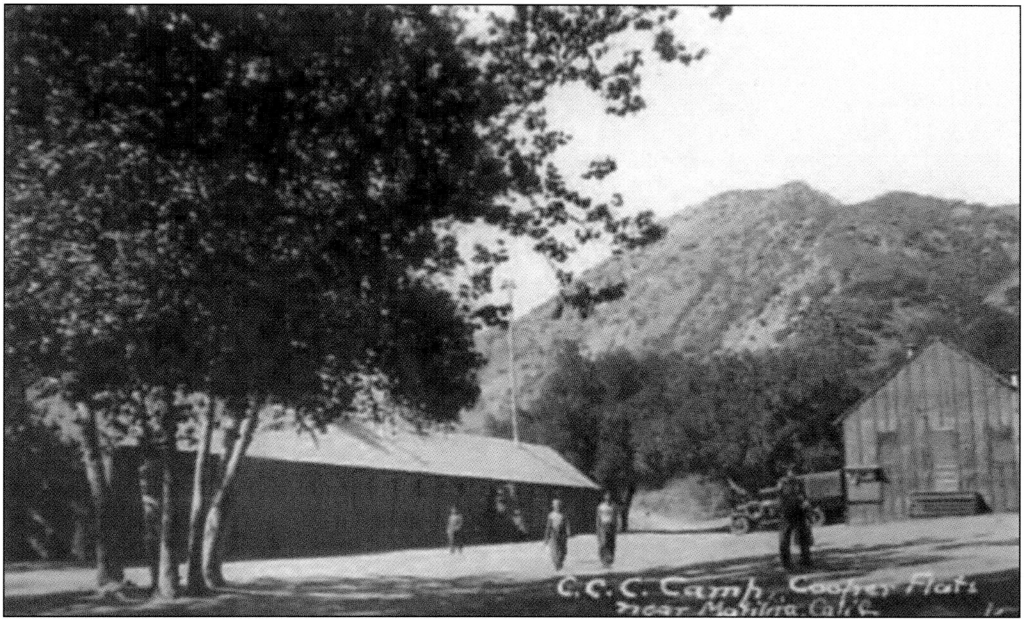

Civil Conservation Corps Camp. The Civil Conservation Corps was created by the federal government in March 1933. There were soon seven camps located in the mountains around the valley. The young volunteers built roads, constructed flood control ditches and dams, and improved campgrounds. They remained in the area until disbanded in March 1940, in advance of World War II. (John Fritsche collection.)

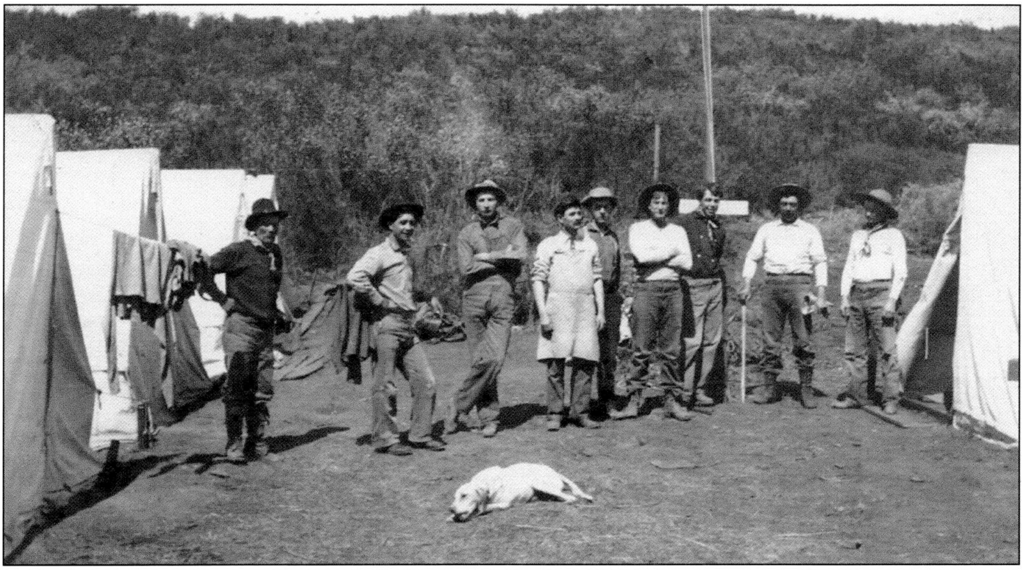

Forest Service Crew. The man second from the right is the renowned forester Jacinto Reyes, after whom the Reyes Scenic Highway is named. His crew stands around him, including George Bald to his left and Robert Clark to his right. Young Robert Clark would later become sheriff of Ventura County. The other men in the picture were members of the Ojai Valley community. (OVM Collection.)

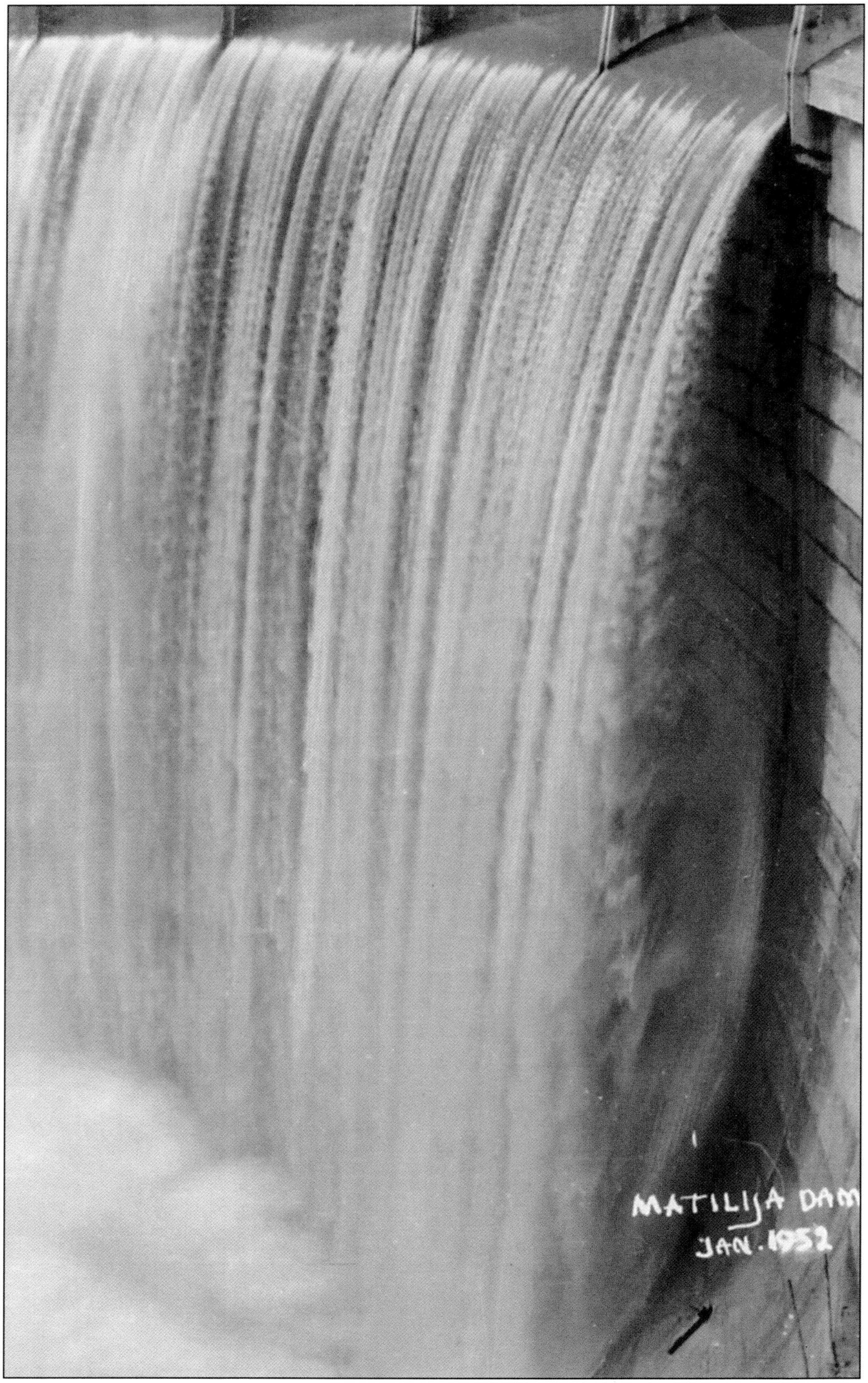

FIRST SPILLOVER AT MATILIJA DAM. Construction of Matilija Dam, near the mouth of Matilija Canyon, began in June 1946 and was completed in June 1948 as both a flood control and a water conservation project. The first spillover, however, did not occur until January 1952. Control of the floodwaters of Matilija Creek seemed assured, for the time being. (George Finn collection.)

Two

WATERS OF LIFE

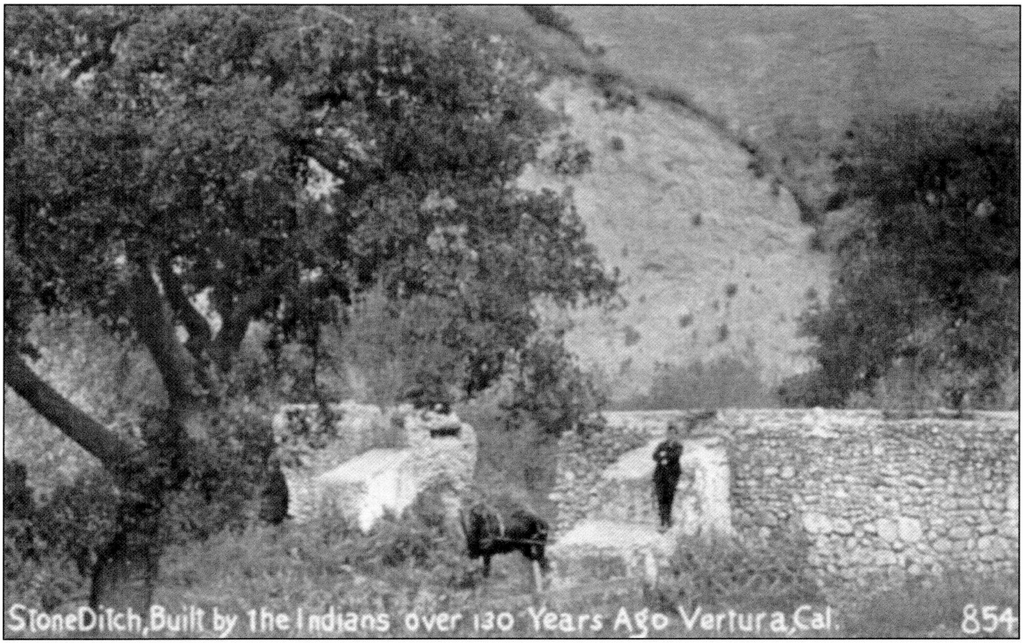

SAN BUENAVENTURA MISSION AQUEDUCT. Remnants of the mission aqueduct can still be seen today in the Ventura River Valley. Constructed over a couple of decades and completed about 1815, the aqueduct drew water from the mouth of the San Antonio Creek, which runs through the Ojai Valley. Securing access to the waters of the river and its watershed has been a persistent theme in the valley's history. (John Fritsche collection.)

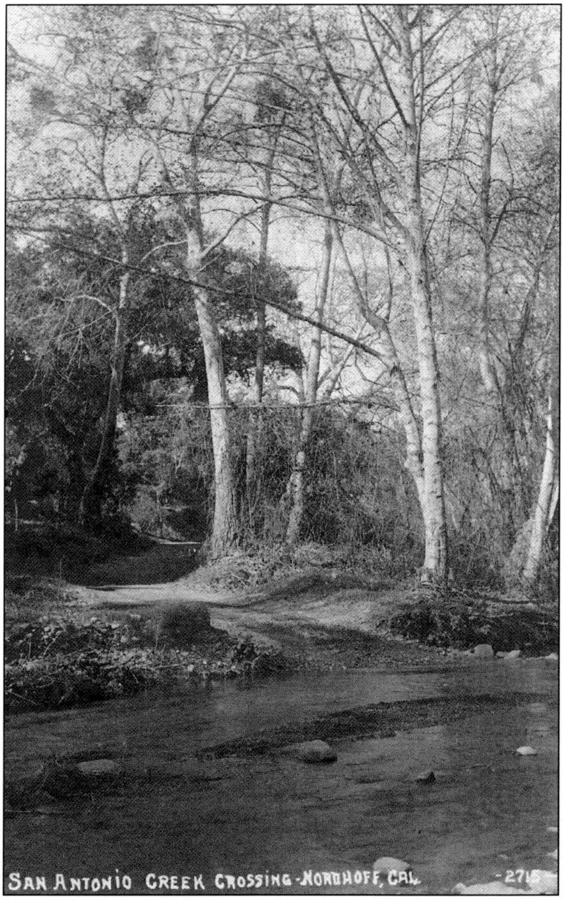

SAN ANTONIO CREEK. San Antonio Creek is the principal waterway coursing through the Ojai Valley. Not only have its waters been used for city, agricultural, and domestic purposes, but it has also been a source of pleasure and enjoyment for travelers. When the first Anglo-American settlers arrived, the only road into the valley from Ventura ran for 6 miles along San Antonio Creek. (Terry Hill collection.)

MATILIJA CREEK IN SPRINGTIME FLOW. Matilija Creek is the primary source of the Ventura River. The creek flows through canyons immediately to the northwest of the Ojai Valley and, once emerging from the canyon, flows effortlessly on as the Ventura River. The appeal of the fresh mountain waters and the wilderness environment of the canyons have provided a source of enjoyment for visitors and residents alike for many years. (Carol Cohen collection.)

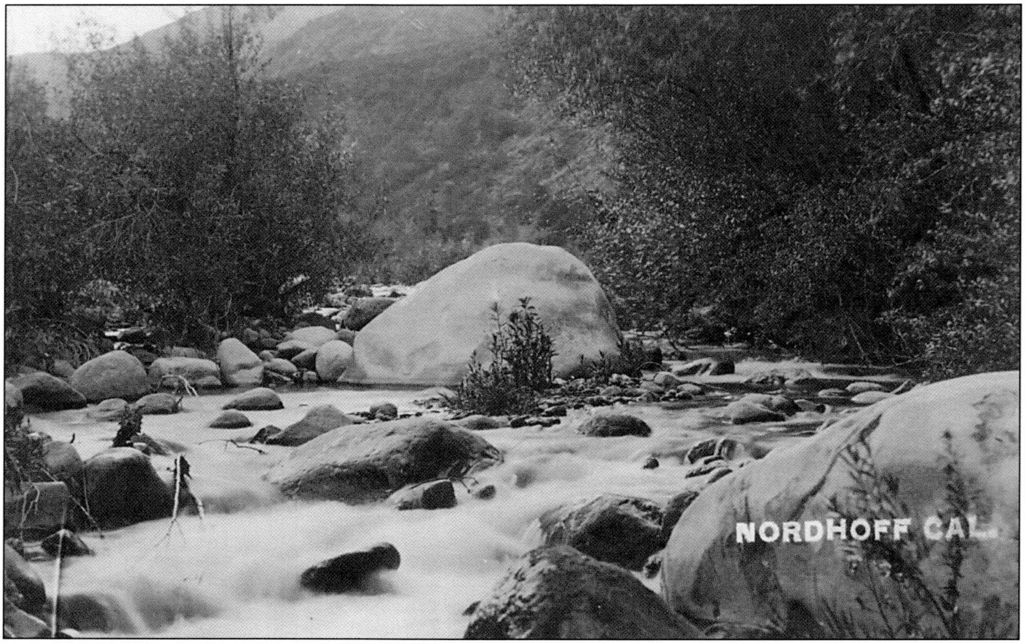

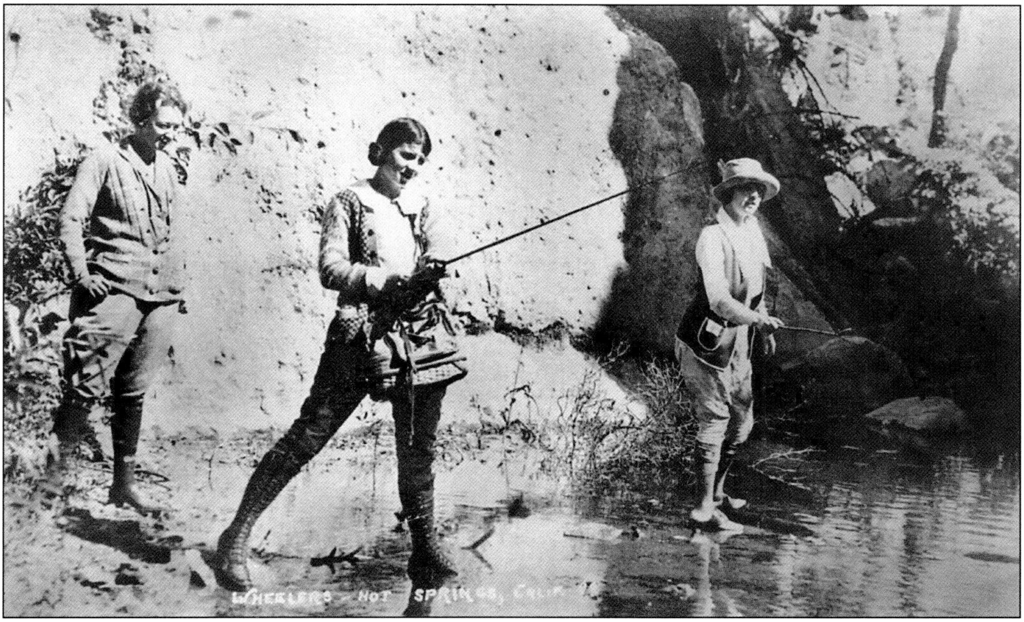

Women Fishing in Matilija Creek. Steelhead trout were once abundant in the Ventura River and the creeks of the Ojai Valley. More than 750 trout were caught in the river and valley streams in a single day in May 1891. Over the years, the abundance of trout has been depleted, and efforts to restore the trout population have begun. (Terry Hill collection.)

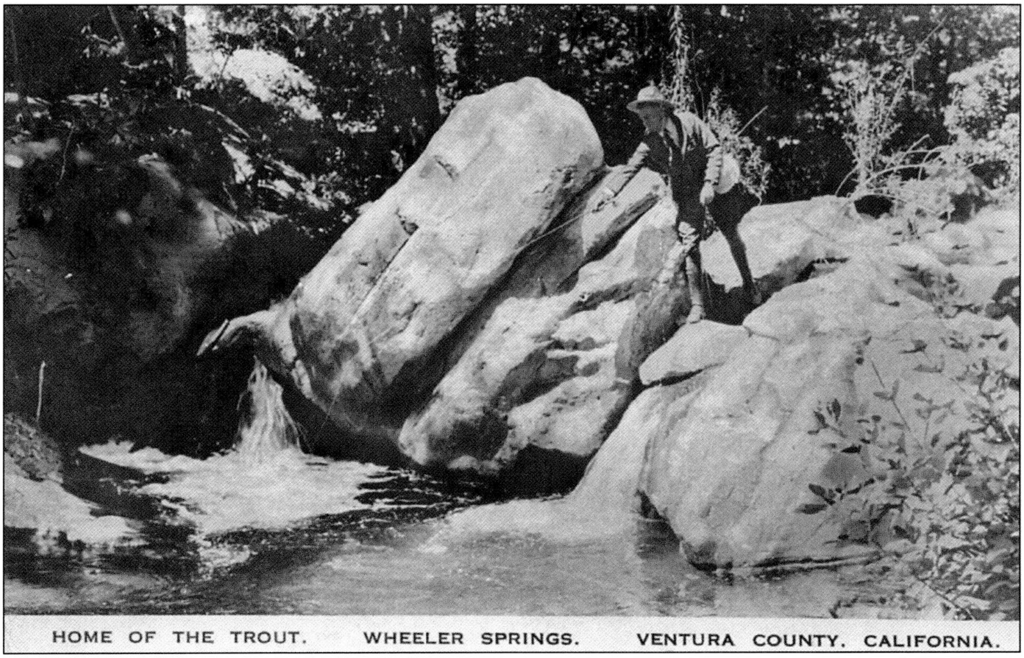

Home of the Trout. Ambitious anglers expected to be out on the streams in the early morning when trout season opened on May Day in the early 1900s, and local businesses were busy in late April to outfit expectant fishermen. Large numbers of people turned out along the river on the opening day. The beginning of the fishing season was a festive and much-anticipated event. (Brian and Connie Aikens collection.)

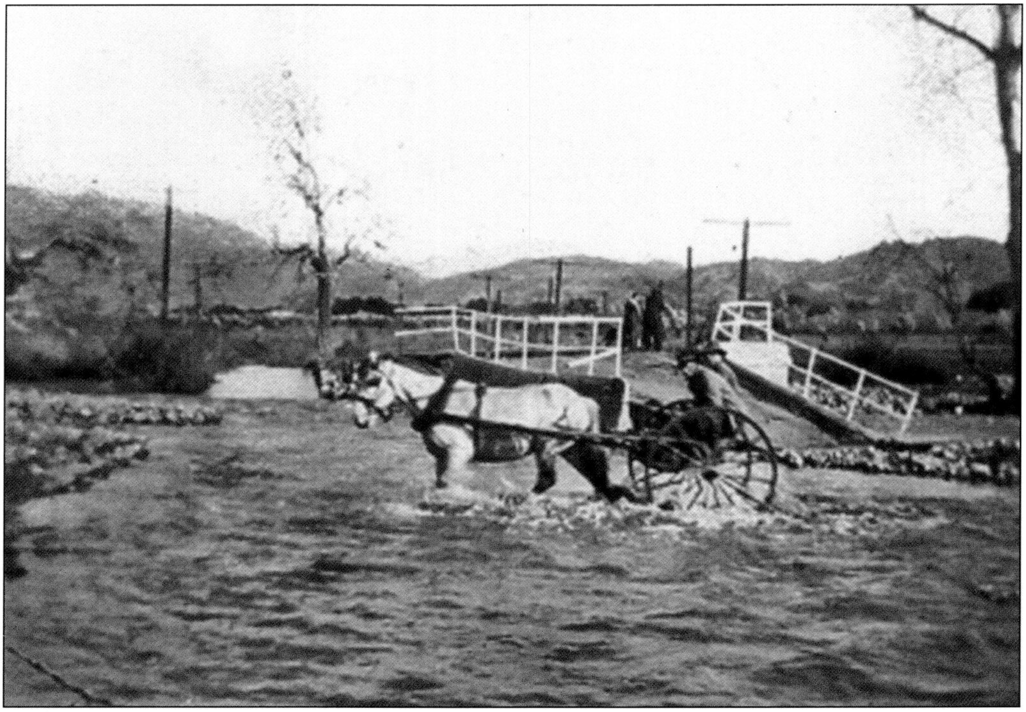

Stream Crossing in 1914. A major rainstorm began in the valley in late January 1914, with rainfall continuing for 54 hours. The resulting flood was called the worst in 30 years, and damage to bridges, railroads, and structures was widespread. A man directs his horse and cart across a flooded stream in the east valley. (OVM Collection.)

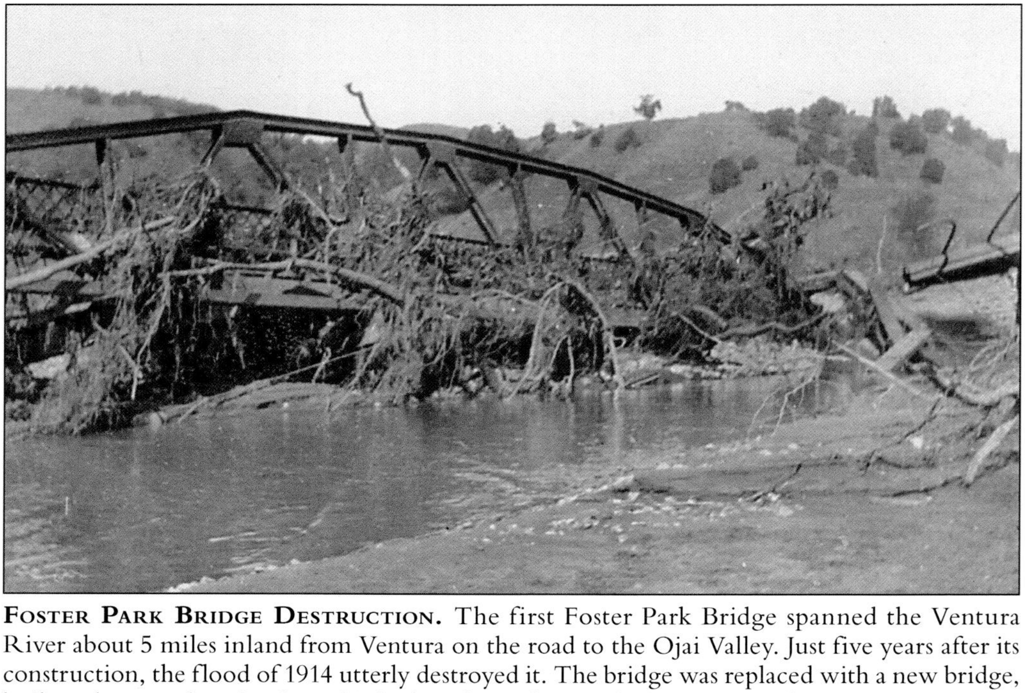

Foster Park Bridge Destruction. The first Foster Park Bridge spanned the Ventura River about 5 miles inland from Ventura on the road to the Ojai Valley. Just five years after its construction, the flood of 1914 utterly destroyed it. The bridge was replaced with a new bridge, built at the same location but a bit higher above the riverbed. (OVM Collection.)

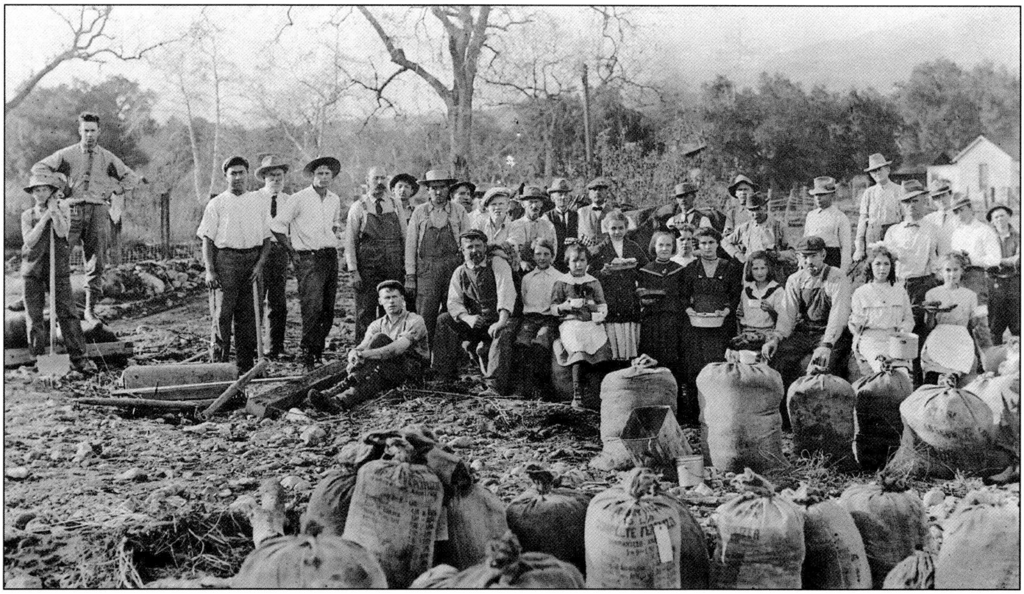

Work Crews on Lunch Break, 1914. Men turned out from all the surrounding ranches to control the 1914 floodwaters and repair the damage they left behind. Here a crew is taking a break for lunch. The river was benign most of the time, but the flood of 1914 galvanized the people of the valley, who worked together to protect their community. (OVM Collection.)

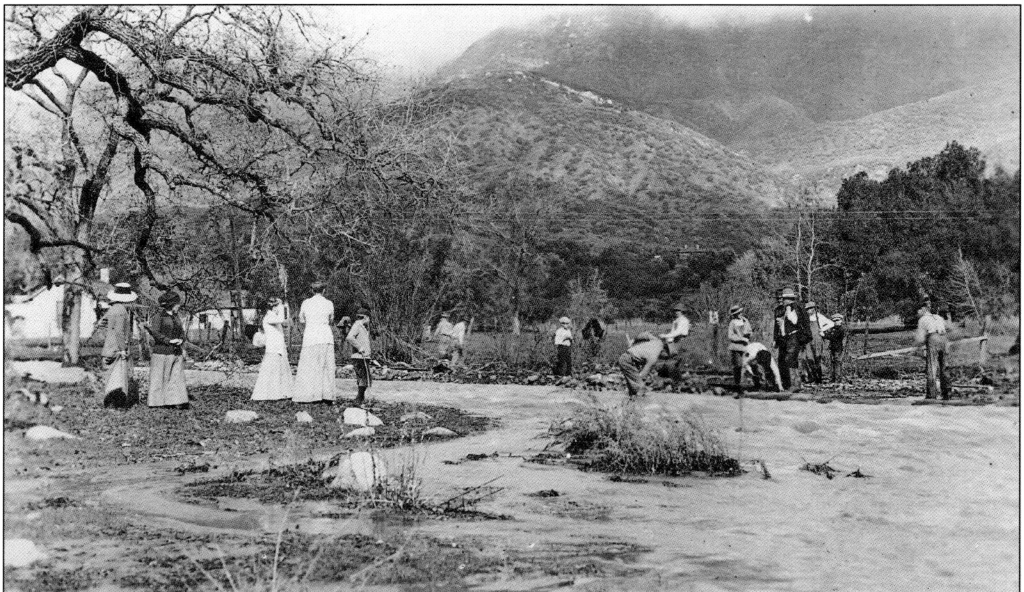

Observers at Floodwaters, 1914. *The Ojai* newspaper reported the 1914 flood with headlines reading, "Damage Results as Streams Burst Their Bonds. All Telephone and Telegraph Lines Down: Train Service Crippled Indefinitely." Repairing damage and restoring the train line to service occupied a good part of 1914. For an area that is accustomed to extended periods of dry weather, the flood was a major and memorable event. (OVM Collection.)

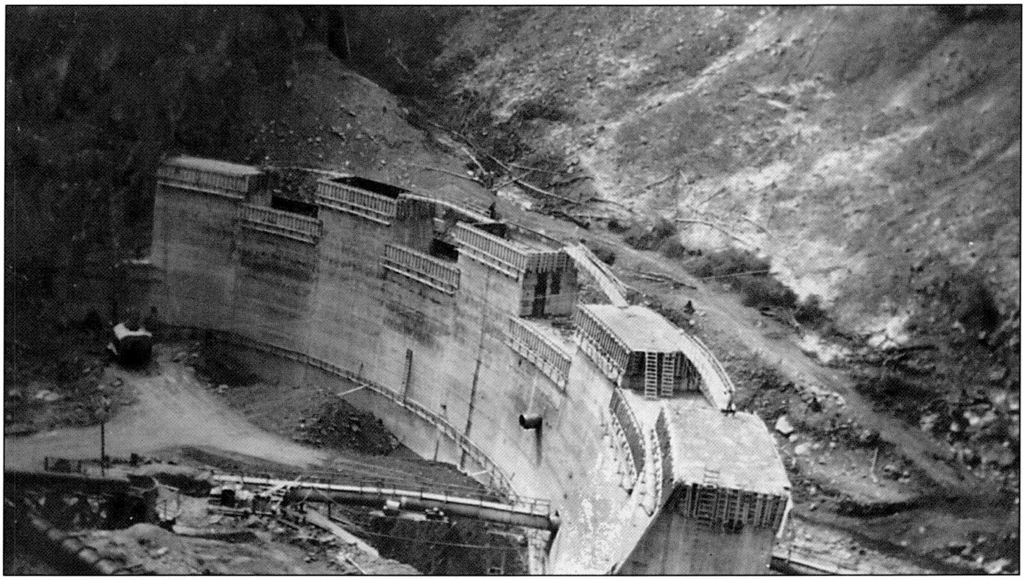

CONSTRUCTION OF MATILIJA DAM, 1947. Residents of the Ventura River watershed approved a bond issue in 1945 for construction of the Matilija Dam to improve flood control, to impound water for agricultural and domestic uses, and to provide a local recreational site. Construction was underway in the summer of 1946, and it drew considerable interest as the largest construction project in the valley to date—at a location that residents knew well and often visited. (Kenneth and Kathryn Williams collection.)

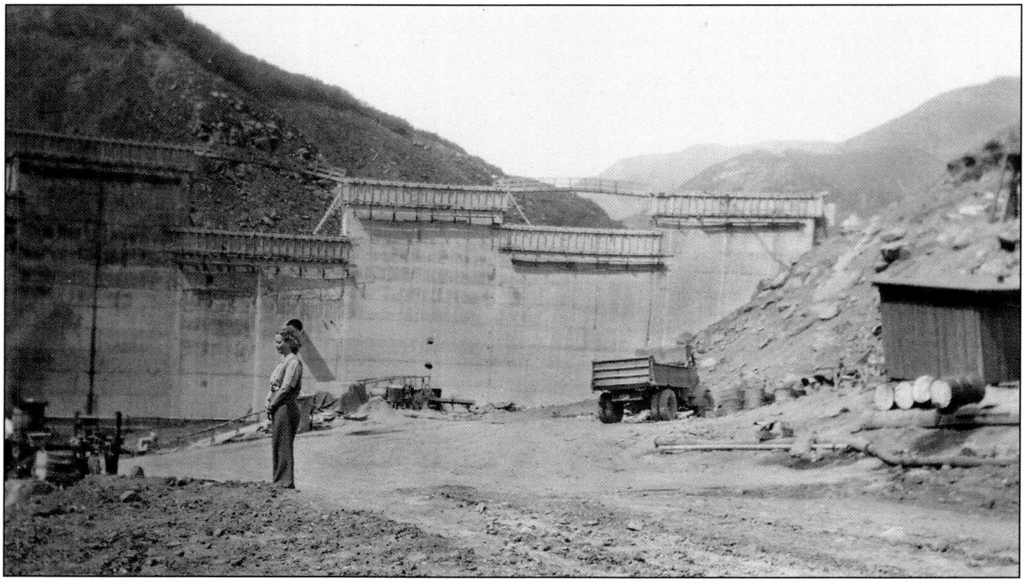

MATILIJA DAM RISING TO FULL HEIGHT. Construction of the dam was complicated by criticisms of its safety, charges of poor workmanship, legal challenges, and labor problems. The local newspaper lamented what it headlined as the "fabulous $2,500,000 headache." Obstacles were overcome or sidestepped, and construction of the dam was completed in the summer of 1948. It had an average height of 190 feet and a crest length of 620 feet. (Kenneth and Kathryn Williams collection.)

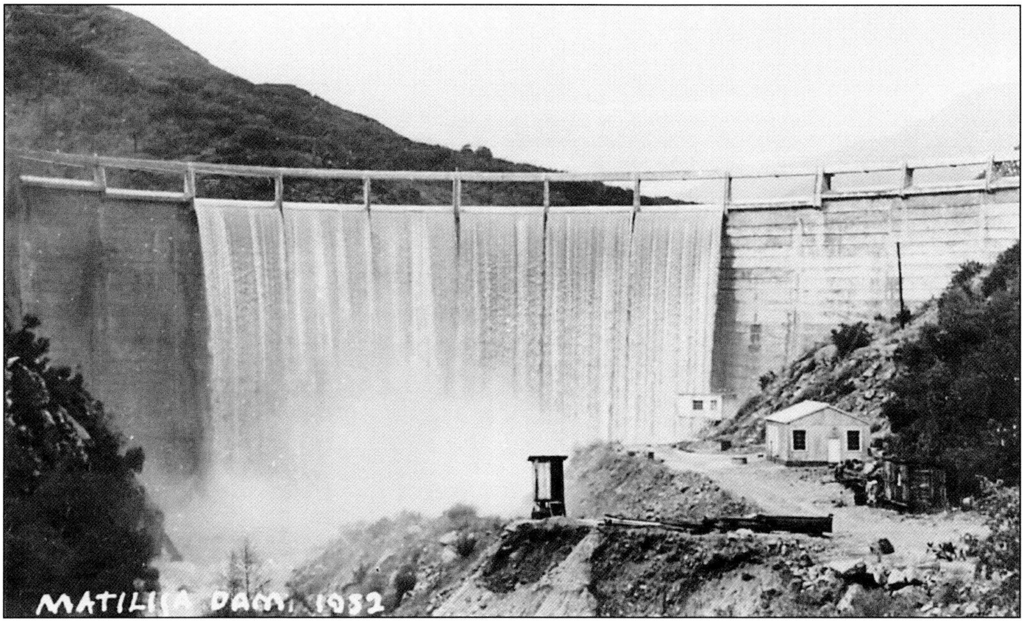

First Spillover at Matilija Dam. A major rainstorm in January 1952 quickly ended dreary months of waiting for water to fill the reservoir. *The Ojai* reported that the lake filled rapidly, and "flood waters" first went over the spillway at 8:40 p.m., Tuesday night, January 15, 1952. Eager sightseers drove their automobiles to the canyon to see the torrent of water falling over the top of the dam. (George Finn collection.)

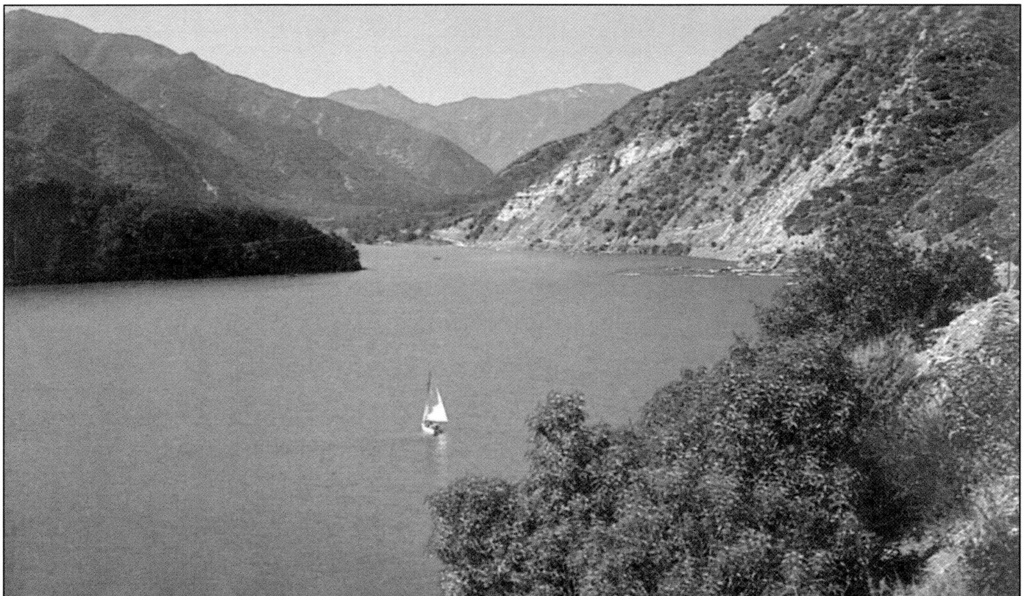

Sailboat on Lake Matilija. Matilija Dam formed a lake in an attractive canyon setting. Gradually, however, the lake filled up with sediment, and by the end of the century, the lake's water storage was reduced to about only five percent of its original storage capacity. The lake disappeared, and the federal government began measures in 2006 to remove the dam and restore the stream to its original state. (George Finn collection.)

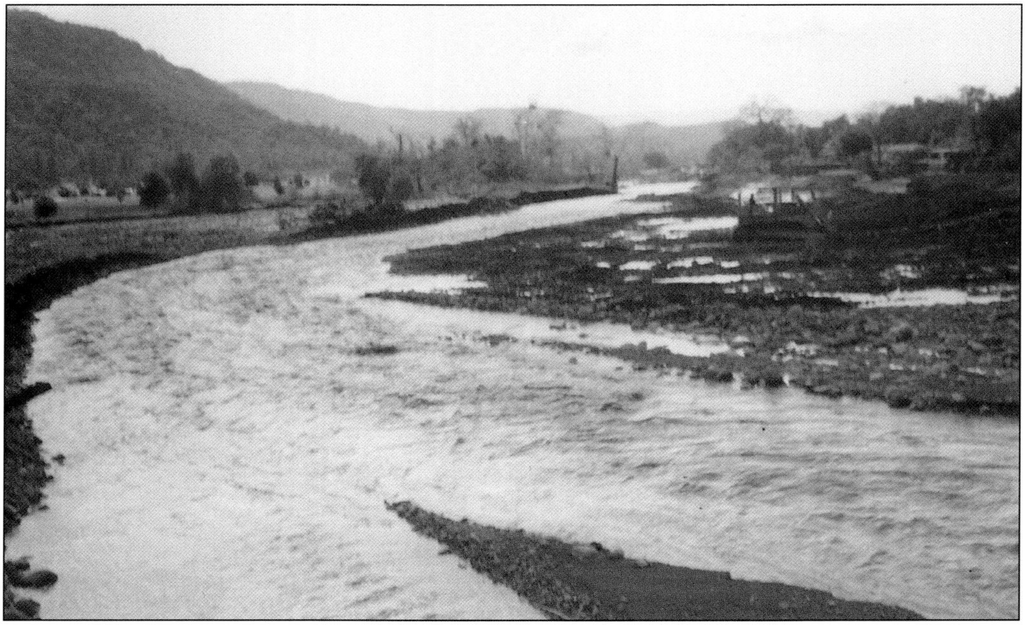

Floodwaters in 1969. A major rainstorm brought floodwaters to the valley once again in January 1969. Matilija Dam and Matilija Lake, now largely filled with sediment, had little effect in reducing the runoff. Once again, roads and fields were washed away, great boulders were washed down mountainsides, and creek beds, bridges, and houses were washed away. (Kenneth and Kathryn Williams collection.)

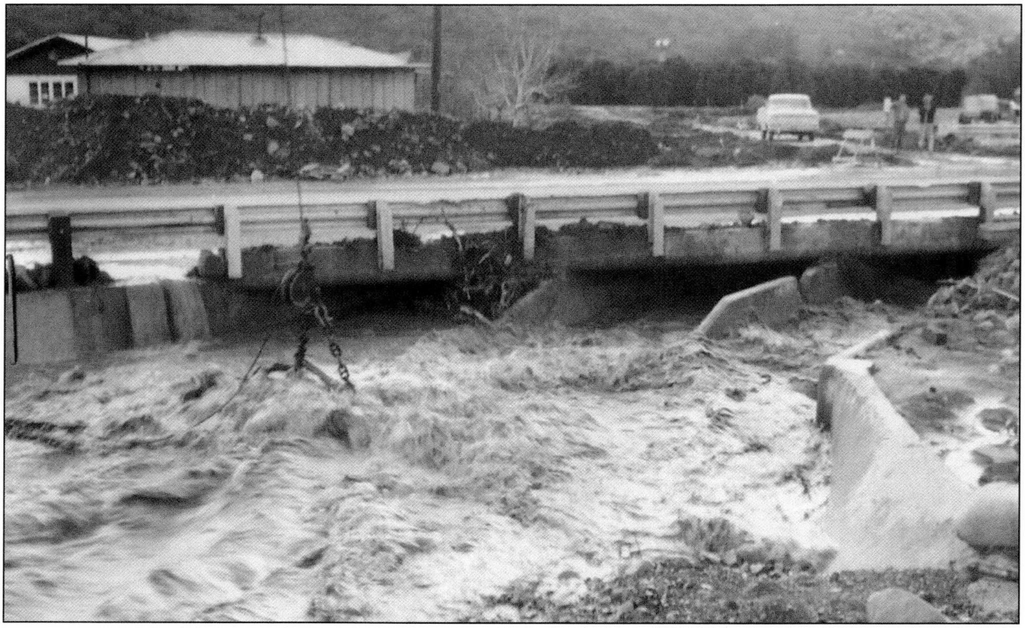

Clearing Debris in 1969 Flood. The *Ojai Valley News* reported on February 26, 1969, that "Unsung heroes of the flood this week were the heavy equipment operators who stayed with their machines night and day in an attempt to channel the waters everywhere." A large scoop is being used here to clear debris in Thacher Creek at the point where it runs beneath Ojai Avenue in the east valley. (Kenneth and Kathryn Williams collection.)

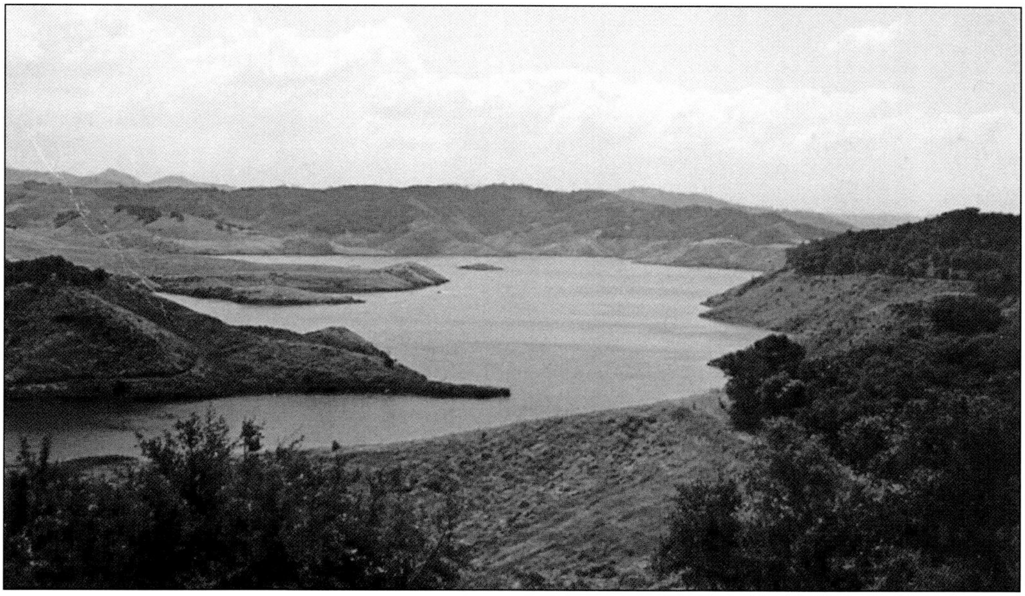

Filling Lake Casitas, 1960. Construction of Casitas Dam on Coyote Creek was "topped out" in November 1958, but the waters behind the dam took several years to fill the lake bed. This photograph shows the filling of the lake. Chaparral was cleaned away from the area that would be flooded, and the eventual height of the waters can be judged by the barren slope at the right center of the picture. (George Finn collection.)

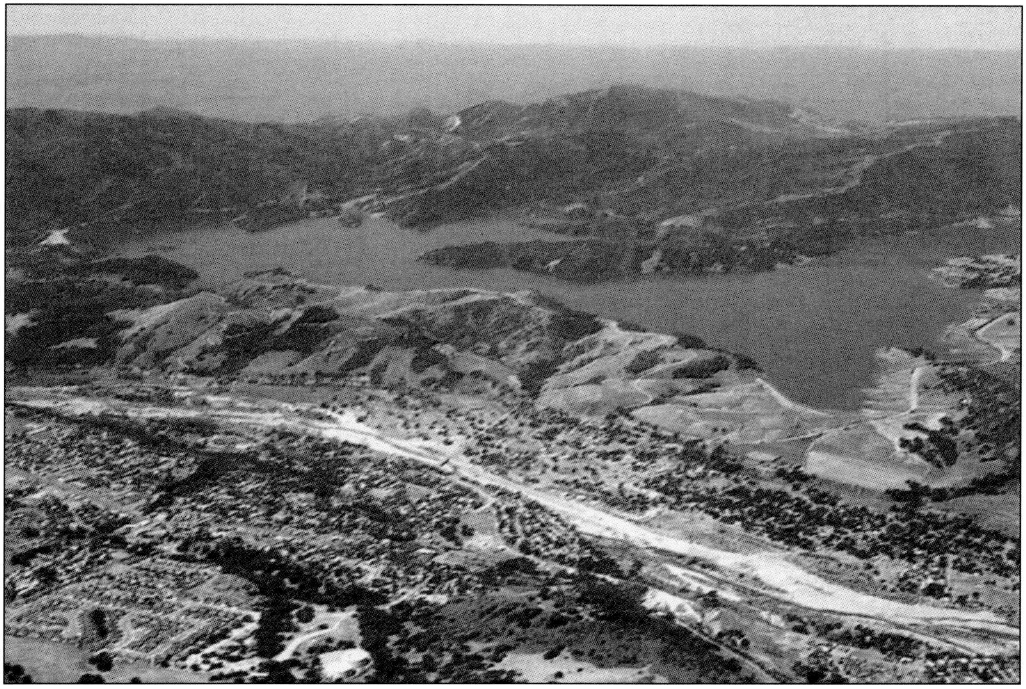

Aerial View of Lake Casitas. Lake Casitas is now a major recreational site as well as a water storage reservoir. Olympic races were staged on the lake in 1984. Casitas Dam is located at left center of this picture, and the complete area of the lake is visible in the photograph. The dry bed of Ventura River runs along the bottom half of the picture. (David Mason collection.)

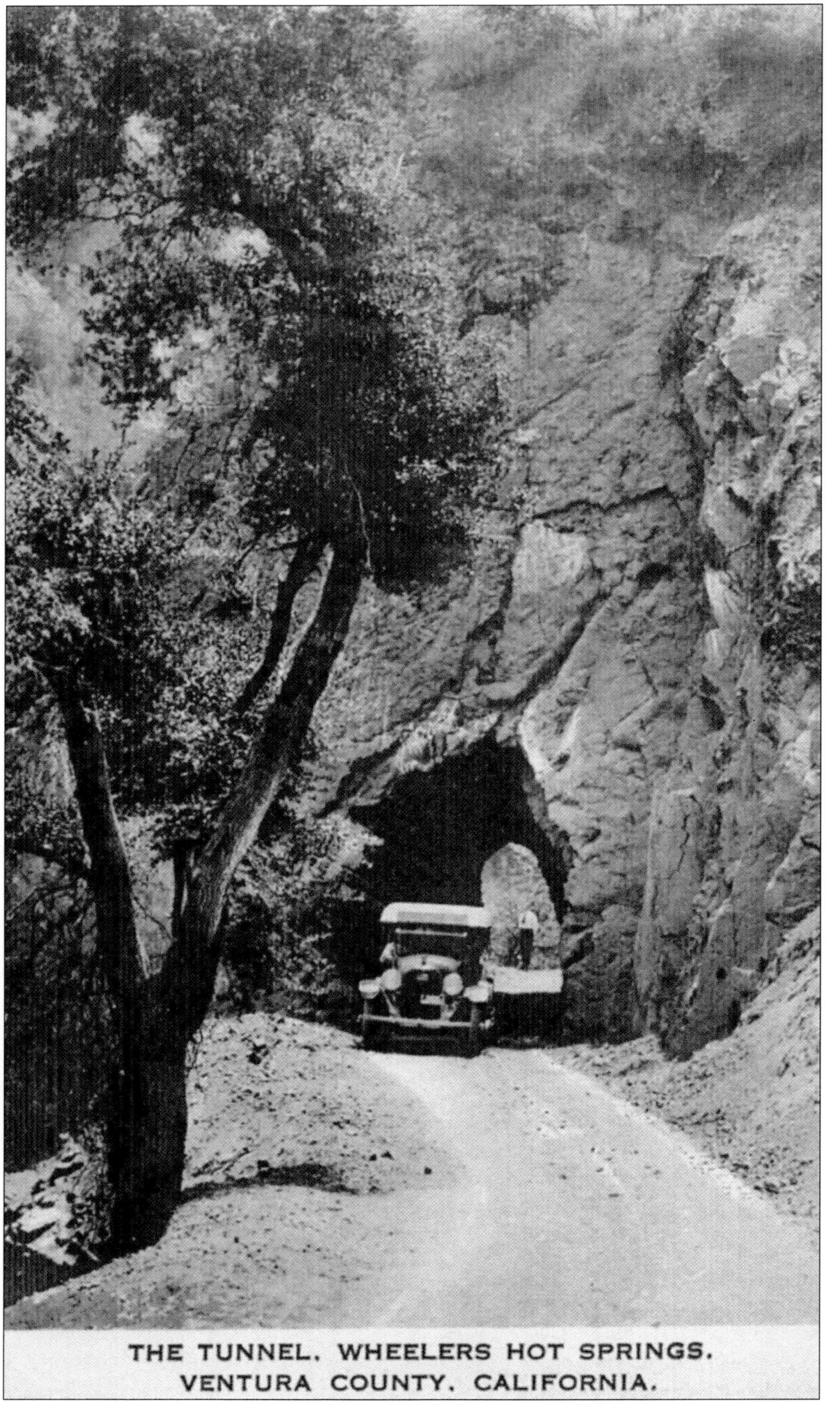

First Tunnel at Wheeler's Springs. Wheeler Blumberg constructed a road to his hot springs in 1888. The same road was improved in 1920, and this tunnel was constructed. It was a much-anticipated feature for travelers headed for the hot springs along the road. This first tunnel was dynamited to enlarge it to a cut-through in April 1931 for construction of the Maricopa Highway. (John Fritsche collection.)

Three

The Road to Ojai

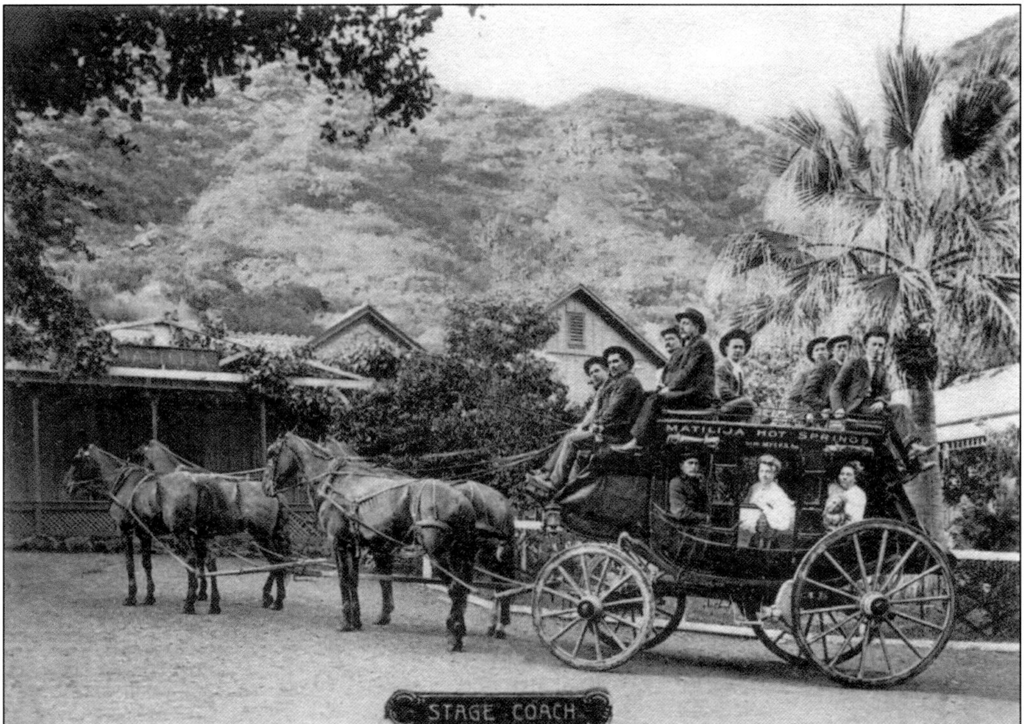

Matilija Stage Coach. The *Ventura Signal* reported on July 26, 1873, that a stage line had been opened between Ventura and Matilija Hot Springs. Andy Van Curen opened a line between Ventura and the valley in the summer of 1875. Various lines operated thereafter. This photograph shows a stage at the second site of Matilija Hot Springs and dates from about 1910. (OVM Collection.)

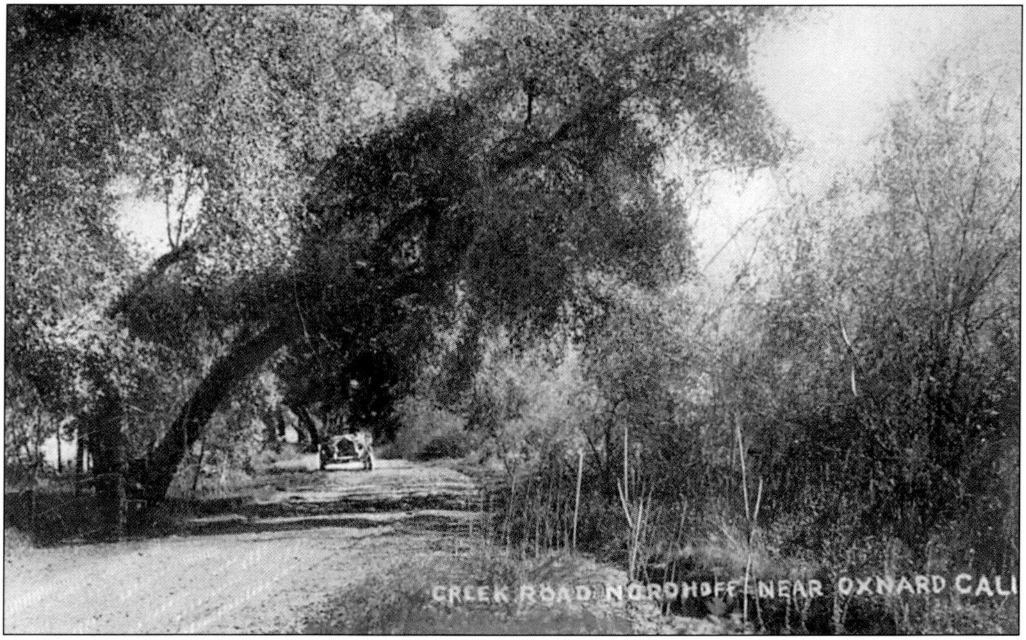

Creek Road in the 1920s. Creek Road stretches southward about 6 miles from Ojai toward Ventura through a long, narrow canyon. When the community of Nordhoff was first established in 1874, Creek Road was the main route to the valley from the coast. (David Mason collection.)

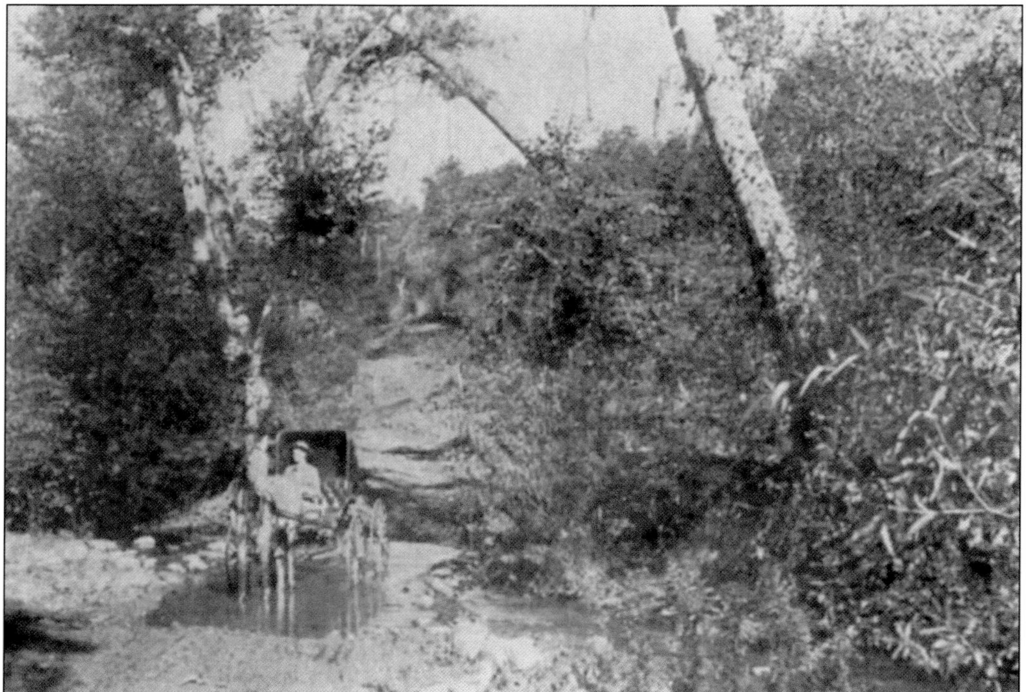

Crossing San Antonio Creek. The *Ventura Free Press* reported on January 22, 1886, that the "creek road between the Arnaz ranch and Nordhoff is somewhat tortuous. The road crosses the creek 16 times within a distance of 6 miles." (Terry Hill collection.)

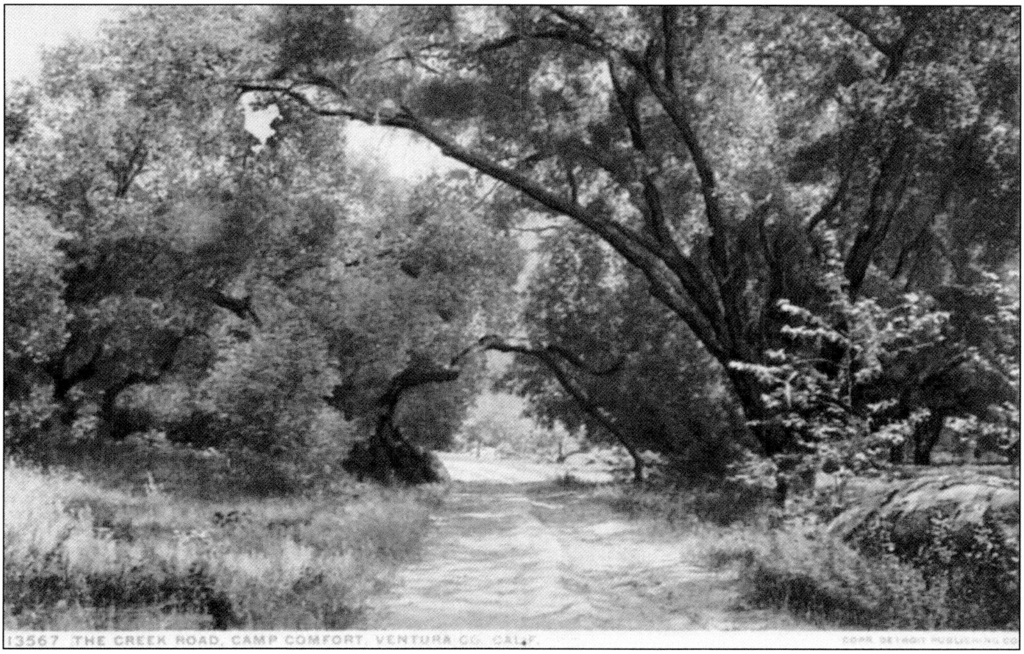

Great Oaks along Creek Road. Even to this day, some stretches of Creek Road are heavily shaded by the limbs of massive oak trees. Nordhoff itself in the 1870s was said to be situated in "White Oak Flats." The abundance and statuesque beauty of the trees attracted many visitors. (Carol Cohen collection.)

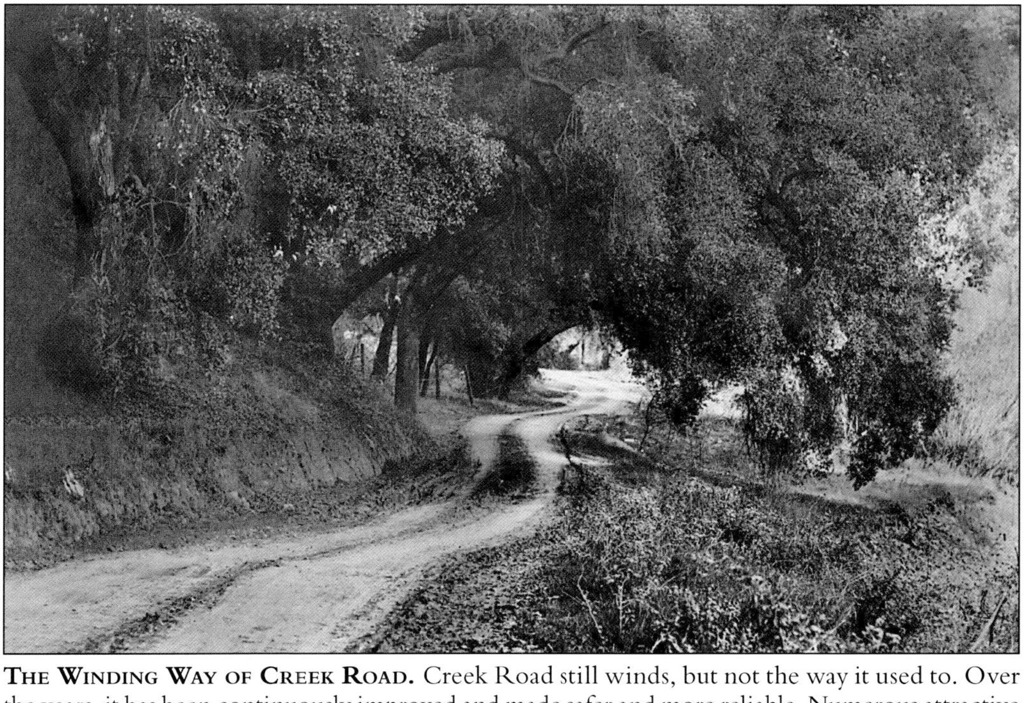

The Winding Way of Creek Road. Creek Road still winds, but not the way it used to. Over the years, it has been continuously improved and made safer and more reliable. Numerous attractive homes and ranches are now located along the road. Direct traffic to Ojai from Ventura presently travels on Highway 33, which parallels Creek Road to the west. (Carol Cohen collection.)

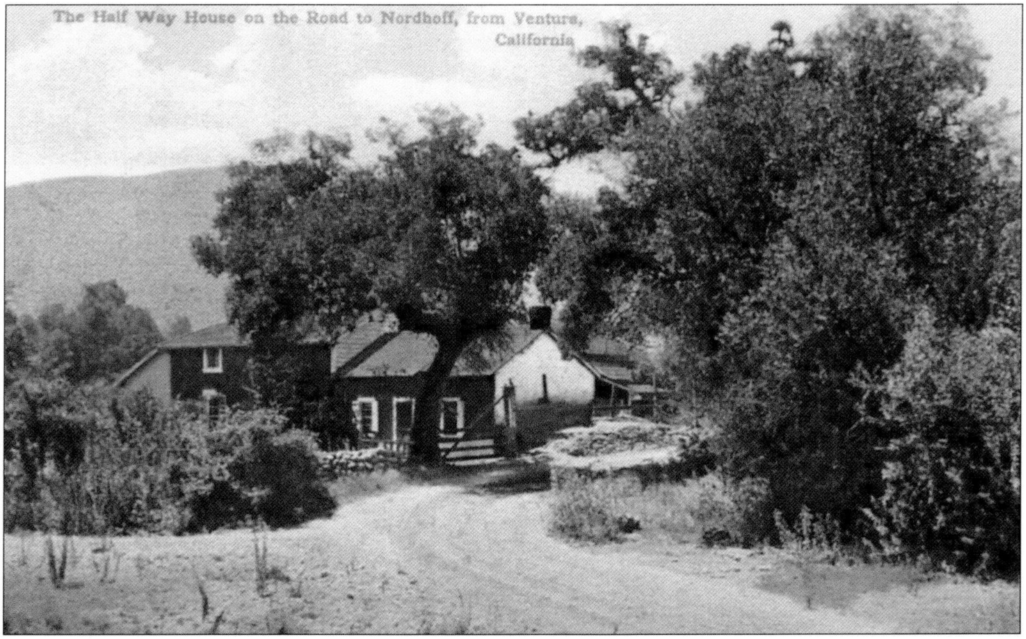

Halfway House in Springtime. These buildings were located at today's Rancho Arnaz, about 7 miles inland from Ventura and halfway to Ojai. The principal house was—and is—an adobe, the home of Jose Arnaz, first owner of the rancho that had been the Mission San Buenaventura. This summertime picture is matched by the winter picture below. (Terry Hill collection.)

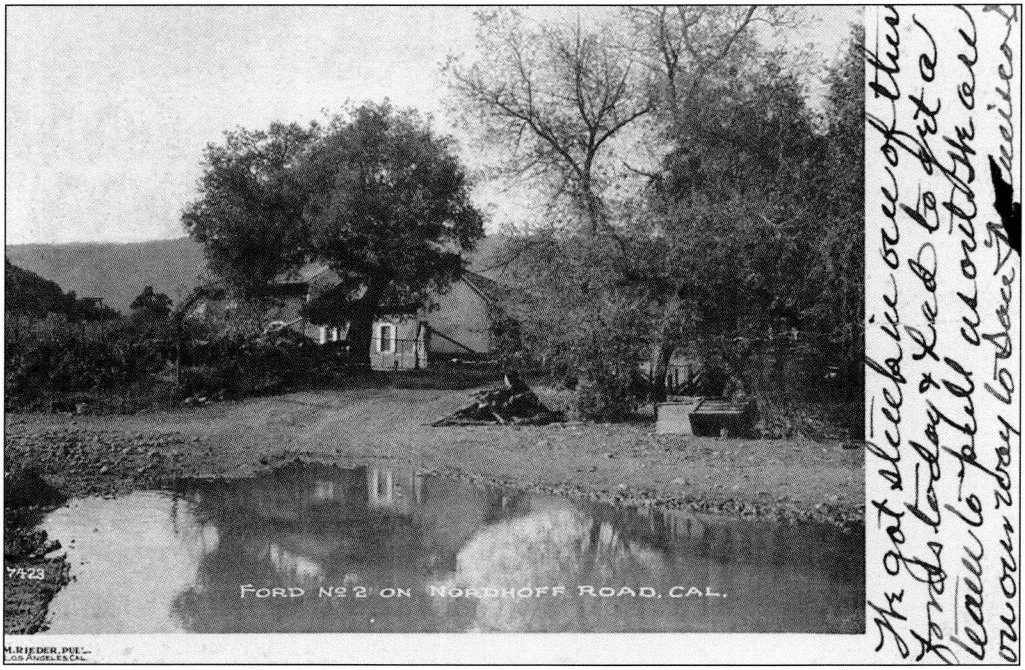

San Antonio Creek at Rancho Arnaz. The person who sent this card remarks, "We got stuck in one of these fords today." San Antonio Creek reaches Ventura River at Rancho Arnaz, and winter flooding was common. Construction of a bridge across the creek near this ford was completed in 1936, replacing an earlier, narrower span. (George Finn collection.)

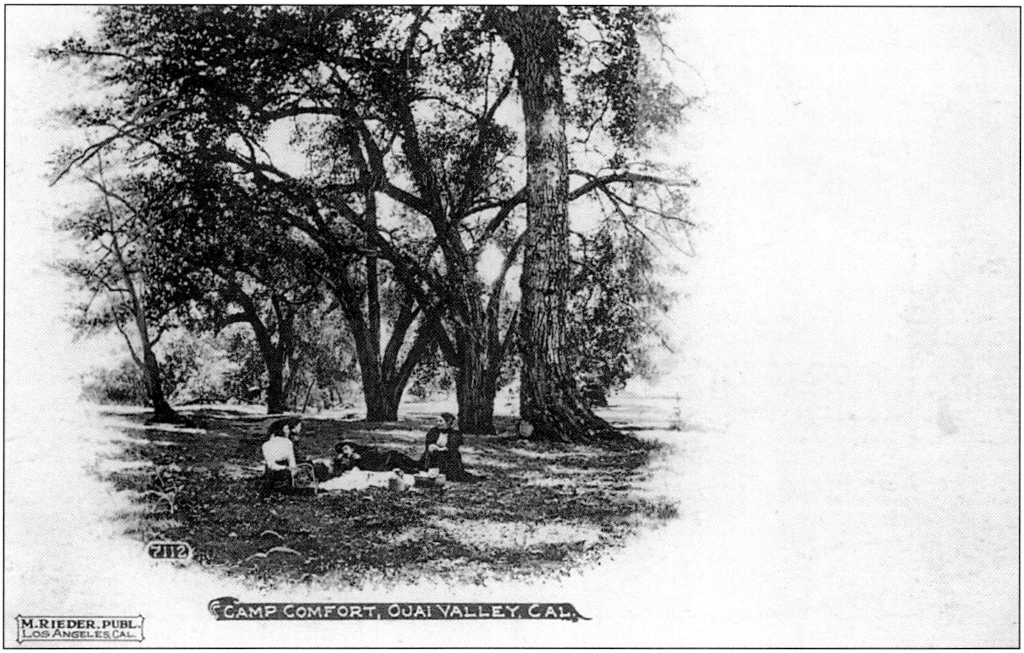

Picnicking at Camp Comfort. A particularly inviting spot along Creek Road convinced travelers to stop for a rest. Sarah McFarland, a minister's daughter, proposed the name Camp Comfort, which the county park at that site retains to this day. This was Ventura County's first regional park, purchased for that purpose in July 1904. (Brian and Connie Aikens collection.)

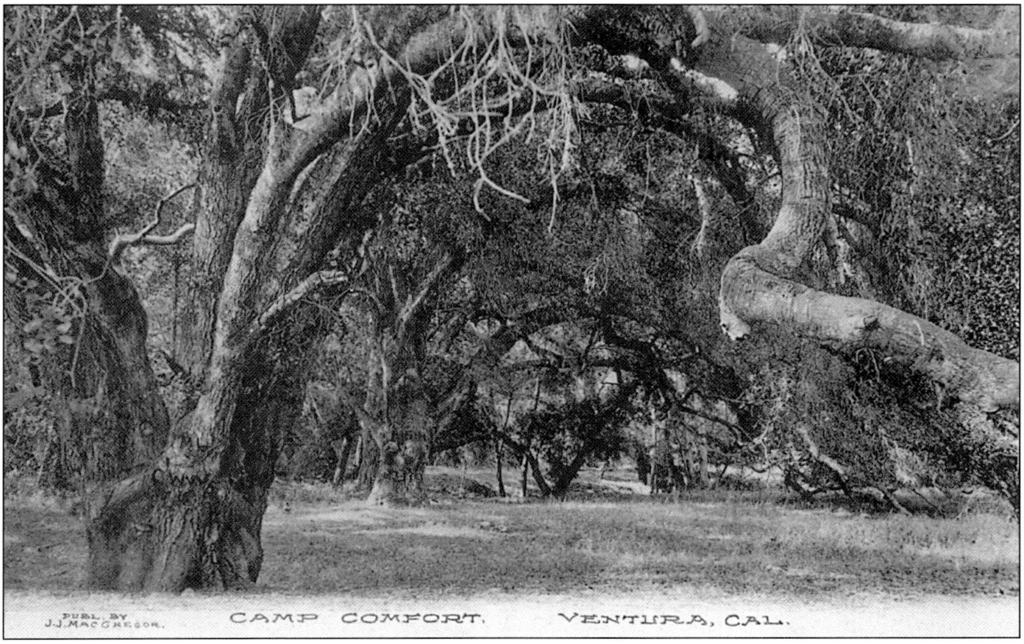

Great Oaks at Camp Comfort. *The Ojai* newspaper reported on May 6, 1900, that "The Nordhoff public school closed Thursday, and yesterday Miss Prudden's pupils had a picnic at Camp Comfort, where they waded in the creek, climbed the live oaks, played outdoor games, and gave all kinds of evidence that they were glad school was out." (John Fritsche collection.)

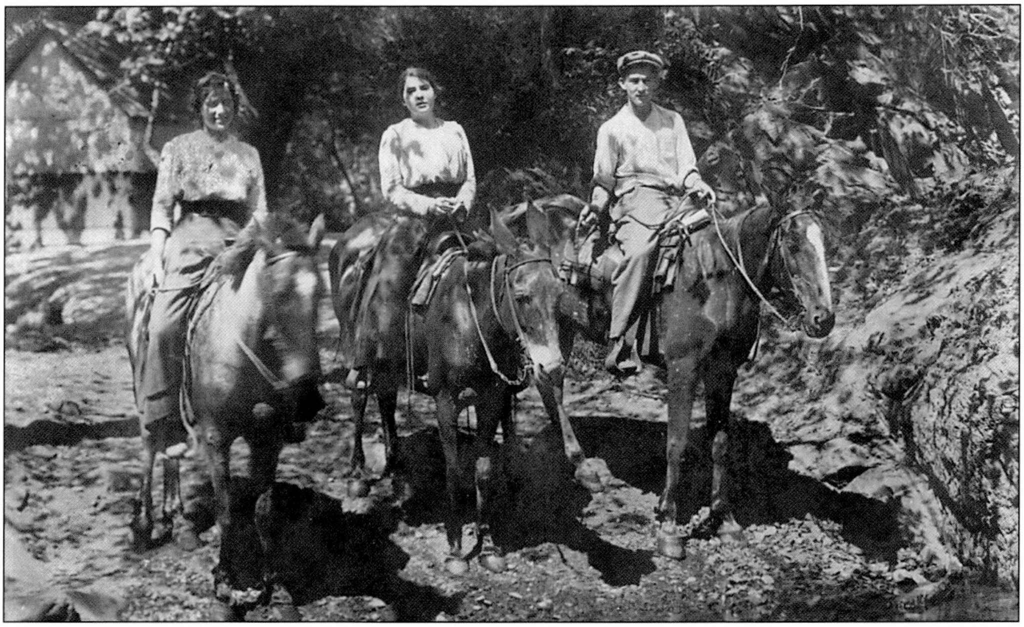

First by Horse. This and the several postcards below illustrate the ways by which people traveled into and through the valley. First, of course, was by foot and by horse. In the 1870s, women and children traveled from their ranches to LaFayette Herbert's general store in Nordhoff by horse and not by buggy, which would have required better roads. In an equestrian community, the village blacksmith was a much-valued community asset. (Terry Hill collection.)

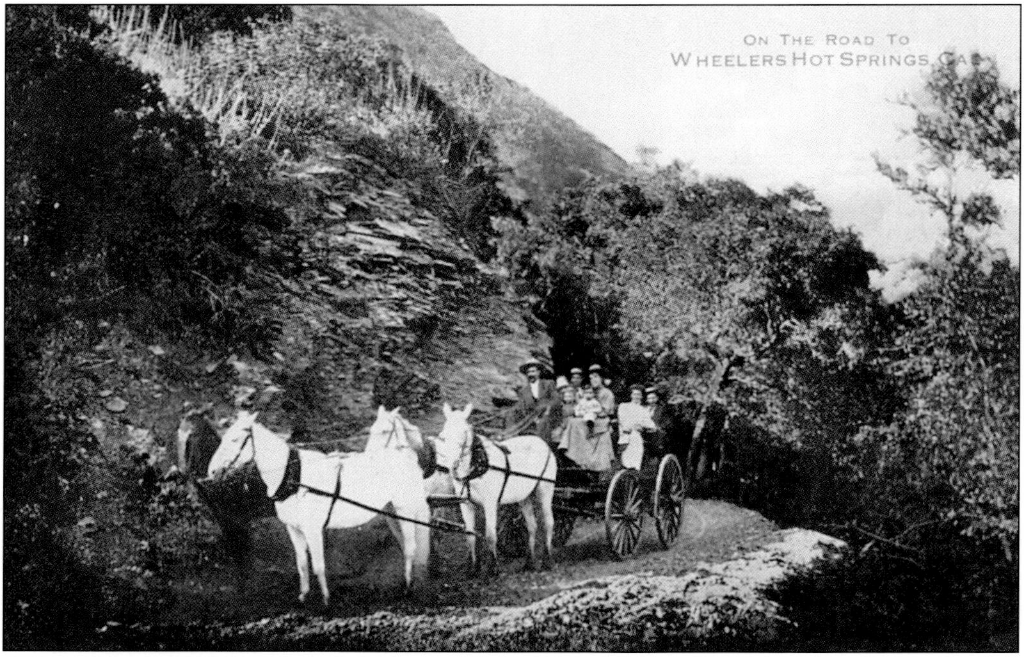

Wagon and Team near Wheeler's. Once improved roads were constructed into and through the valley, it was possible to bring in all kinds of horse-drawn conveyances: carts, buggies, wagons, stagecoaches, and more. Here is what appears to be an extended family in their sturdy wagon on the mountainous canyon road leading to Wheeler's Hot Springs. (George Finn collection.)

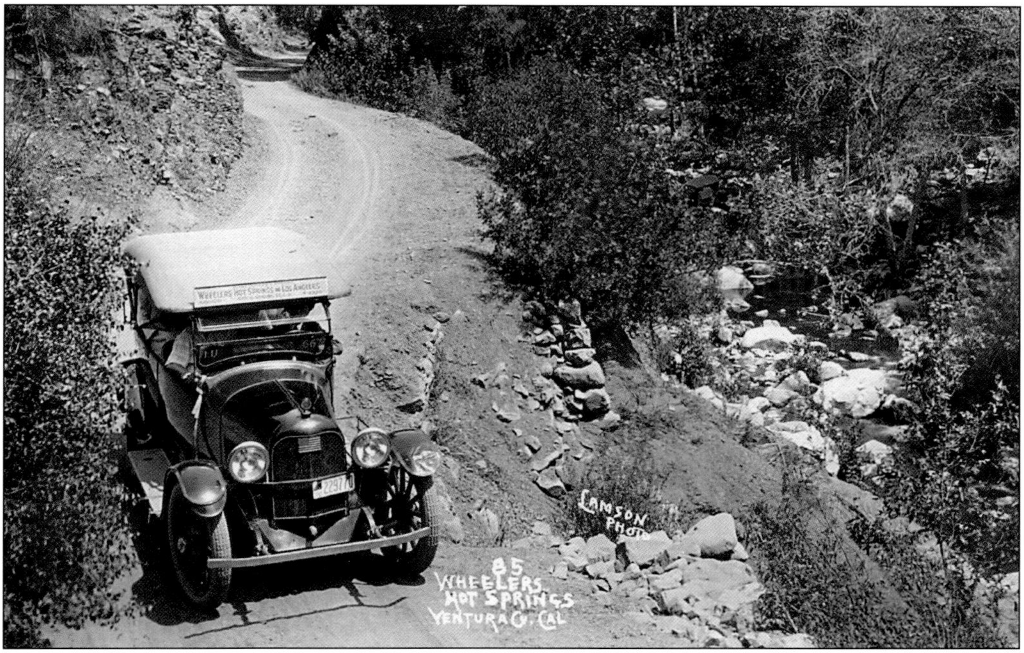

Auto on the Wheeler Road. There is more in this photograph than is immediately apparent. First, the road is washed out, and the auto is gingerly moving past the washout. Second, there is a sign along the roof of the vehicle reading, "Wheeler's Hot Springs to Los Angeles." It was possible at the time to obtain direct shuttle service all the way between Los Angeles and Matilija Canyon. (Terry Hill collection.)

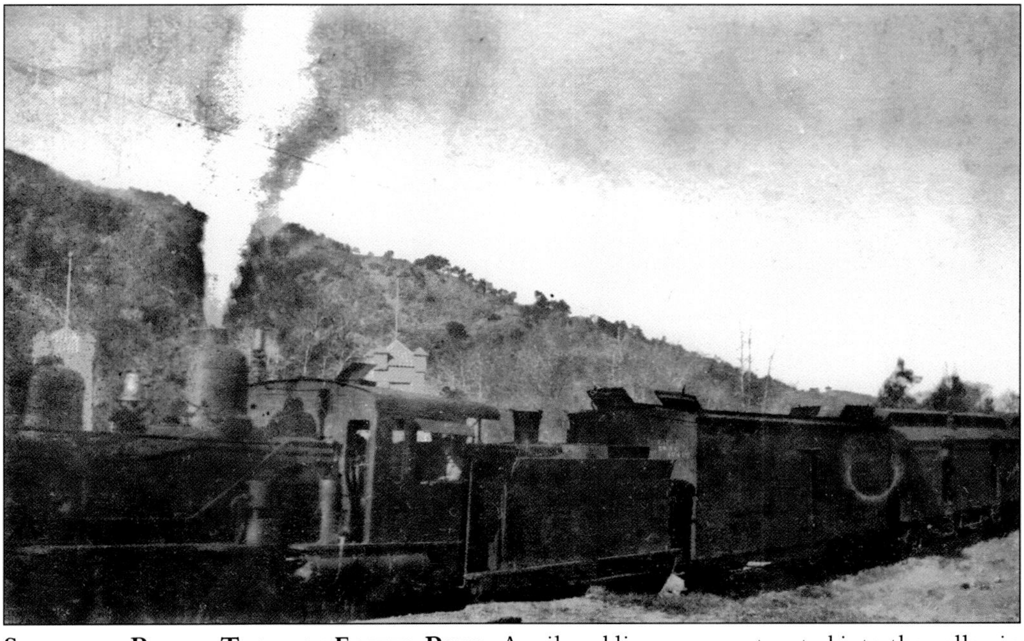

Southern Pacific Train at Foster Park. A railroad line was constructed into the valley in 1897 and 1898. Valley residents held a "Jollification" on March 12, 1898, to welcome completion of the line. The railroad continued service until 1969, and the course of its tracks is still seen today as the Ojai Valley Trail, running largely along Highway 33. (OVM Collection.)

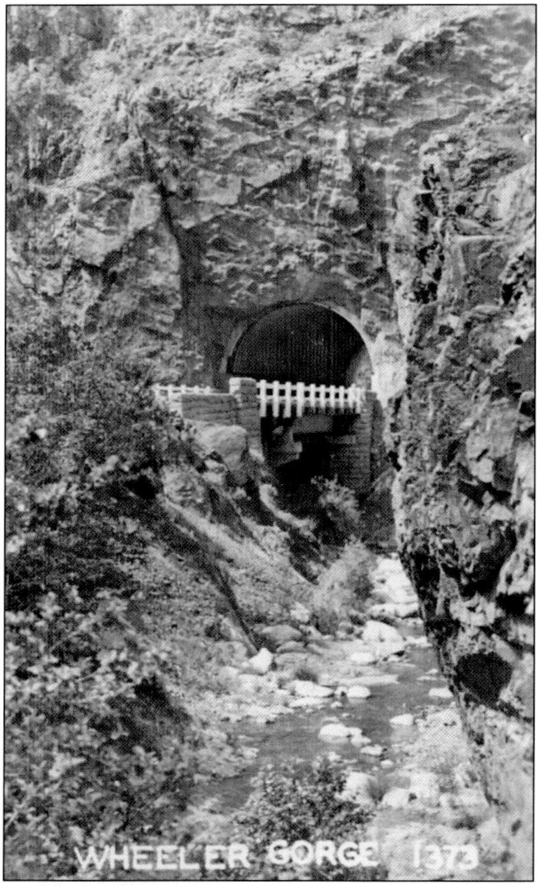

Maricopa Highway Tunnel at Wheeler Gorge. Desire for a road to connect the county seat of Ventura with the county's northernmost reaches was not realized until 1933 with construction of Maricopa Highway. Ground was broken on April 19, 1929, for the construction. A grand celebration was staged on October 22, 1933, to mark the highway's completion. (John Fritsche collection.)

Double Tunnels on Maricopa Highway. The first tunnel constructed on the road leading into Matilija Canyon in 1920 was blown up and replaced by three new tunnels, the one shown at left and the two below. Each of the tunnels in narrow Wheeler Gorge is short, but they add drama to the trip. (Terry Hill collection.)

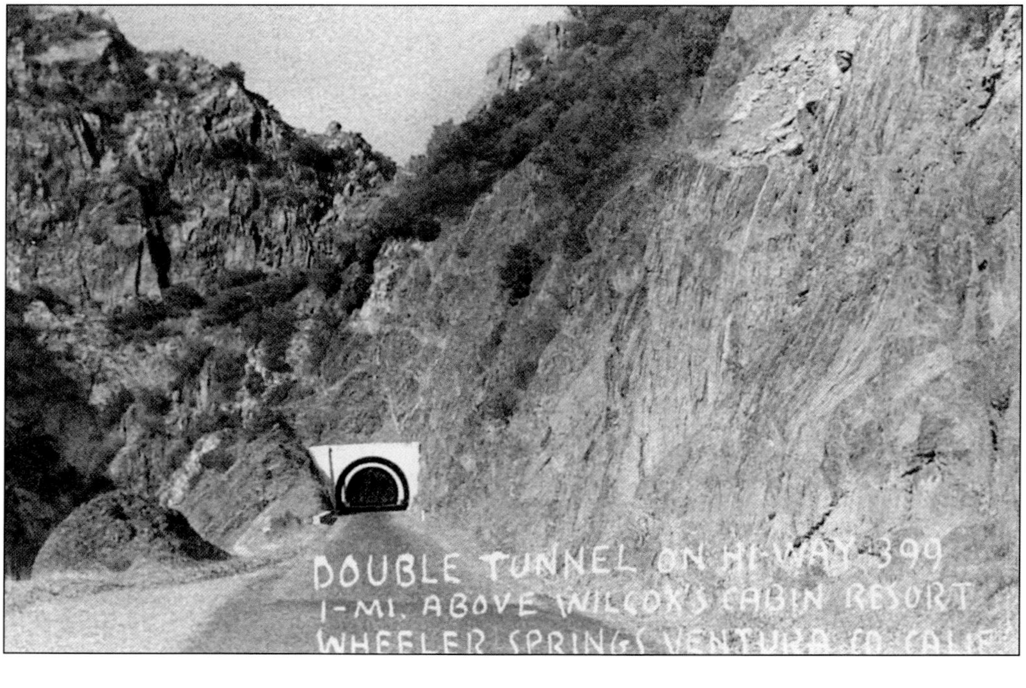

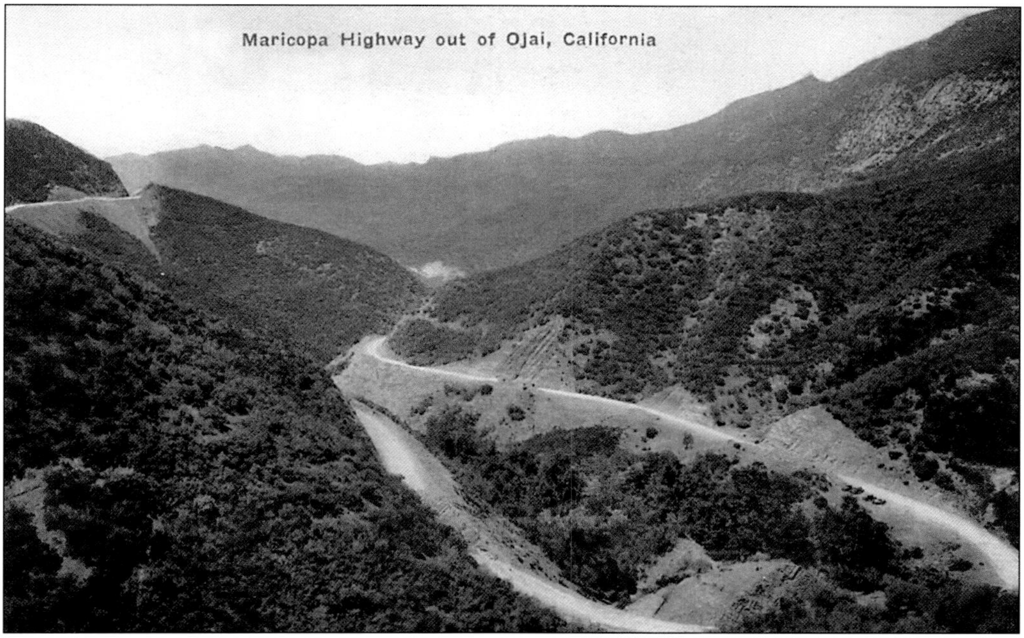

ASCENT OF MARICOPA HIGHWAY. This photograph is taken from near the summit of the highway, looking southward toward the Ojai Valley. On a clear day, it is possible to see a narrow portion of the ocean from this location. The highway is now designated the "Jacinto Reyes Scenic Highway" in honor of a much-esteemed early forest ranger. (David Mason collection.)

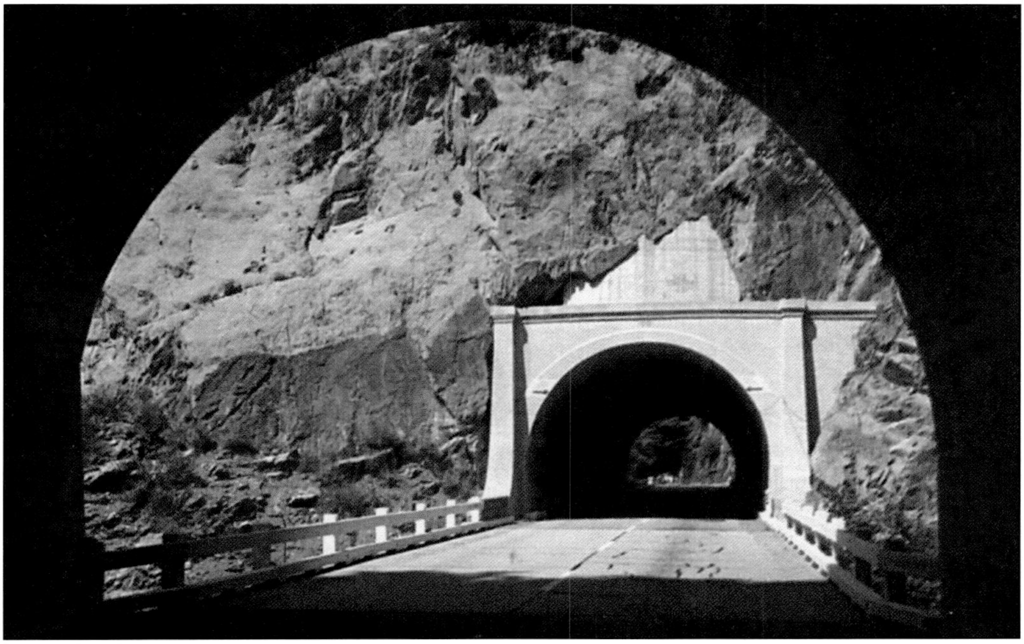

INSIDE A DOUBLE TUNNEL. This photograph is taken within one of the spans of the double tunnel on Maricopa Highway. In the early months of World War II, dynamite explosives were fixed around these tunnels. If an invasion occurred on the coast, the population of the valley was to be evacuated up Maricopa Highway and the tunnels blown up behind the fleeing population. (OVM Collection.)

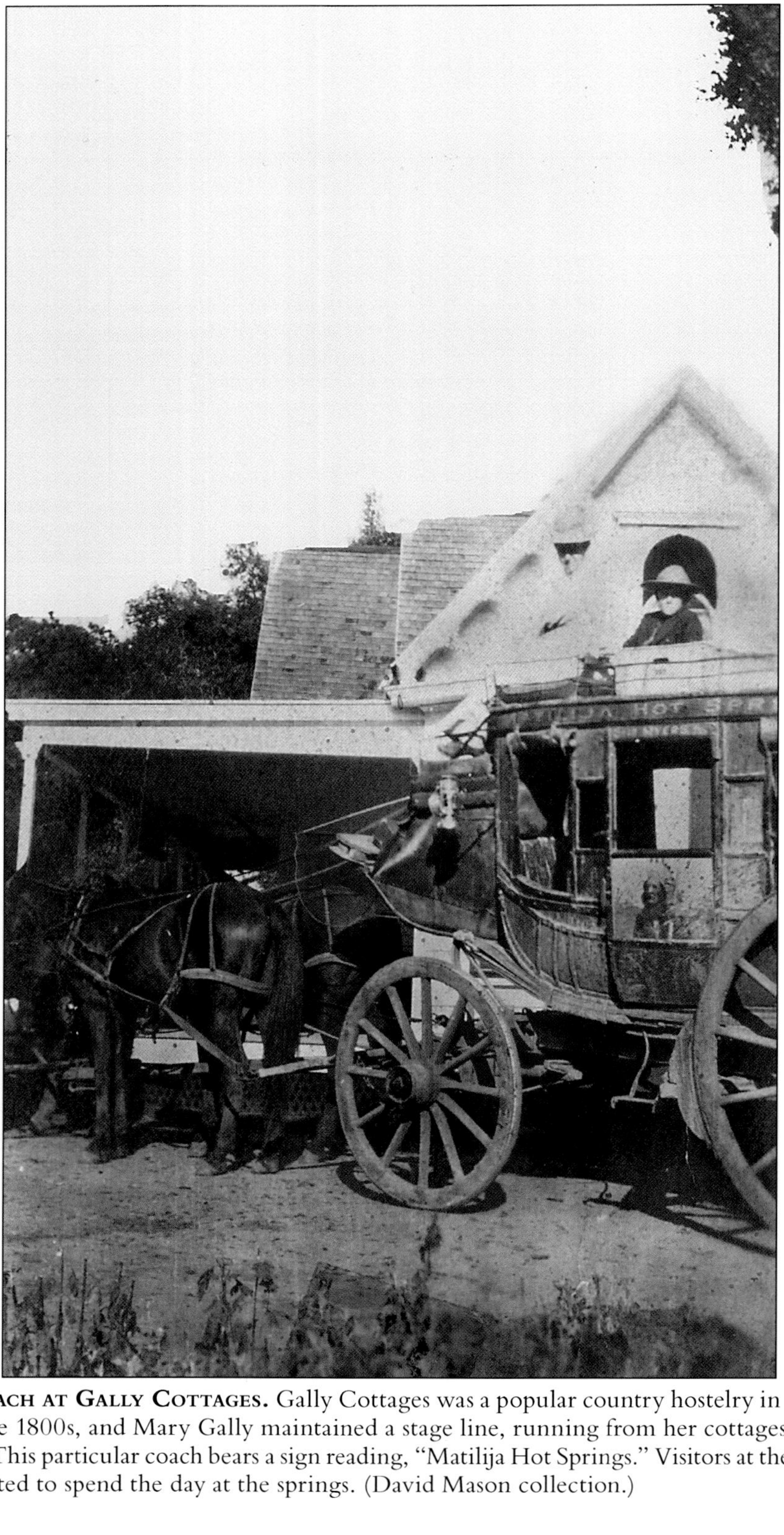

Stagecoach at Gally Cottages. Gally Cottages was a popular country hostelry in the latter part of the 1800s, and Mary Gally maintained a stage line, running from her cottages to Santa Barbara. This particular coach bears a sign reading, "Matilija Hot Springs." Visitors at the cottages were invited to spend the day at the springs. (David Mason collection.)

Four

Old Town Nordhoff

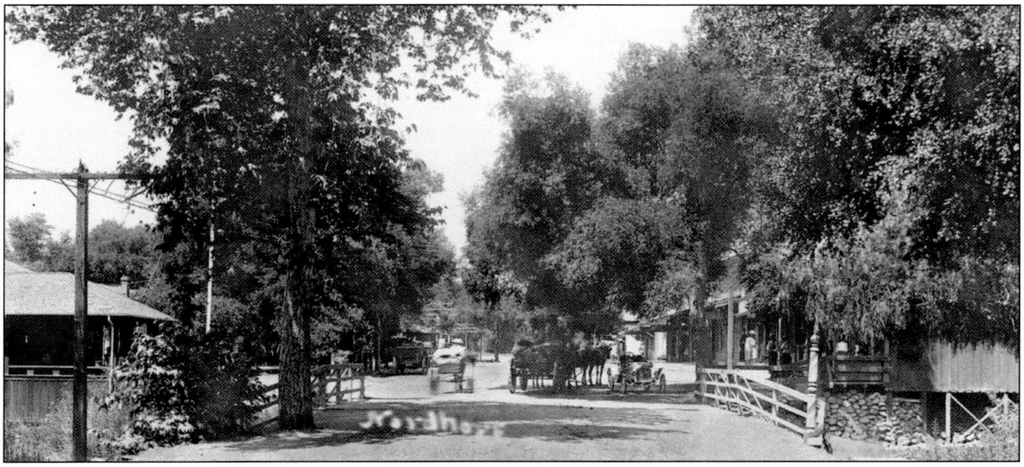

Main Street, Nordhoff, around 1908. The founding of the village of Nordhoff was celebrated on April 6, 1874, by over 300 people at a "grand ball" at the Blumberg hotel (hidden behind trees at the left center of this picture). The business district was constructed across the street from the hotel (at the right center of this picture). Stewart Canyon Creek (now often called Ojai Creek) ran beneath Main Street. (Mary Lee Eaton collection.)

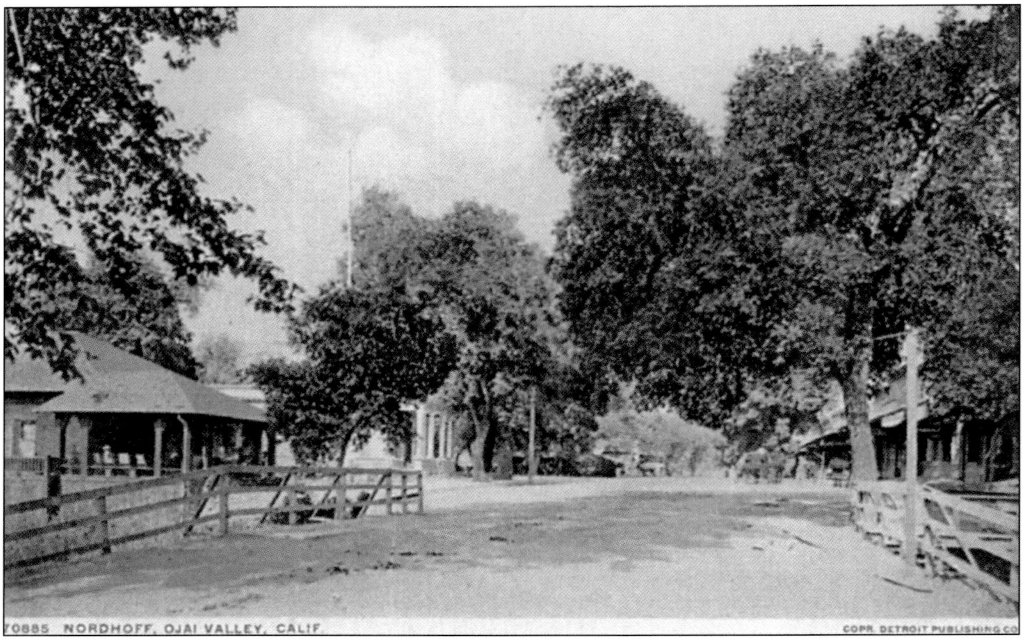

MAIN STREET, NORDHOFF, AROUND 1912. What is now called Ojai Avenue was, in the early part of the 1900s, called Main Street. Two buildings are shown in this postcard that serve to date the image: the Boyd Club (far left, constructed in 1903) and the Ojai State Bank building (in the trees just beyond the Boyd Club, constructed in 1910). Awnings of the business block can be seen across the street. (OVM Collection.)

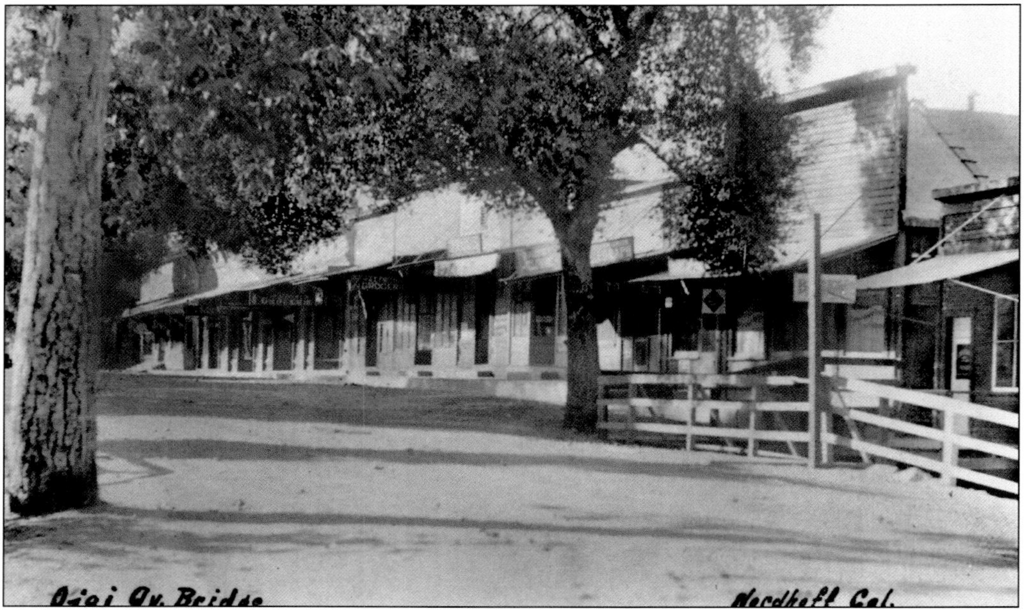

NORDHOFF BUSINESS DISTRICT. These buildings stood across Main Street from the Boyd Club and Bank of America. Businesses included general merchandise and clothing stores, a drugstore, and a telephone and telegraph office. It is anyone's guess how it was possible for the postcard to be taken in the afternoon without a person in sight. The Ojai arcade was later constructed at the front of these buildings. (OVM Collection.)

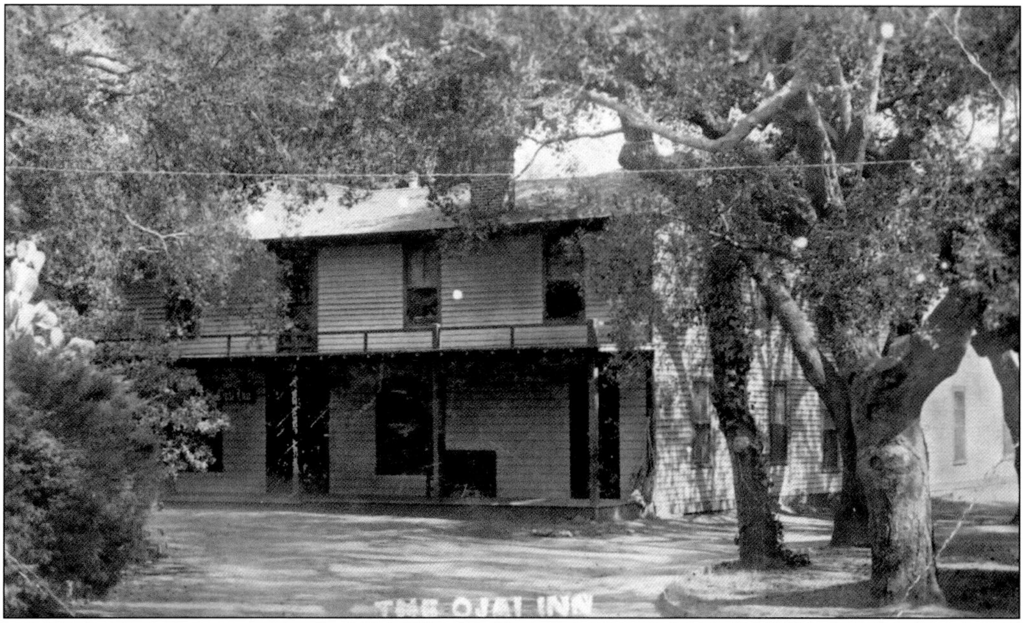

The Ojai Inn, around 1910. Abram Blumberg constructed the first section of this building in 1874, but ownership passed from hand to hand until new owners renamed it the Ojai Inn in 1901. It was in this building that a grand ball was staged in April 1874 marking the beginning of the town that was to become the city of Ojai. (Brian and Connie Aikens collection.)

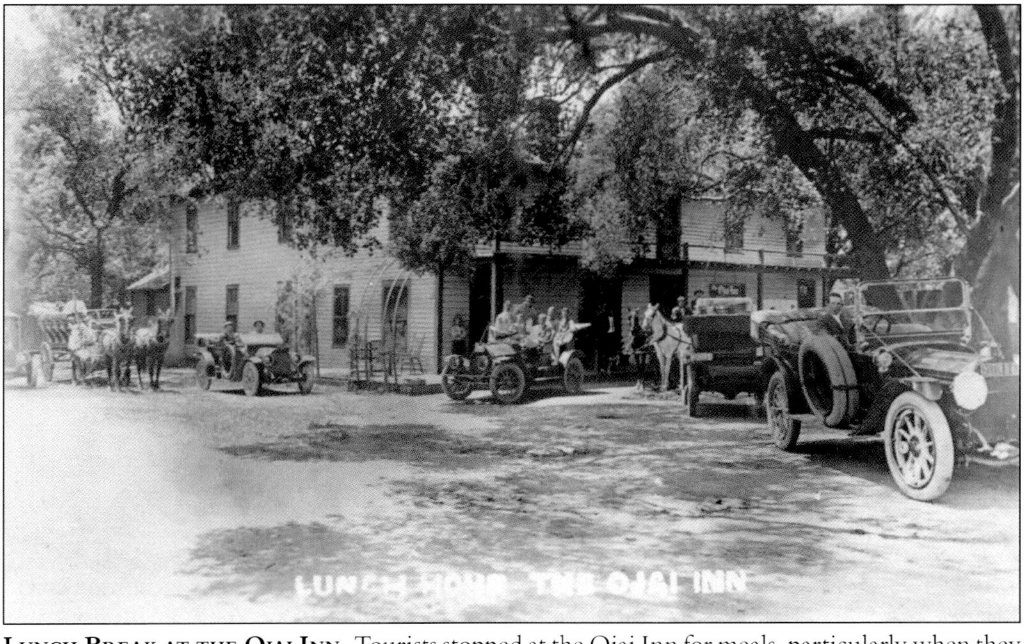

Lunch Break at the Ojai Inn. Tourists stopped at the Ojai Inn for meals, particularly when they drove what was called "the Triangle," from Ventura to Santa Paula and then through the Upper and Lower Ojai Valleys. The automobiles here date from about 1916, shortly before the hotel was bought by Edward Libbey and razed for creation of today's Libbey Park. (OVM Collection.)

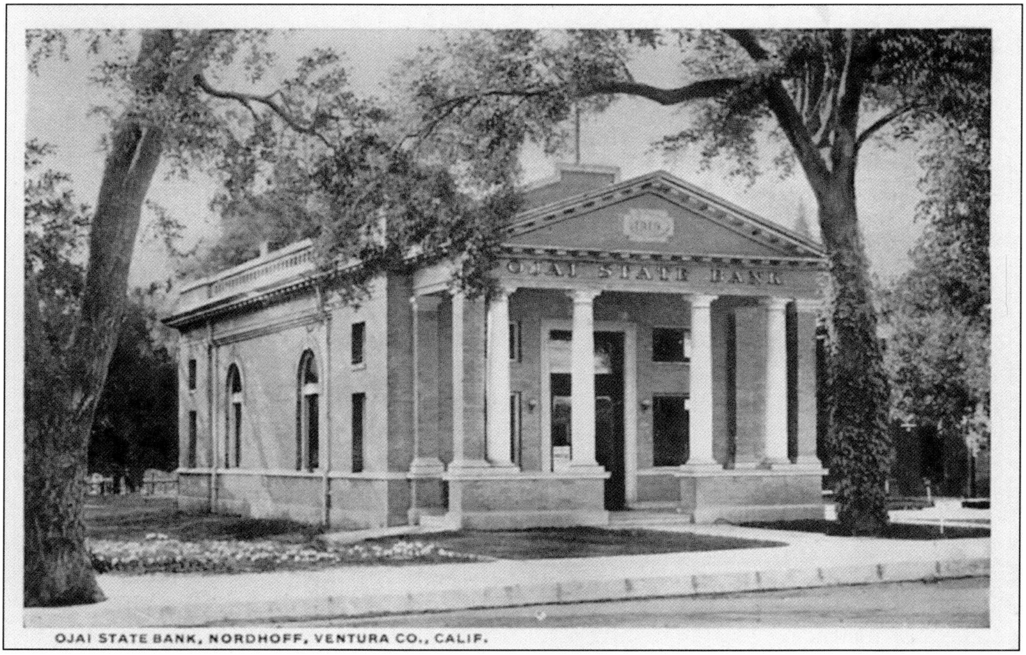

OJAI STATE BANK. This remarkable building with its classical columns was constructed in 1910 and retained that name until 1927, when it was purchased by the Bank of Italy (subsequently, the Bank of America). Even though the false-fronted businesses of Nordhoff had the appearance of any frontier Western town, this elegant building stood facing them across the street. It was razed in 1960. (OVM Collection.)

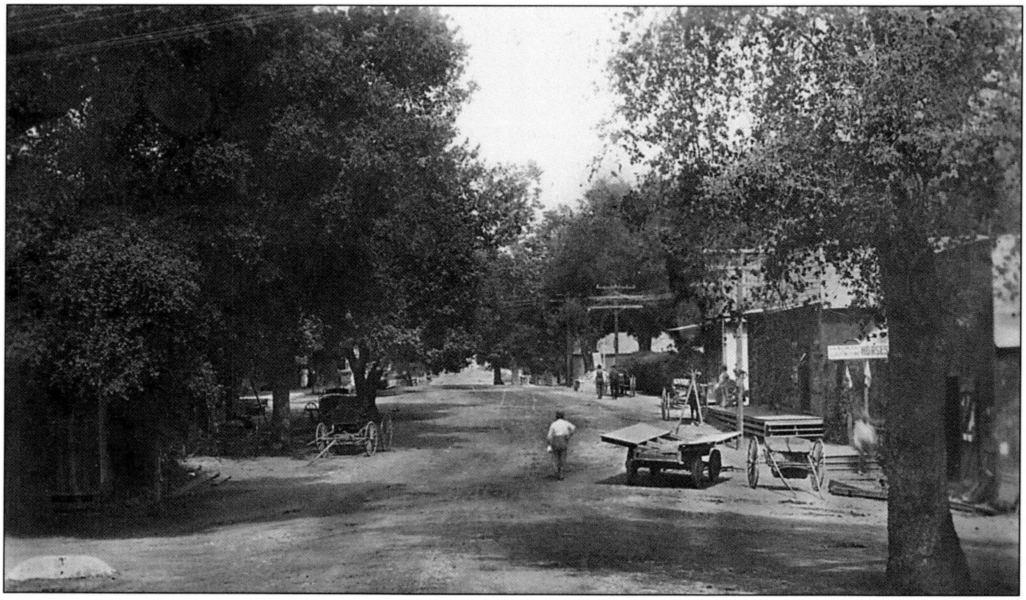

SOUTH SIDE OF OJAI AVENUE. This postcard shows the businesses that stood on the south side of Ojai Avenue, across the street from the present arcade. The first business, at the left, was a blacksmith. Other businesses included a barber, grocer, and plumbing shop. Electric service was started in the valley in 1913, so this photograph was taken some time between that year and the construction of the arcade in 1917. (David Mason collection.)

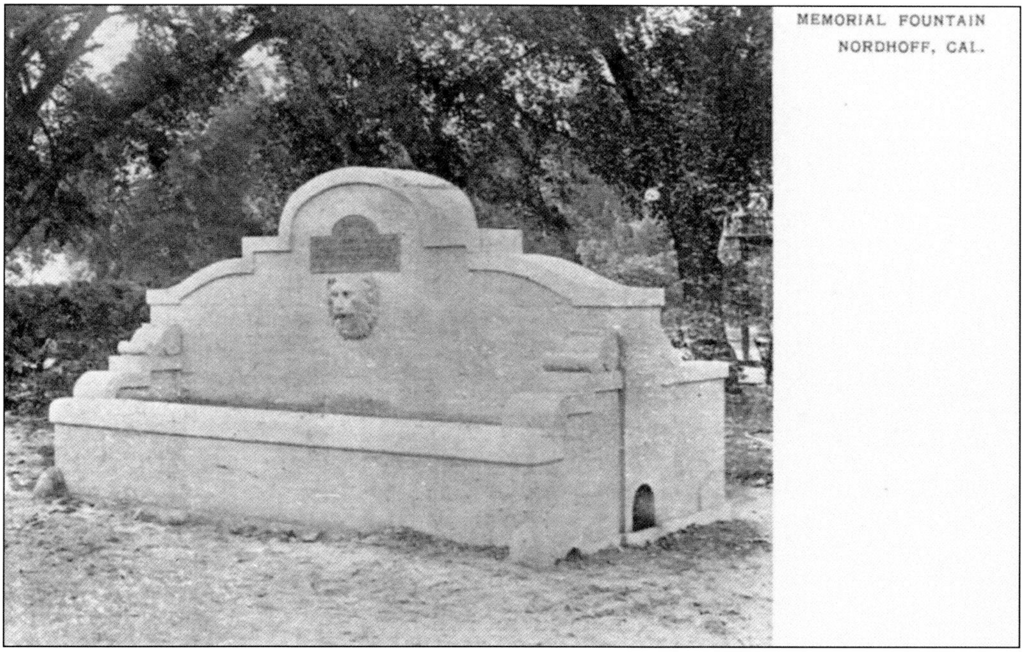

EVELYN NORDHOFF MEMORIAL FOUNTAIN. This horse trough was constructed in 1904 in memory of Charles Nordhoff's daughter, who died suddenly not long before she was to be married. The architect for the fountain was S. M. Ilsley, who also designed the Foothills Hotel. A reconstruction of this fountain (with the original plaque) can be seen today at the center of the pergola, across Ojai Avenue from the arcade. (George Finn collection.)

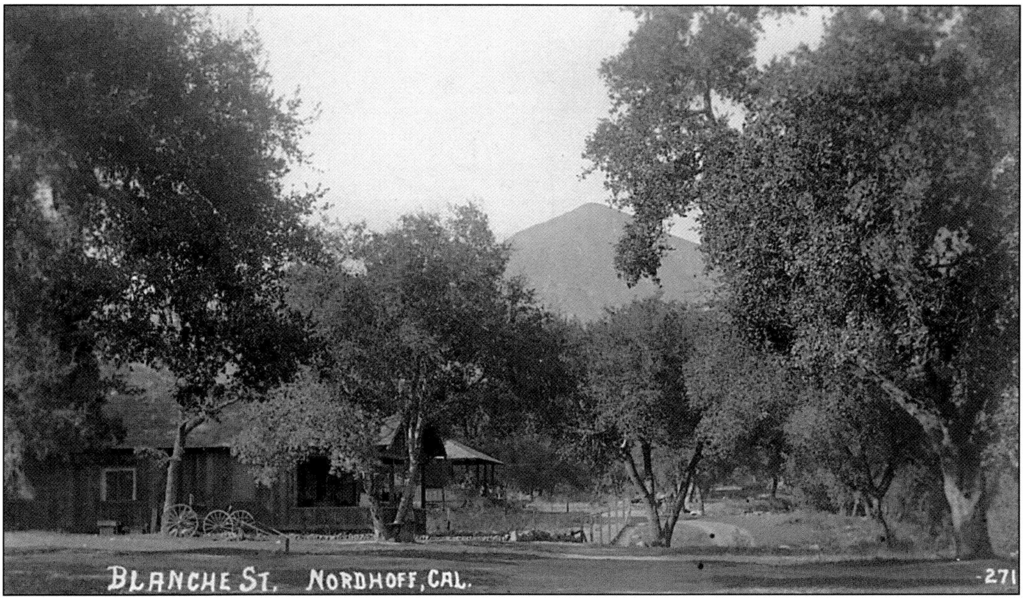

BLANCHE STREET RESIDENCES. This postcard shows what the residential section of Ojai (then called Nordhoff) looked like around 1900. The entire community was built into a forest of coastal live oaks (*Quercus lobata*) and valley oaks (*Quercus agrifolia*). It was the abundance of the valley oaks that led to the naming of the valley floor as White Oak Flats in the 1800s. (OVM Collection.)

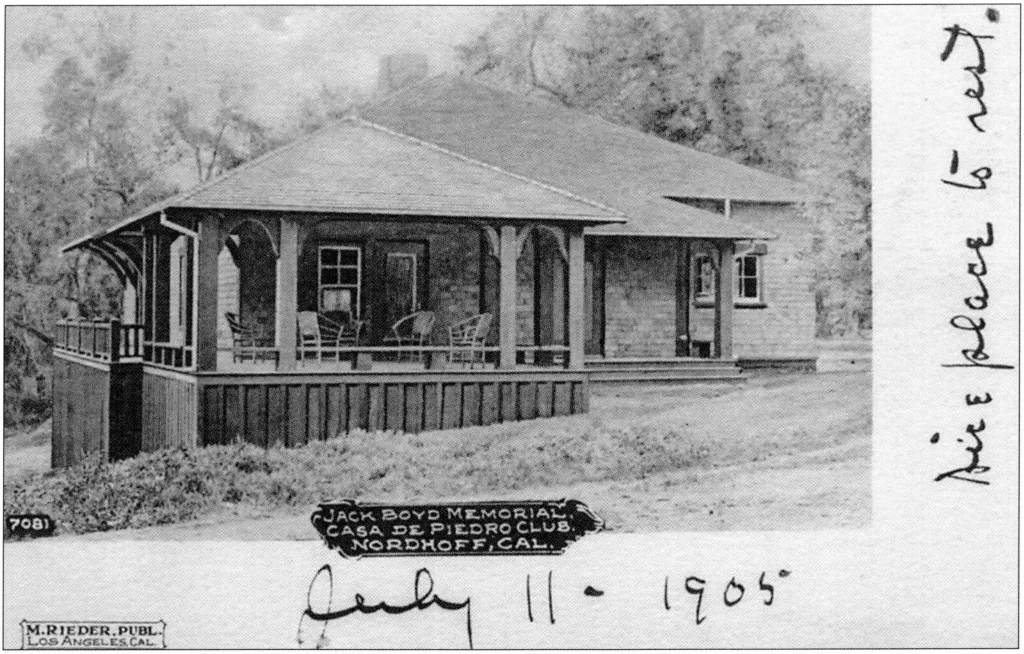

THE BOYD CLUB, 1905. This men's clubhouse was built in 1903, just two years before this postcard was sent. It was founded in memory of Jack Boyd, a Thacher School student who died at a young age. The club served as a social and recreational center for the men of the valley. (Terry Hill collection.)

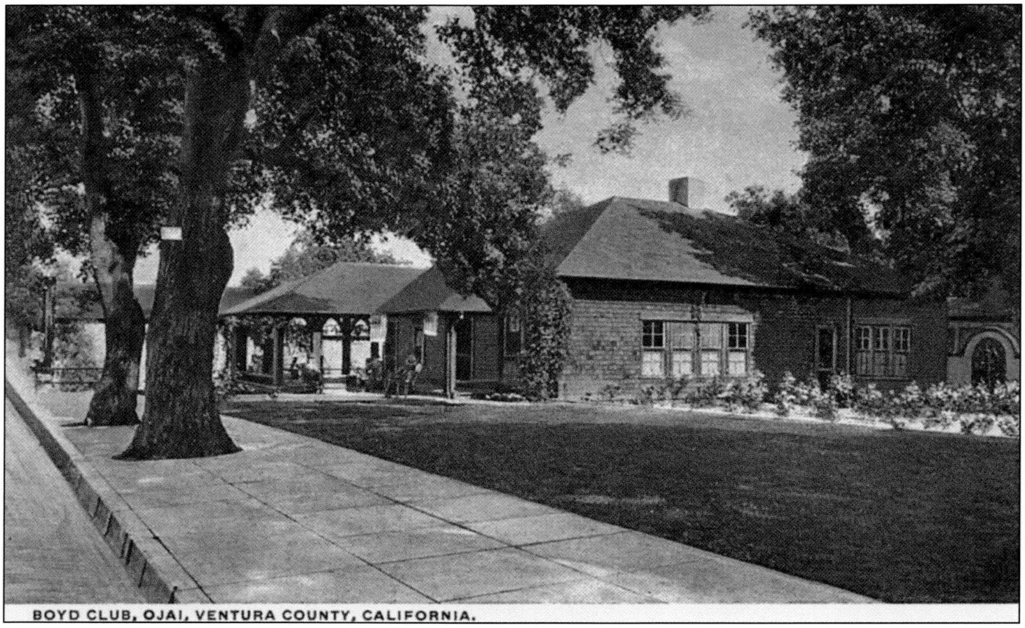

THE BOYD CLUB, AROUND 1940. This is a later photograph of the Boyd Club, with well-constructed sidewalks and a rose garden. Also shown as an extension at the rear of the original building is a gymnasium that was a gift of Charles Pratt in 1912. The planting of the rose garden was funded by Edward Libbey. The building was moved from this site in 1957 to Sarzotti Park, where it can be seen today. (Carol Cohen collection.)

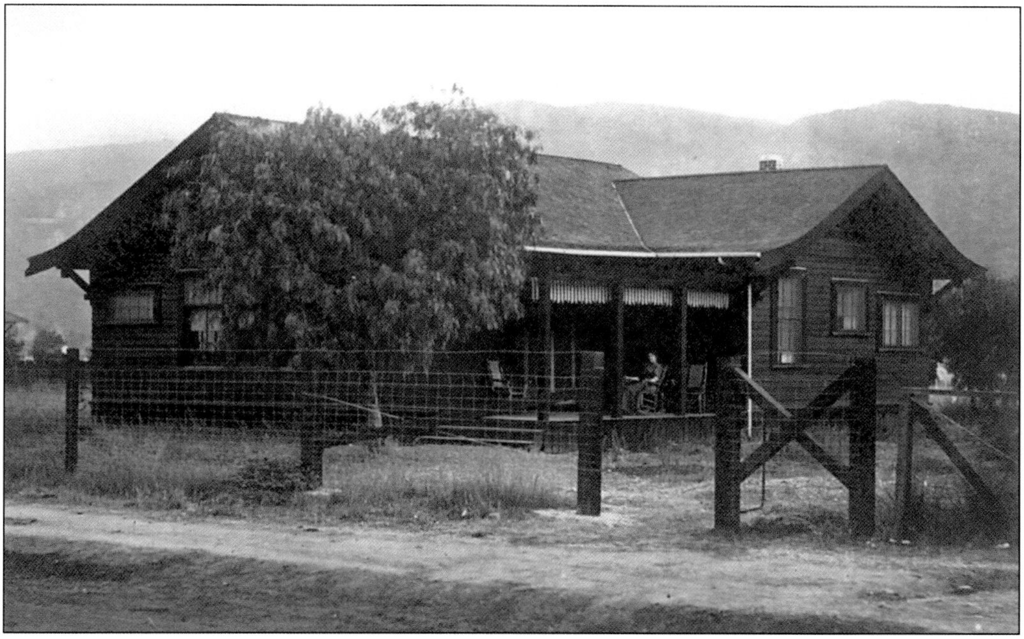

The Woman's Club. Josephine Pierpont-Ginn funded the construction of this building in 1911 as a gift to the King's Daughters, a predecessor organization to the Woman's Club. The building, which still stands today a block east of the arcade block, has a long history as a place for women's activities, community events, and community service. (OVM Collection.)

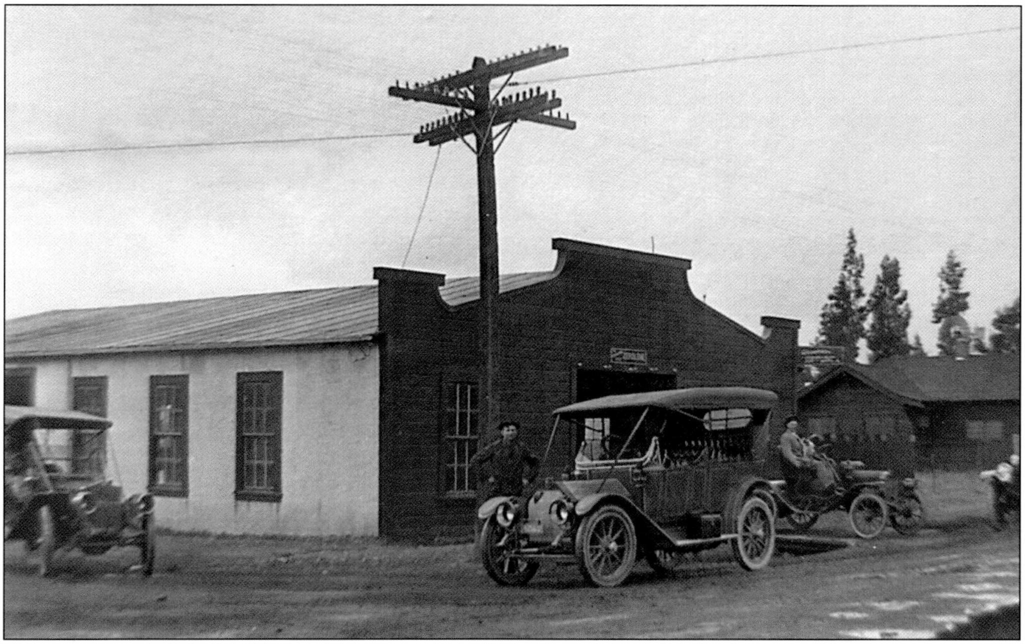

An Ojai Garage. This garage was located near the intersection of Ojai Avenue and Fox Street, east of the center of town. The sign over the entrance advertises Zerolene lubricants, which would continue to flow in zero-degree temperatures. Electric service to the community started in 1913, so the photograph probably dates to a little later in that decade. (David Mason collection.)

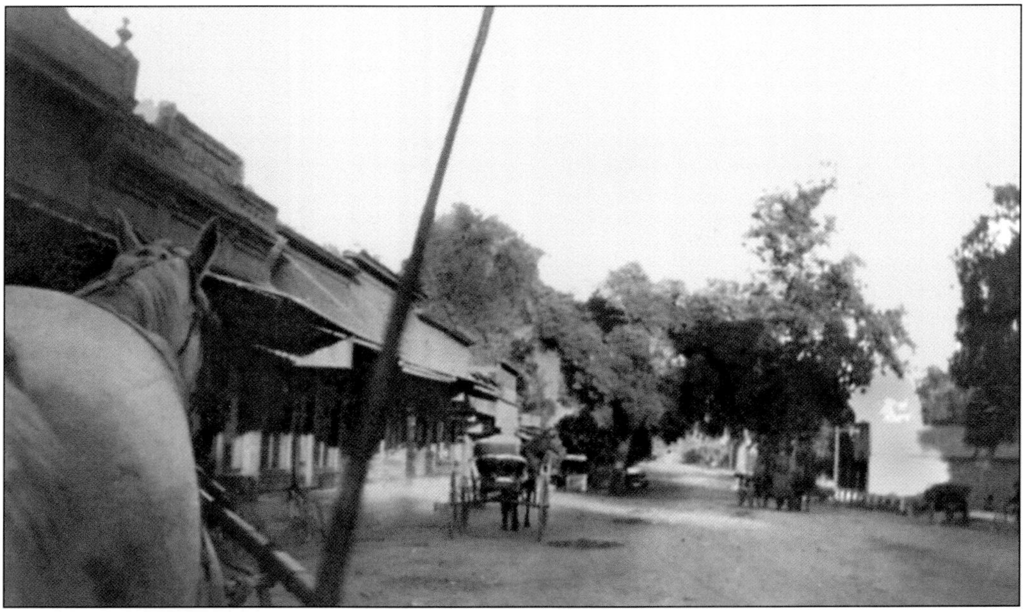

View from an Ojai Buggy. This postcard provides a unique view of central Nordhoff, looking east prior to 1917. The false fronts of the line of stores, which would shortly be faced with an arcade, appear on the left. A bicyclist enters from the right. It is a quiet late afternoon in a country village. (David Mason collection.)

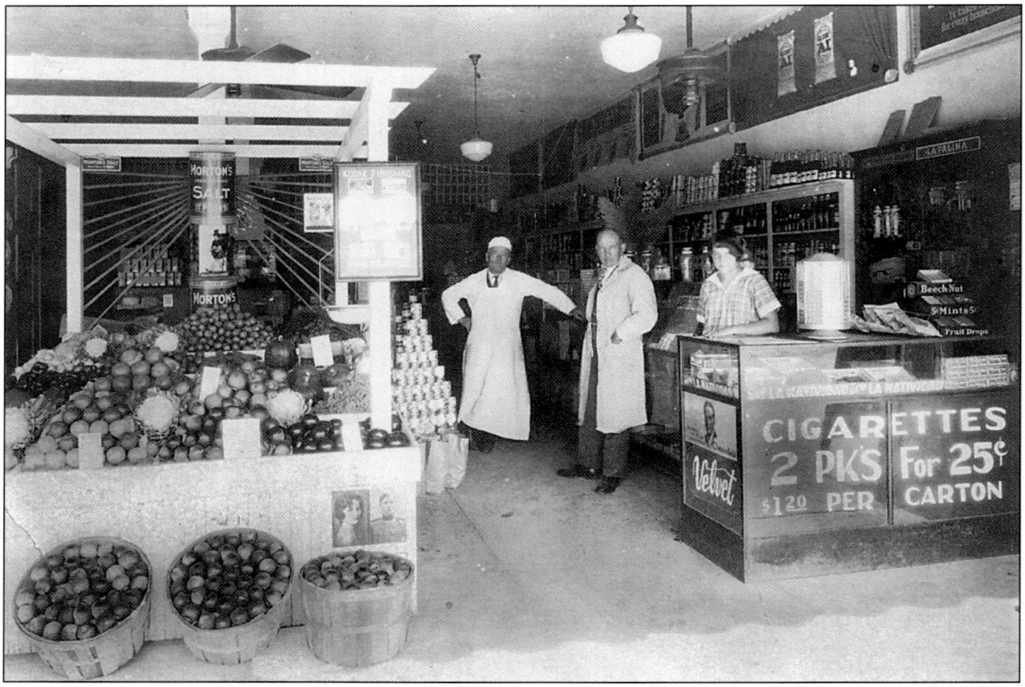

Interior of a Nordhoff Market. The actual name of the store depicted in this photograph is uncertain, but it may be the Ojai Cash Grocery, owned by L. B. Henry and F. H. Stewart. The sign on the post at the center of the picture advertises "Kodak Finishing" and displays some examples. (Kenneth and Kathryn Williams collection.)

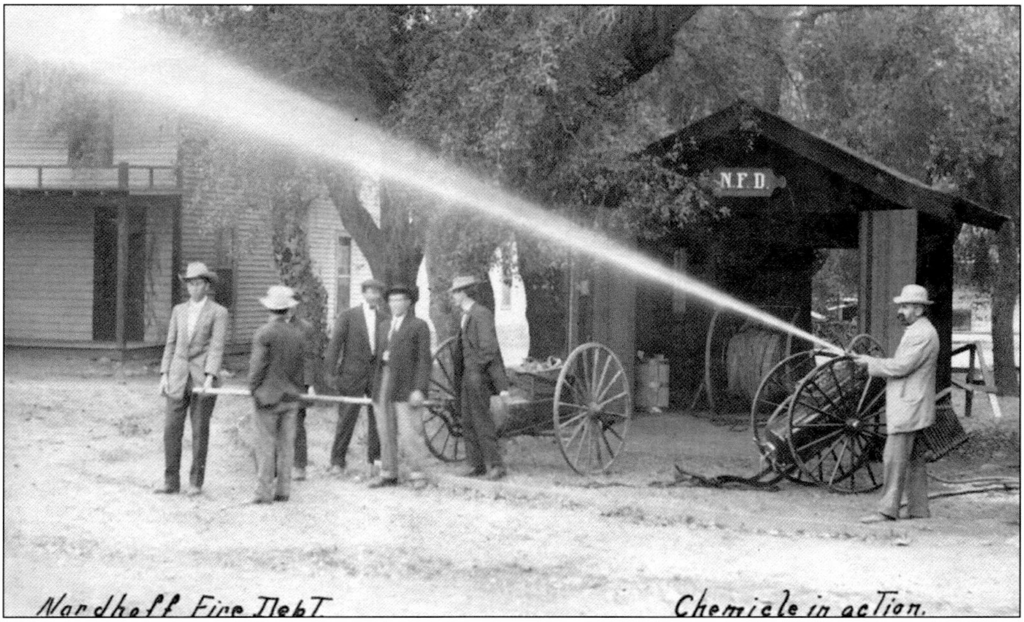

The Nordhoff Volunteer Fire Department. The building shown in this photograph was constructed in 1904, not far from the Ojai Inn, shown at the left. The volunteer fire department was organized in February of that year. The company obtained a soda and acid extinguisher in 1910, shown here being demonstrated. The wheeled extinguisher, next to the man holding the hose, is still on display in front of the fire station on East Ojai Avenue. (OVM Collection.)

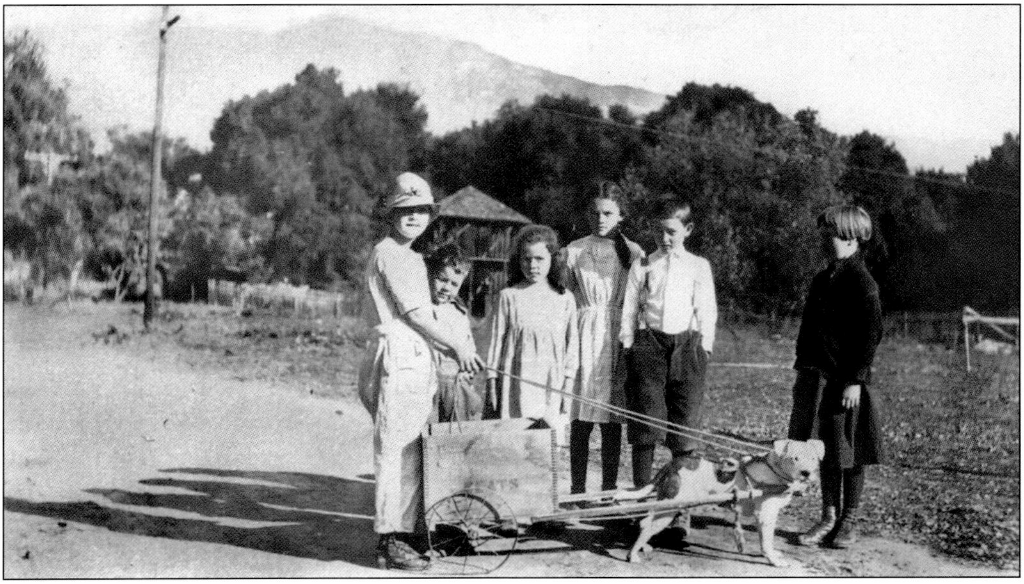

A Nordhoff Dog Cart. This photograph dates from about 1920 and depicts what appears to be a docile dog attached by children to a cart. Dacy Linder holds the reins. The names of the other children have not been identified. Dacy later attended San Jose Teacher's College and majored in art and music. Children participated in community parades at the time, and this dog cart may have been an entrant. (OVM Collection.)

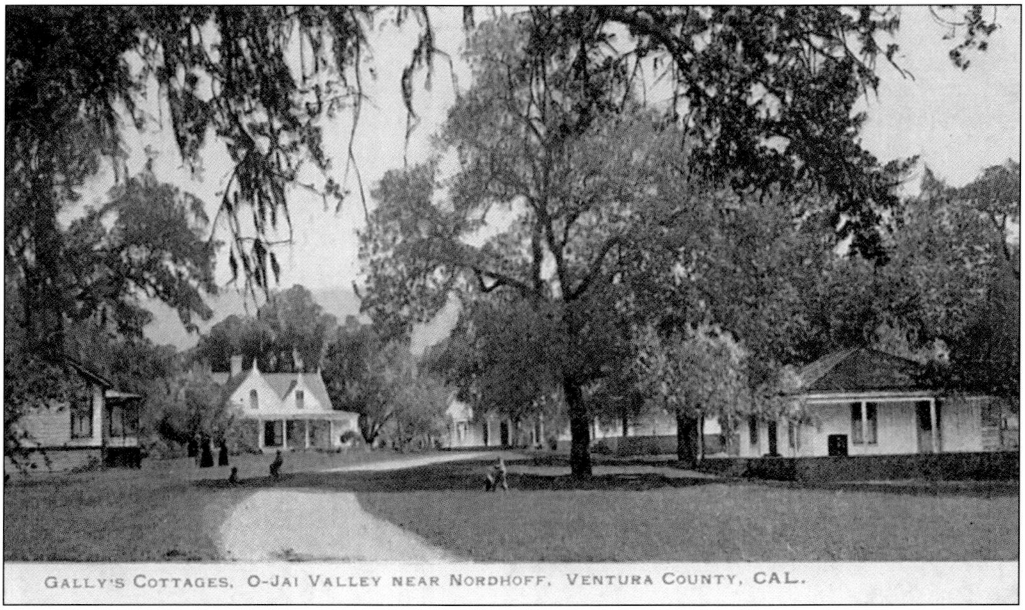

A WELCOMING VIEW OF GALLY COTTAGES. Gally Cottages were a principal accommodation for travelers in the valley for many years. Mary and William McKee first opened the cottages to visitors in 1874, the same year that the community of Nordhoff was founded. At that time, they called it Oak Glen Cottages and welcomed "invalids" who were seeking a cure in the fine Ojai Valley weather and environment. (Brian and Connie Aikens collection.)

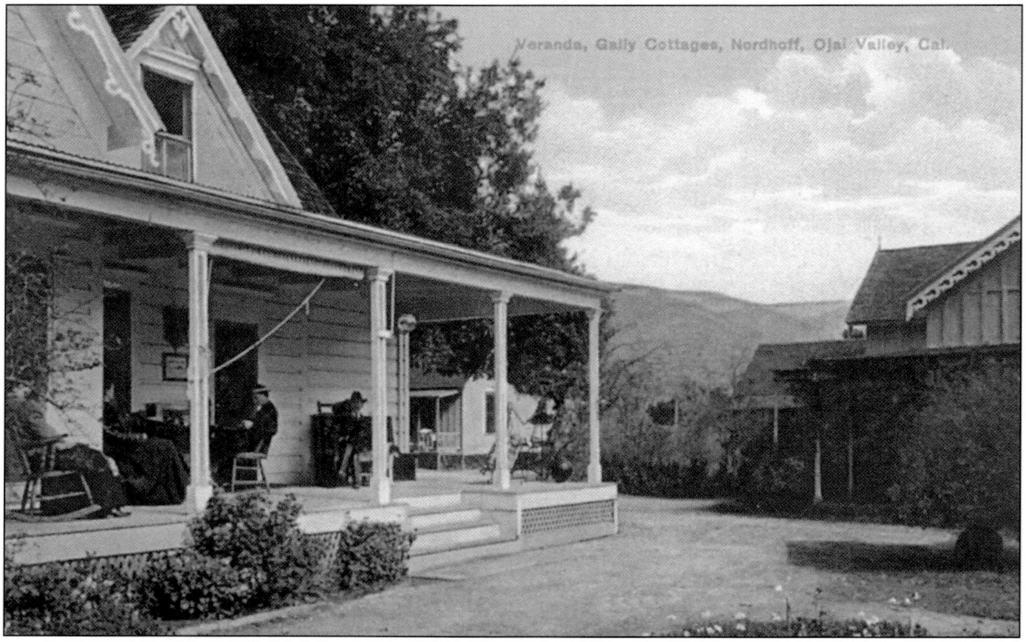

MAIN HOUSE AT GALLY COTTAGES. Benjamin Gally bought an interest in Oak Glen Cottages in 1883; by the time of his early death in 1893, he was sole owner. His wife, Mary, changed the name of the cottages to Gally Cottages, the name by which they were known for most of their existence. The main house at Gally Cottages included a common dining room and sitting room. (OVM Collection.)

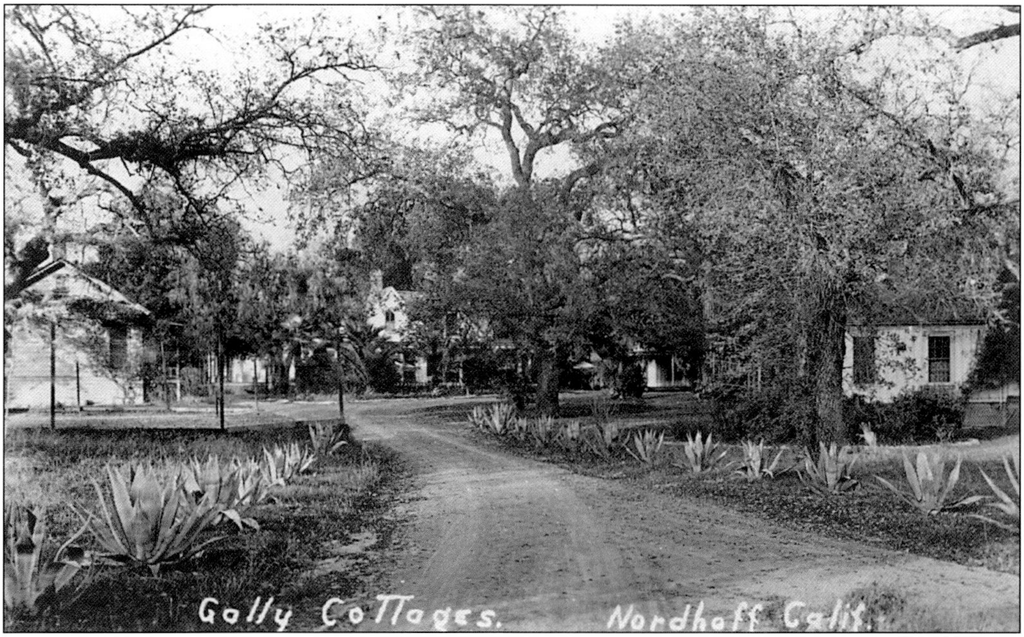

Landscaping at Gally Cottages. Mary Gally managed the cottages after her husband's death. They were no longer simply a place for invalids. Mary operated a stagecoach line from her cottages direct to Santa Barbara. Golf was first played in the valley at Gally Cottages in 1899. The local newspaper reported that "the golf links were cared for by a one-horse lawn mower." (Carol Cohen collection.)

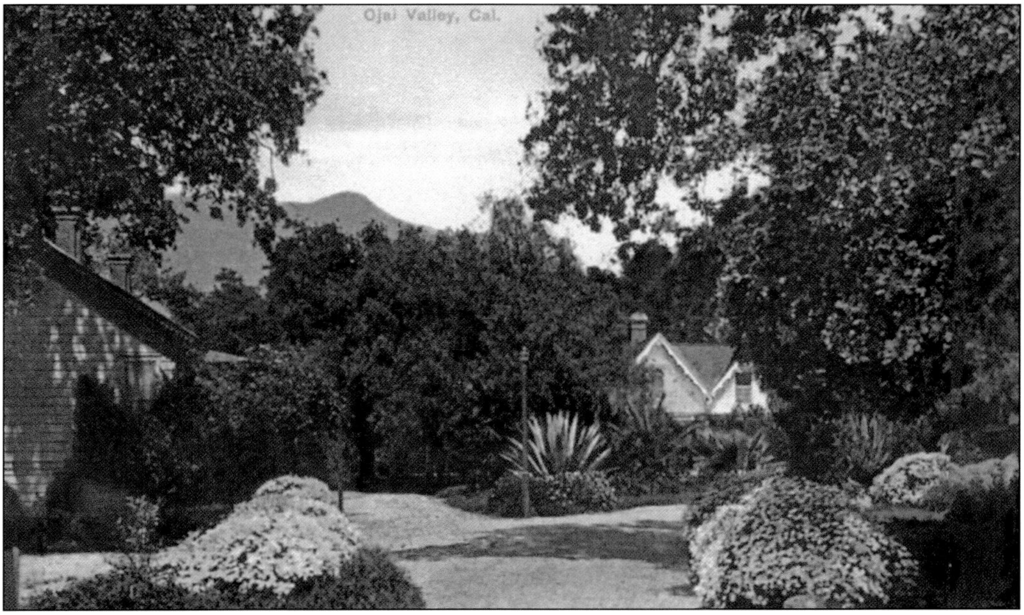

Gally Cottages in Full Glory. Charles Nordhoff and his family stayed here each time that he visited the valley. His first visit, in company with William Hollister and Dixie Thompson, was made in an overnight stay on October 22, 1881. He returned in 1889 and 1894. Good food was probably one of the cottages' strong points. A listing in the telephone directory for Gally Cottages in 1910 claimed that they served a "table unexcelled." (OVM Collection.)

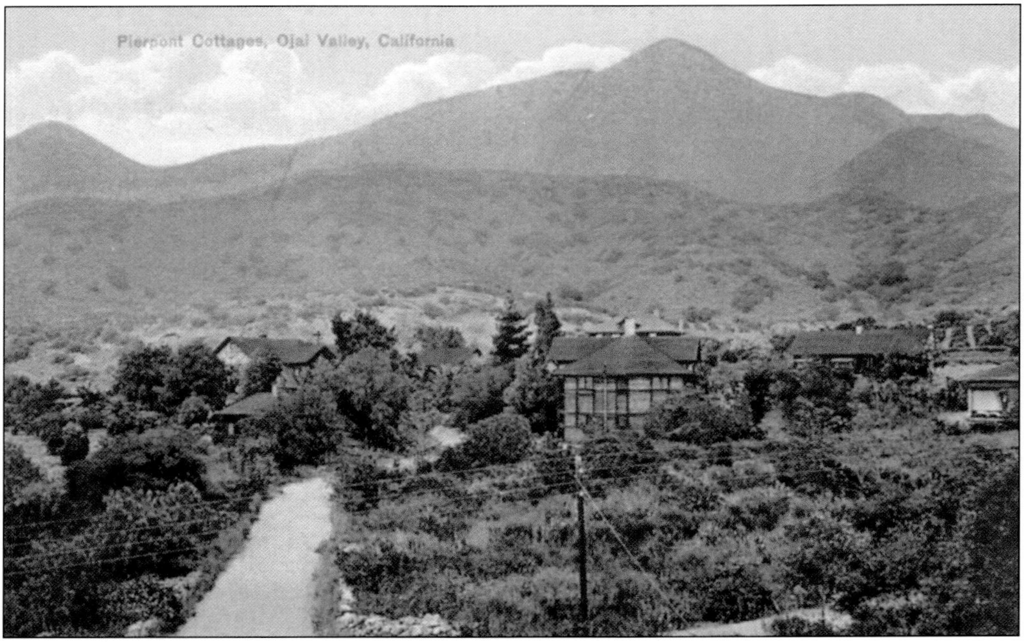

Overview of Pierpont Cottages. Pierpont Cottages were first opened in 1892 at the east end of the valley by Ernest and Josephine Pierpont, primarily to provide accommodations for parents visiting students at the Thacher School. In that year, eight cottages were constructed and at first were given the collective name The Overlook. The name was changed to Pierpont Cottages in 1900. (Brian and Connie Aikens collection.)

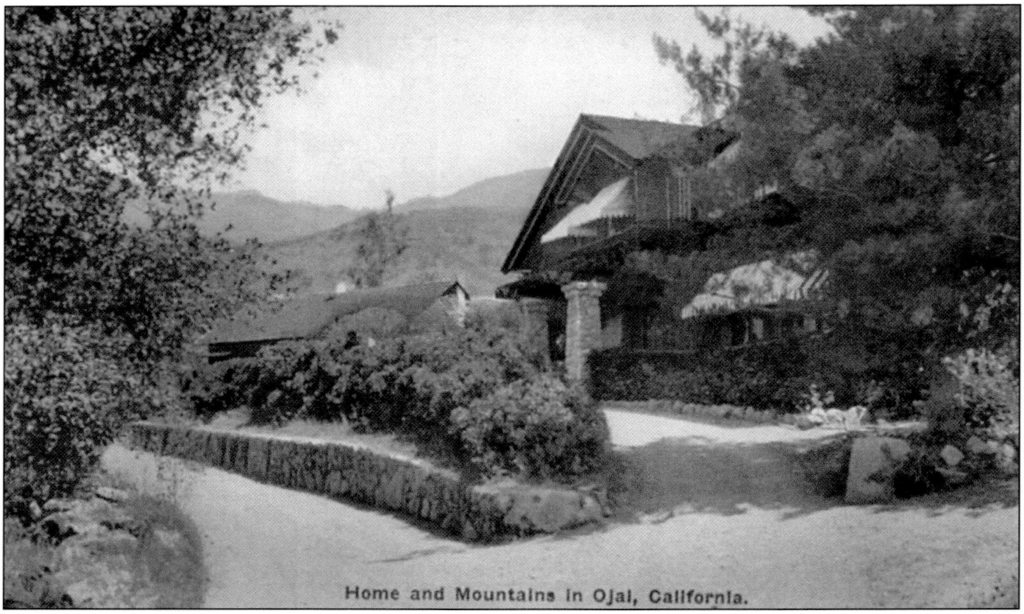

The Pierpont-Ginn House. After the death of her husband in 1905, Josephine Pierpont married San Francisco publisher Frederick Ginn. She commissioned the famous California architect Julia Morgan to design a house for her in 1908. Seen here is the house that resulted, one of Morgan's first residential works. The family's first home then became the main house for Pierpont Cottages. (David Mason collection.)

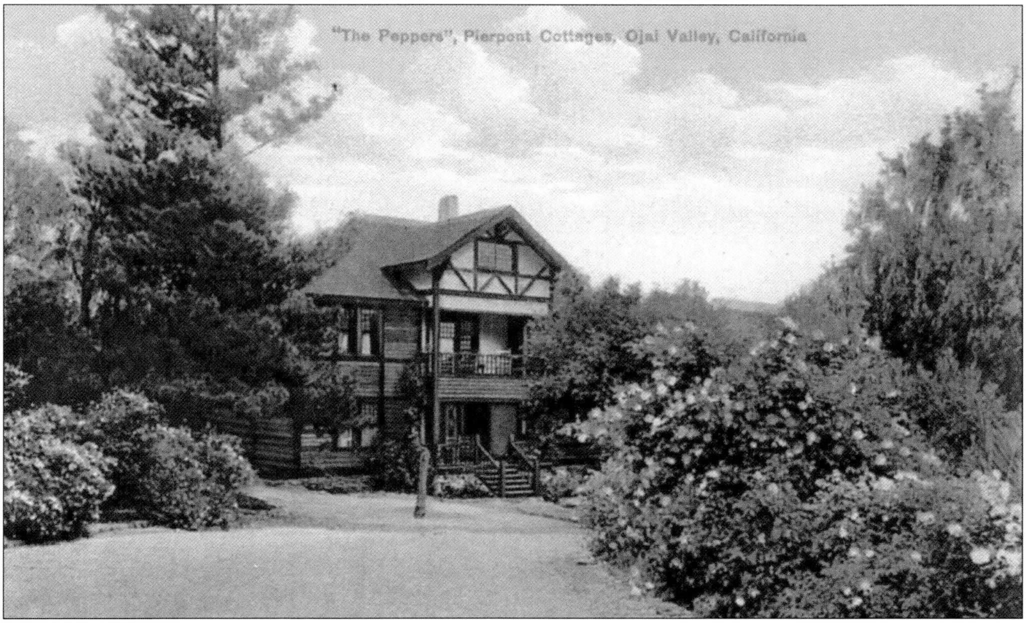

THE PEPPERS AT PIERPONT COTTAGES. This Tudor/craftsman building shows the architectural style typical of Pierpont Cottages. Numerous famous visitors stayed here. Lucretia Garfield, widow of assassinated president James A. Garfield, visited in 1904. Wendell Willkie stayed in 1940, the year that he announced his candidacy for U.S. president. (George Finn collection.)

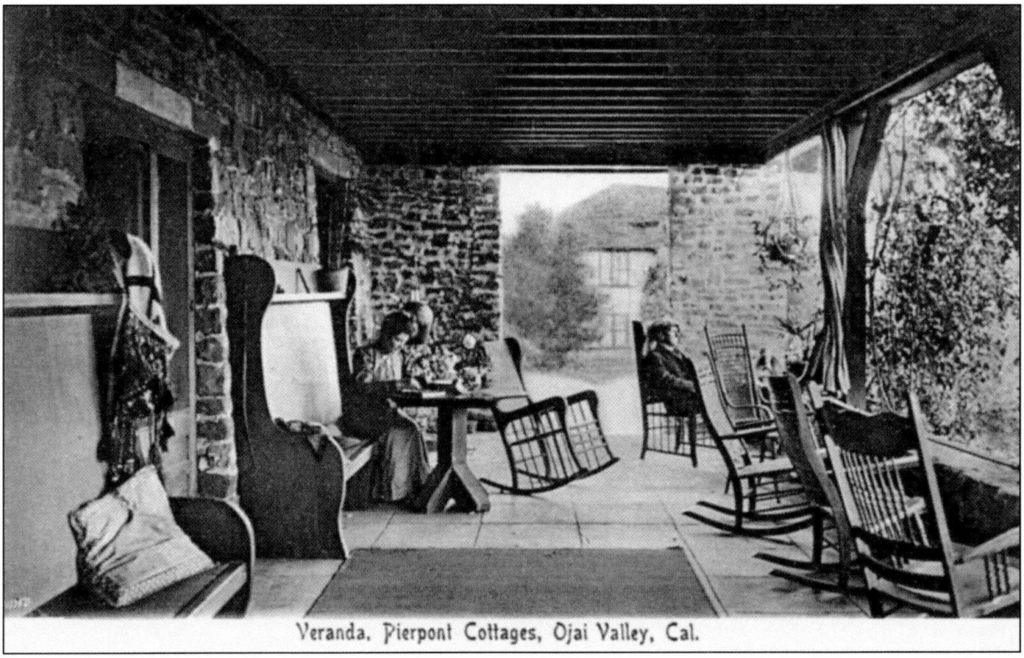

PORCH OF THE MAIN HOUSE AT PIERPONT COTTAGES. In 1908, the maximum charge for a night's stay at Pierpont Cottages was $3. They were popular with valley visitors in town for the Ojai Tennis Tournaments. The cottages remained in service until the start of World War II. Josephine Pierpont-Ginn also commissioned construction of the Woman's Club in Ojai and the Pierpont Inn in Ventura. (George Finn collection.)

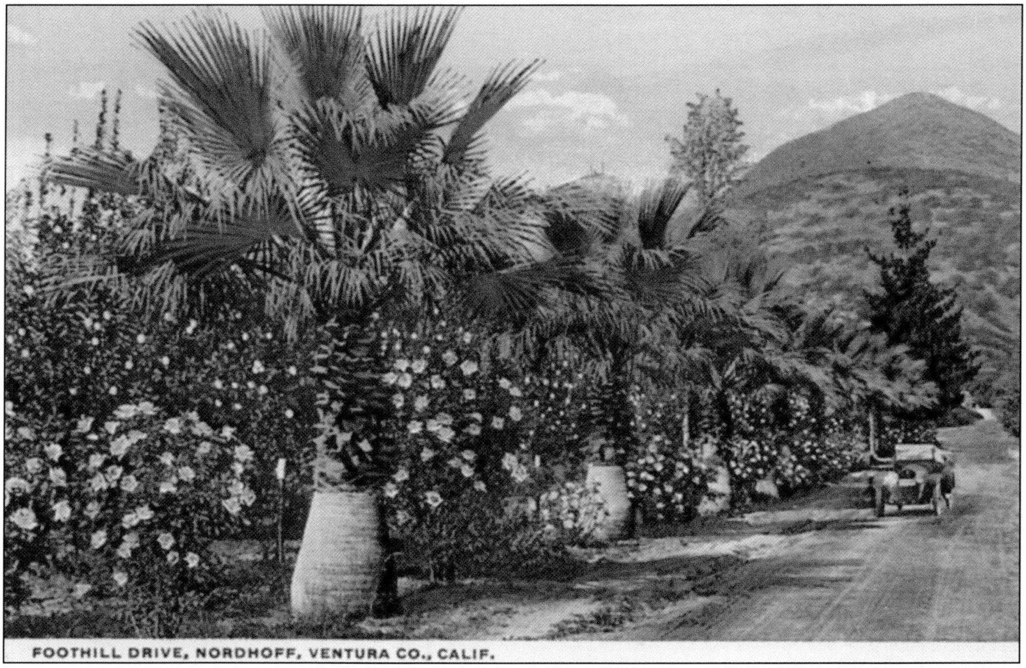

ON THE WAY TO FOOTHILLS HOTEL. The Ojai Improvement Company commissioned construction of the first Foothills Hotel in 1903, and the hotel opened on January 19, 1904. It was located in the hills immediately to the north of what was then still called the community of Nordhoff. Foothill Drive, shown in this picture, is now named Foothill Road, and the hotel was at the road's northern end. Even the road itself bespoke luxury. (OVM Collection.)

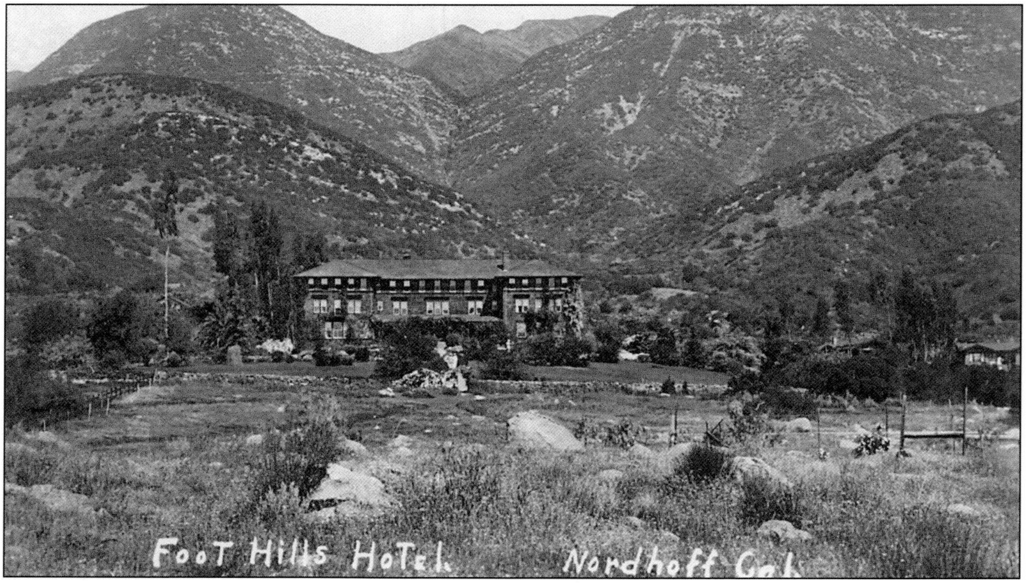

FOOTHILLS HOTEL, AROUND 1905. The hotel was a luxury hotel but was located nowhere near a main highway. Its rugged mountain setting was part of its appeal. Visitors to the hotel might take horseback rides up trails that were cut into the mountains. The Charles Pratt Trail was constructed to ascend the canyon at the center of the picture. The grounds were eventually developed to include a golf course. (Carol Cohen collection.)

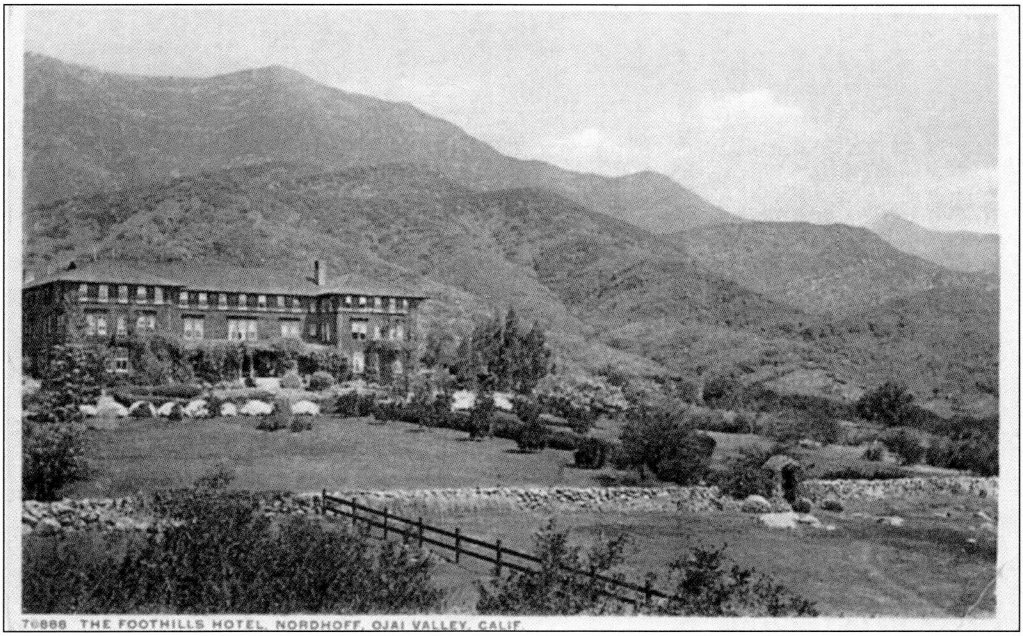

EDWARD LIBBEY AND THE FOOTHILLS HOTEL. Edward Libbey, the famous glass manufacturer, was drawn to the Ojai Valley in 1908 because of the enjoyable accommodations of the Foothills Hotel. In the following year, he commissioned construction of a house near the hotel. This was the beginning of the profound impact that would result from Libbey's interest in development projects in the valley. (David Mason collection.)

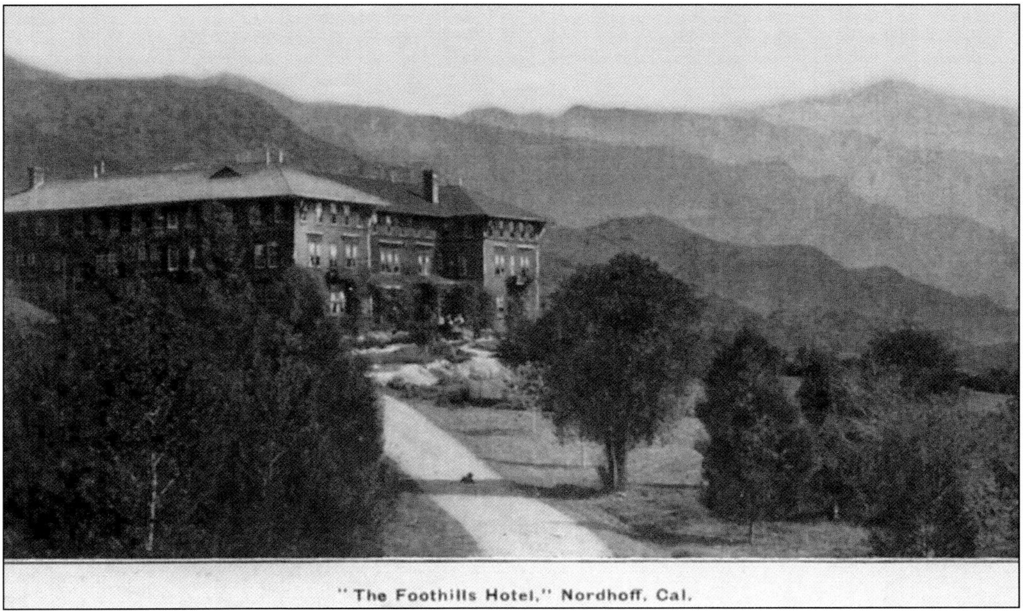

BRIEF LIFE OF THE FIRST FOOTHILLS HOTEL. A great fire roared through the valley in 1917, destroying everything in its path. This building burned to the ground. Its demise marked the end of early development in the valley but at the same time began a new phase in the valley's history. A second Foothills Hotel was built on the same site, and it followed not the craftsman design but the Mission Revival design promoted by Edward Libbey. (OVM Collection.)

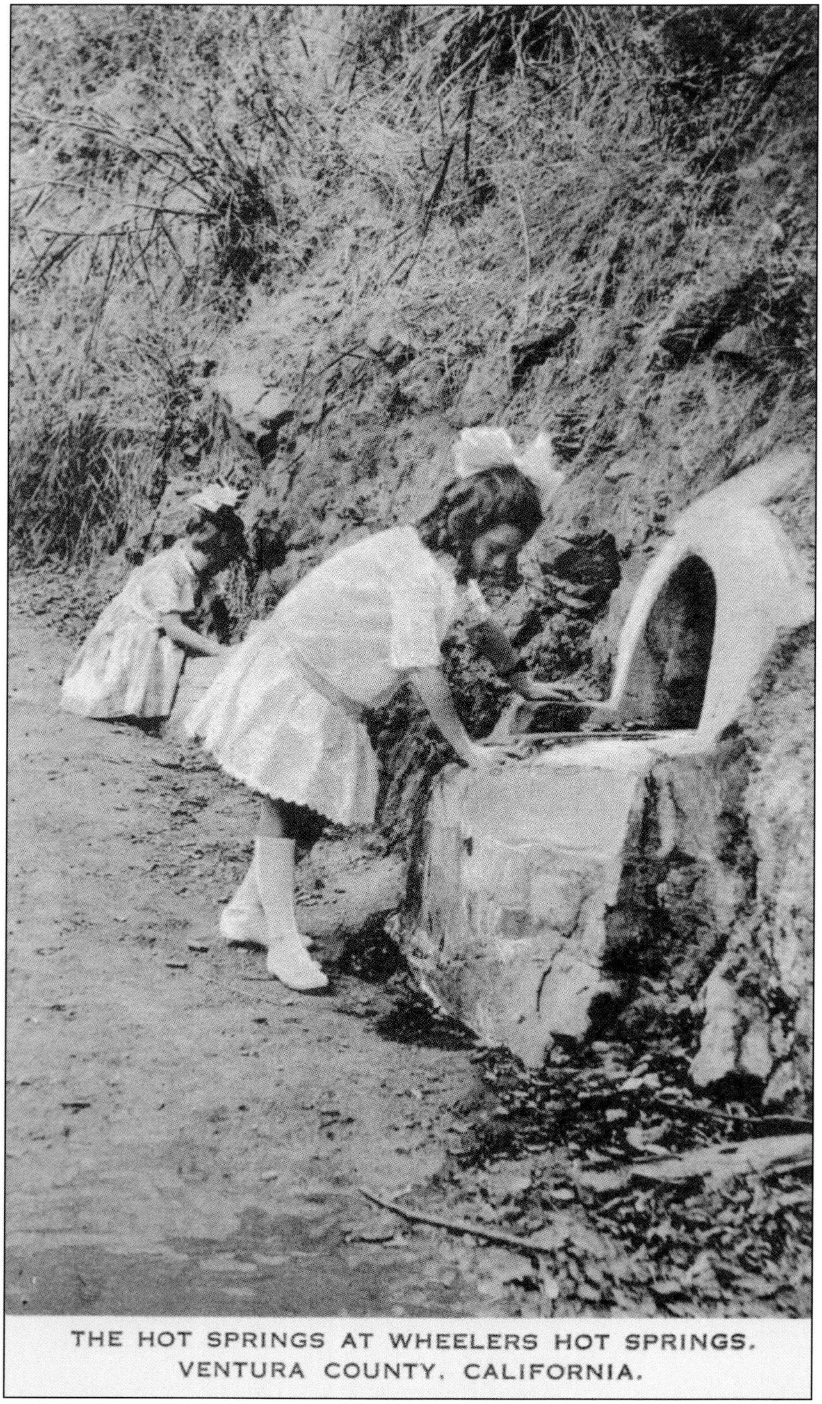

SAMPLING WATERS OF THE HOT SPRINGS. The camps in Matilija Canyon were established to take advantage of natural mineral water springs. One visitor to Matilija Hot Springs in 1935 reported, "We slid into three separate tubs . . . filled with hot, strong-smelling sulfur water. Beside each tub was a small table with a large glass full of the pungent water. It was supposed to be good for you, very cleansing, the management told us." (John Fritsche collection.)

Five

Hot Springs and Mountain Resorts

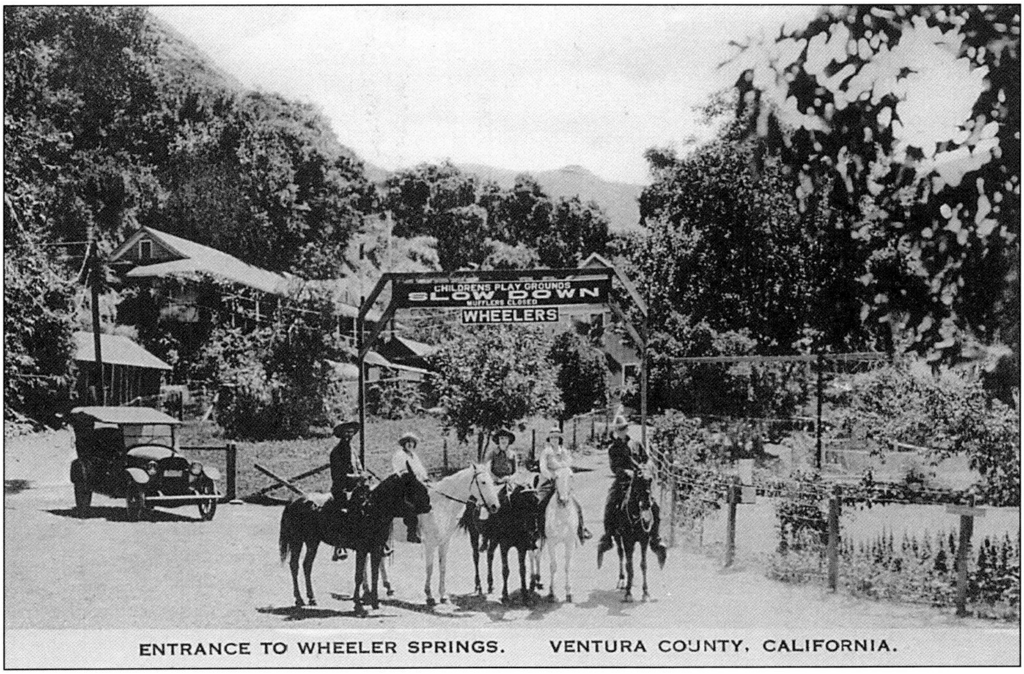

Entrance Gate at Wheeler's Springs. One of the first tourist attractions of the Ojai Valley were hot springs in Matilija Canyon. A series of camps were constructed in the canyon and promoted for their medicinal springs and refreshing mountain settings. Lyons Camp, Matilija Hot Springs, Wheeler's Hot Springs, Wilcox Cabins, Ojala, and Soper's Camp drew great numbers of visitors. (John Fritsche collection.)

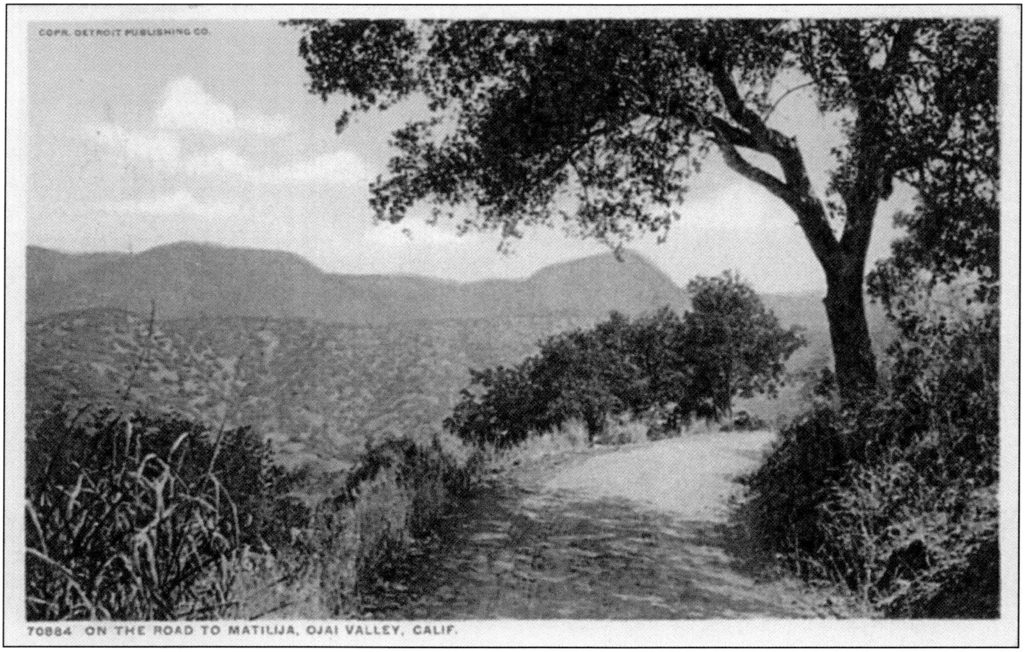

THE ROAD INTO MATILIJA CANYON. In the early years, access to Matilija Canyon was a problem. The *Ventura Signal* reported in May 1872 that "Five or six miles of the route is through a narrow mountain defile barely passable for a skillful horseman or hardy foot traveler." A road was opened by the summer of 1873, and stagecoach service soon began. (David Mason collection.)

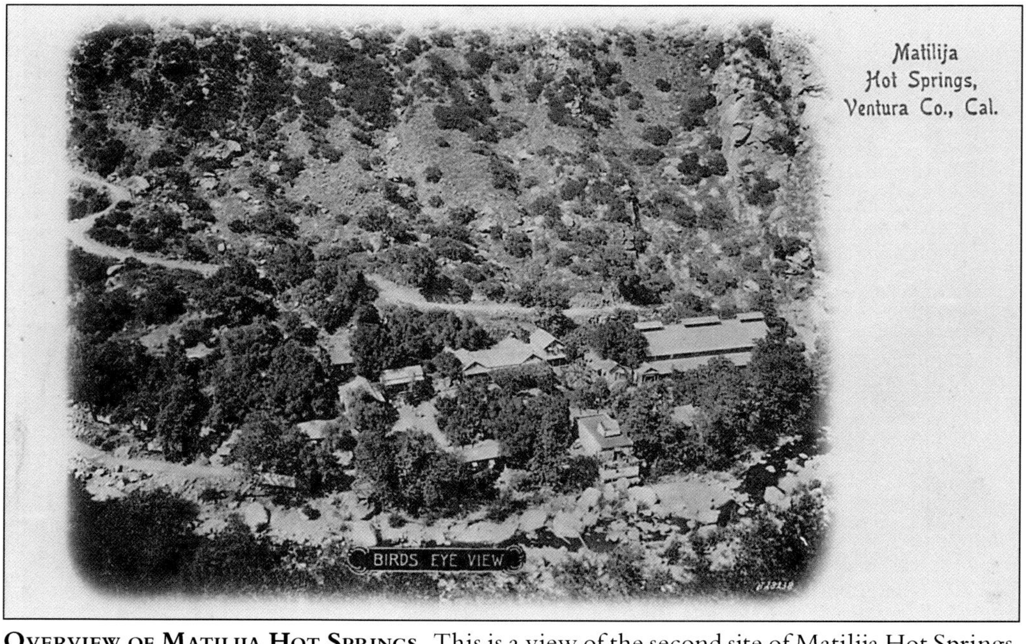

OVERVIEW OF MATILIJA HOT SPRINGS. This is a view of the second site of Matilija Hot Springs. The first site, established in 1871, was located several miles upstream. After damage from major flooding in 1884 and the death of the owner, the site was relocated downstream. The springs were located in a steep-sided canyon, which the photographer must have climbed to take this picture. (Brian and Connie Aikens collection.)

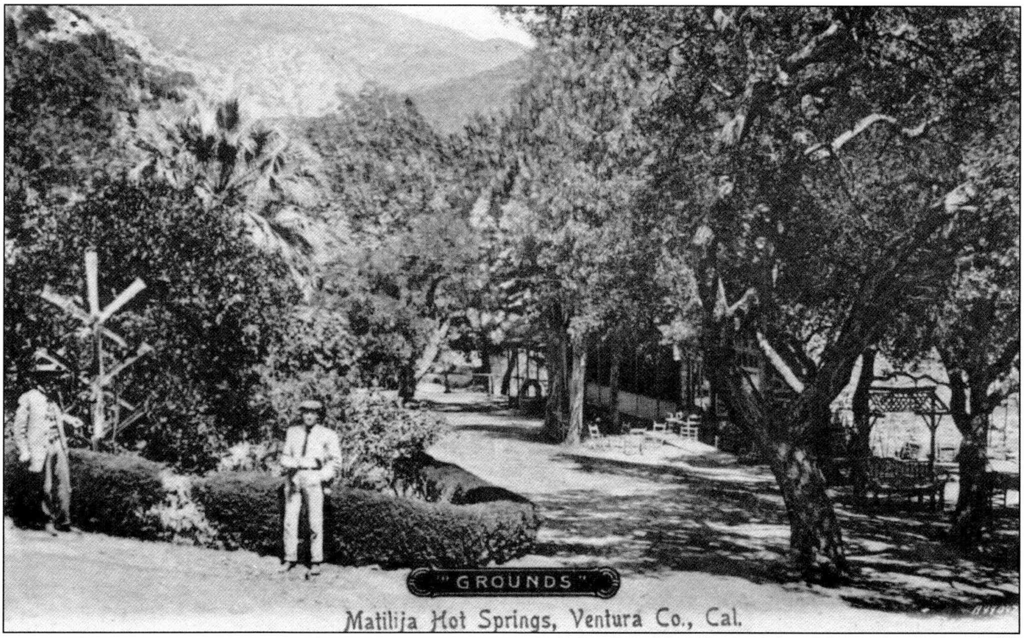

GROUNDS OF MATILIJA HOT SPRINGS. The *Ventura Daily Democrat* commented in May 1905 that Matilija Hot Springs was a place of "unmarred beauty . . . touched with a charm of comfort and restfulness." The article added, "Matilija Springs still holds first rank among California resorts famous for beauty, comfort, cleanliness, and ideal management." The function of the object at left center is uncertain. (OVM Collection.)

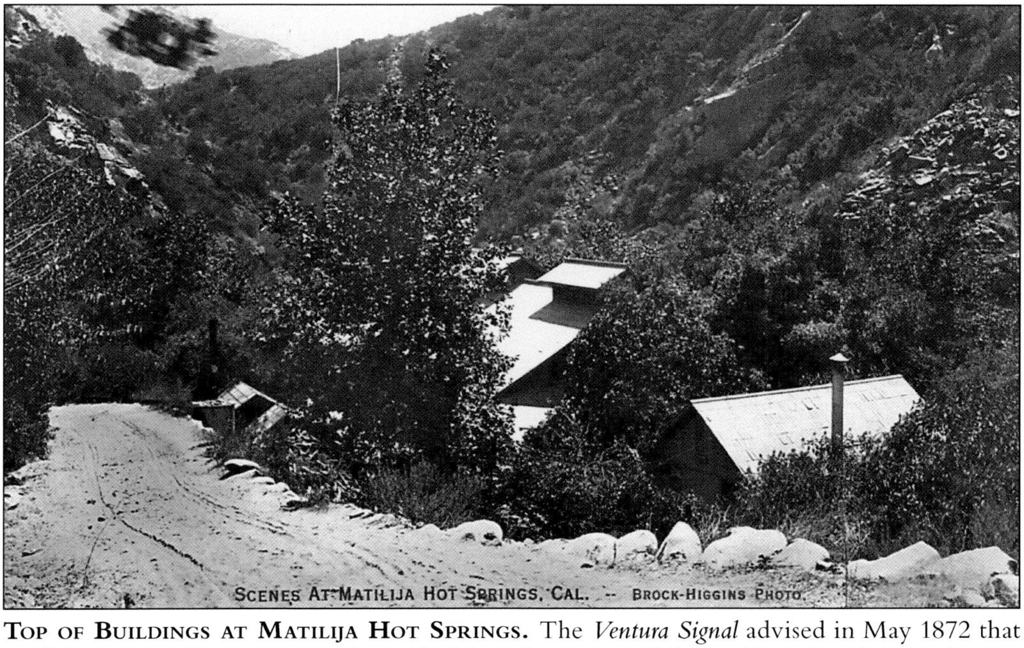

TOP OF BUILDINGS AT MATILIJA HOT SPRINGS. The *Ventura Signal* advised in May 1872 that until the canyon "is made passable and bathing places erected, it would not be advisable for any one to pay these springs a visit for pleasure." Perhaps it was good timing, for the wharf at Ventura went into operation for the first time in October of that year. Delivery of lumber from Northern California became much easier, and construction could proceed. (David Mason collection.)

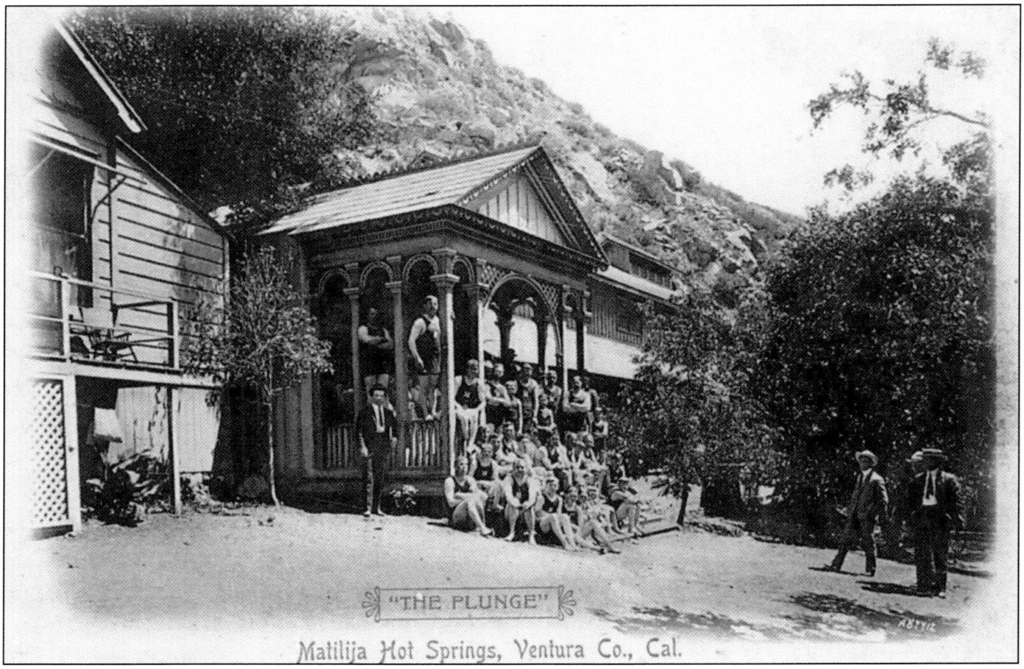

Bathers on the Steps of the Plunge. *The Ojai* newspaper reported in March 1902 that "Work on the building to surmount the plunges at Matilija Hot Springs has been begun, and the frameworks will be up in a couple of weeks with propitious weather." The indoor pool was 150 feet long and 65 feet wide. Individual dressing rooms accommodated 70 people. Electric lights illuminated the grounds, and there was a covered dance pavilion. (Terry Hill collection.)

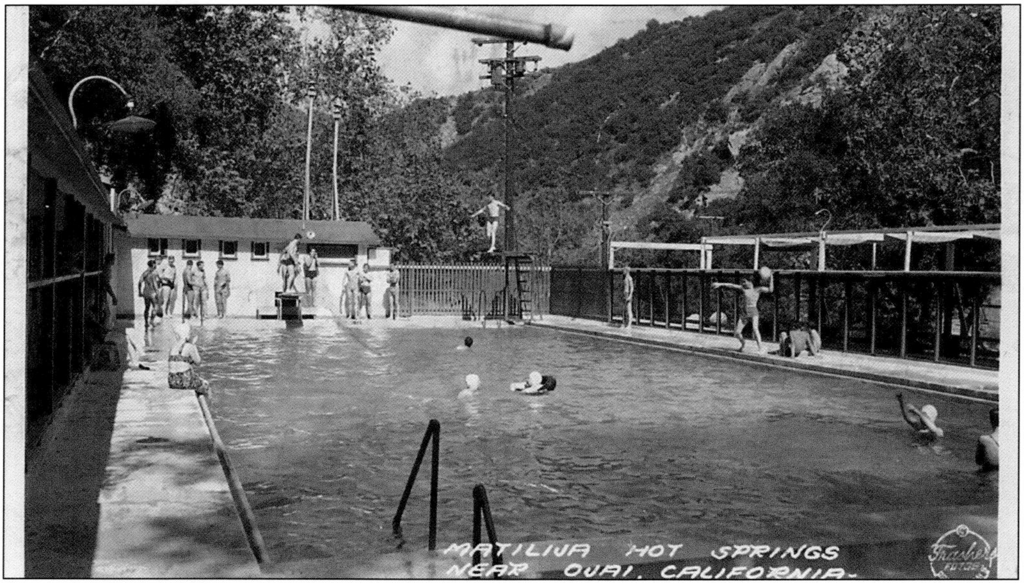

Later Open Pool at Matilija Hot Springs. Buildings and facilities at each of the Matilija Canyon camps were replaced over time, often due to the fact that one or the other had been destroyed by floodwaters. Here is a replacement to the earlier plunge at Matilija Hot Springs. The scarcity of swimming pools elsewhere in the county resulted in lots of summer traffic to the pools in Matilija Canyon. (Kay Renuis collection.)

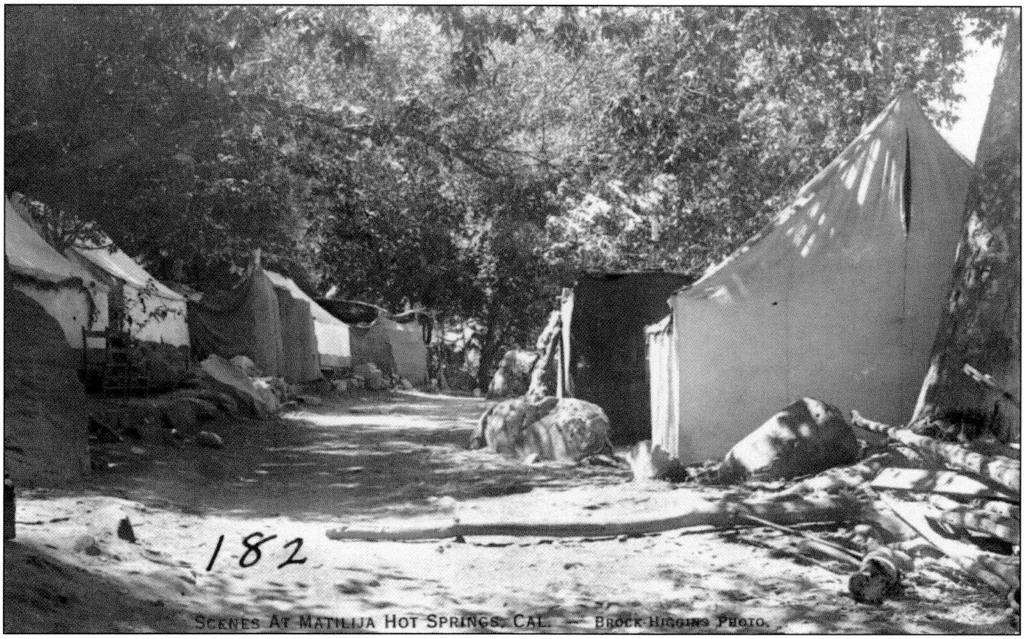

Tenting at Matilija Hot Springs. Tents have been set up in a Sycamore grove at Matilija Hot Springs. The tents are large enough to accommodate families, and they appear to have been placed on wooden frame platforms. A bird feeder hangs in the tree at center right. Some families at the time would spend the better part of a summer camped at the springs. (Terry Hill collection.)

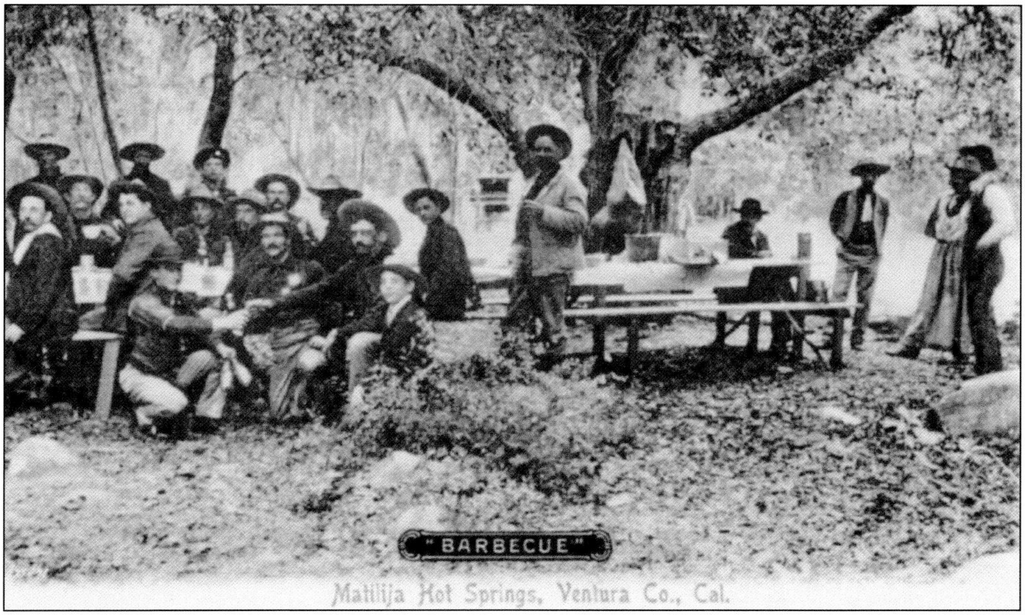

A Barbecue at Matilija Hot Springs. Men with broad-brimmed hats gather at picnic tables at Matilija Hot Springs for a barbecue. Is this a special celebration? One man at the center left appears to be wearing a badge. Are these men associated with law enforcement? The cook stands at the right with his long apron. Are the bottles being opened at the left full of sarsaparilla? (Terry Hill collection.)

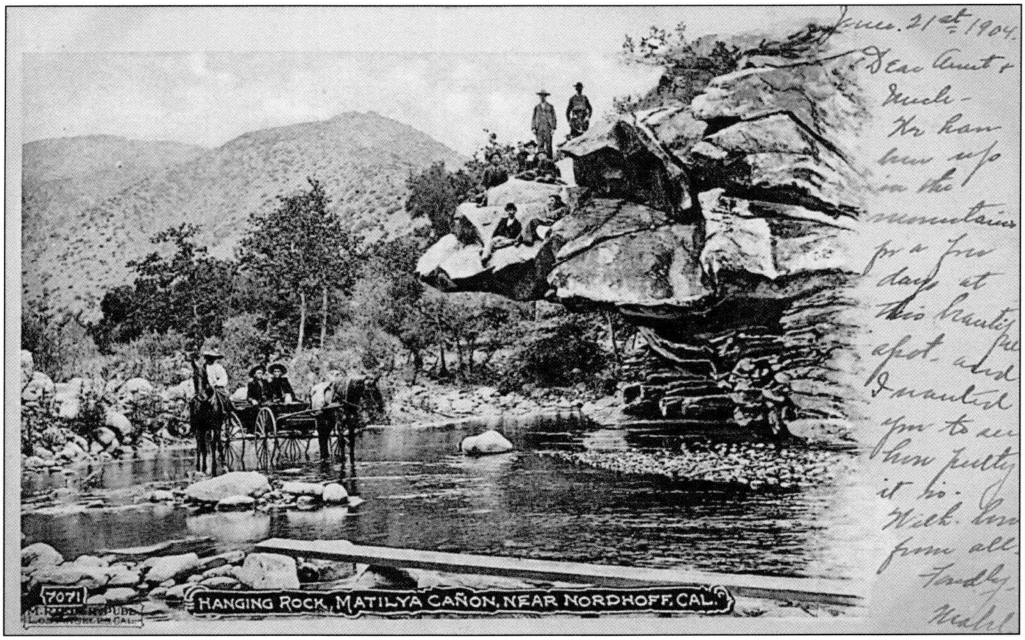

Hanging Rock, Looking Upstream, 1904. Hanging Rock was one of the principal attractions of Matilija Hot Springs, and climbing up on top of it was a great pastime. Here a group of men poses on top of the rock. The spelling of Matilija on the postcard is incorrect. The word is derived from the name of a Native American village that was once located at the mouth of the canyon. (Brian and Connie Aikens collection.)

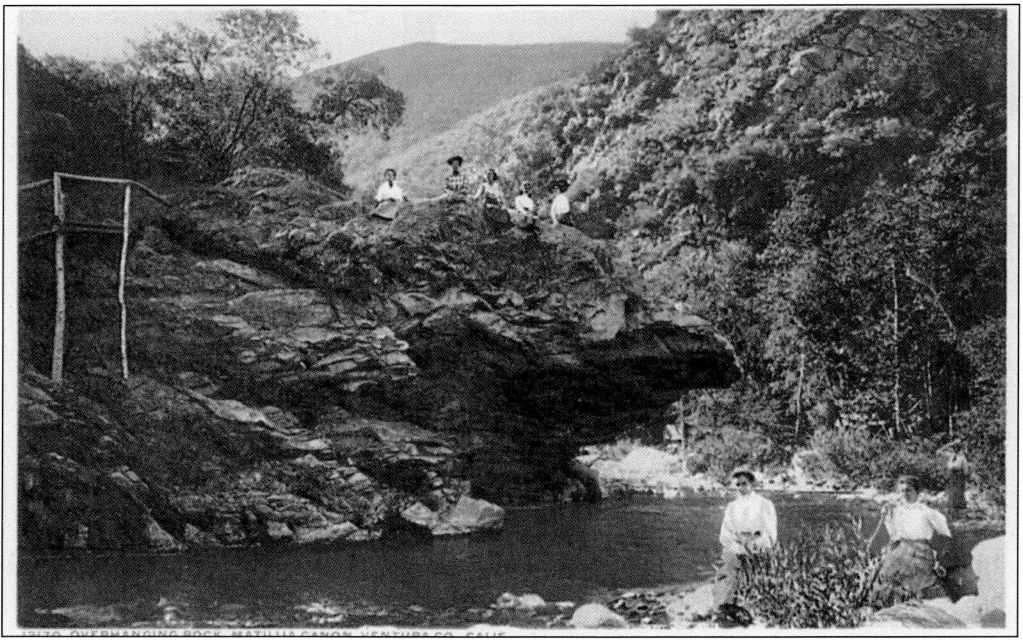

Hanging Rock, Looking Downstream. These women are perhaps the other half of the party seen above. The springs were open only during summer months, and May 1 was usually opening day. A newspaper in 1905 reported on preparations for the opening day, adding that 50,000 trout had been seeded into the waters of Matilija Creek. (Brian and Connie Aikens collection.)

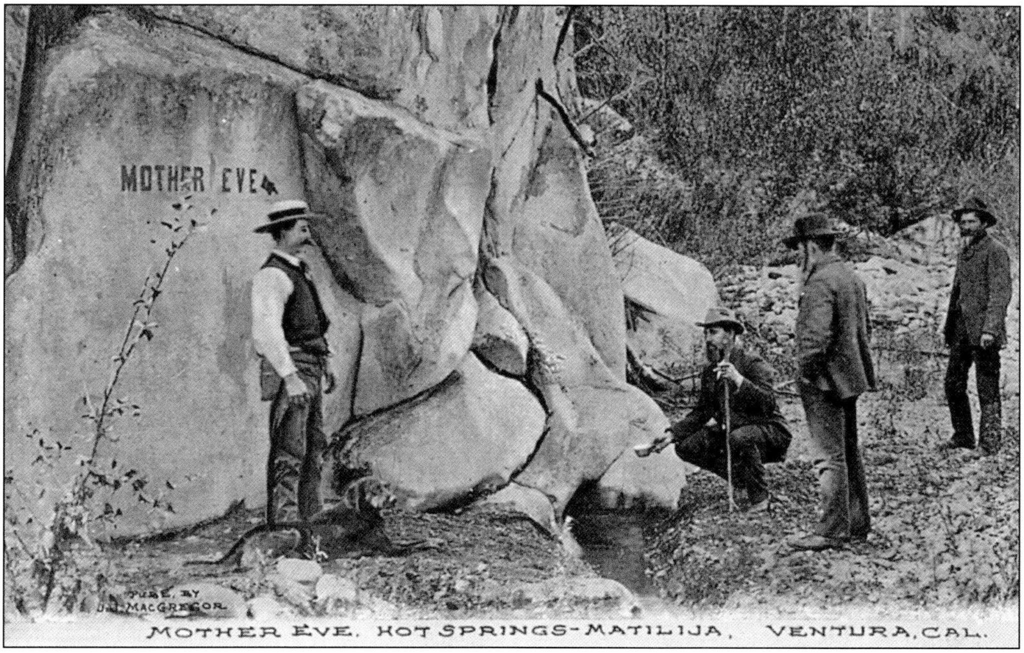

The "Mother Eve" Spring. An article in the *Ventura Signal* in November 1873 was headlined, "The Ojai—The Sanitarium of the World." In that year, the owner of the springs advertised his camp as having a hotel "ready for invalids." The mineral waters, of course, were reputed to be effective in curing a host of ailments. (John Fritsche collection.)

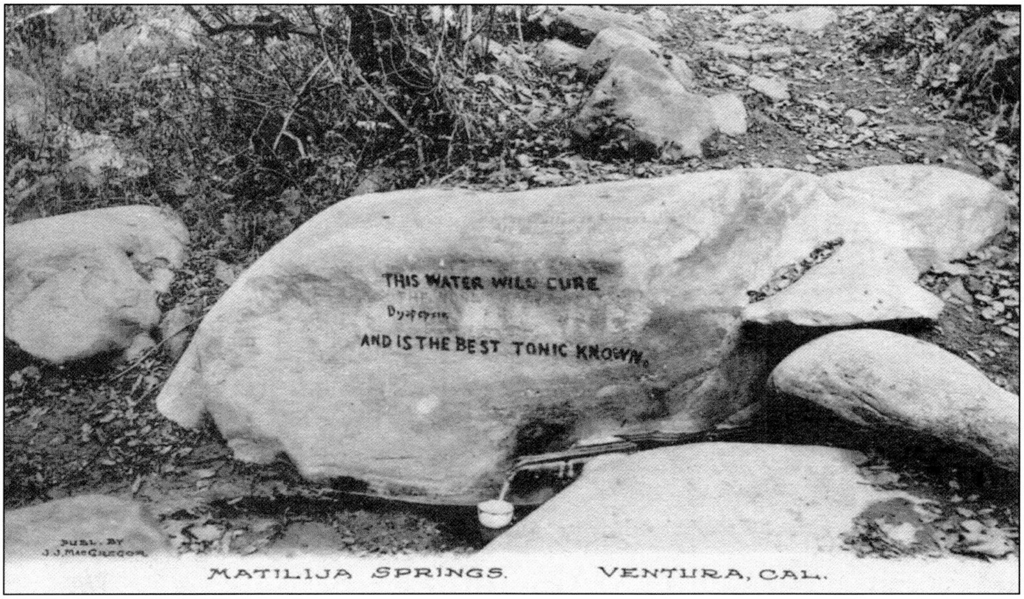

"The Best Tonic Known." An anonymous journalist for the *Santa Barbara Press* wrote in August 1874, "I have found a place of happy seclusion, a quiet retreat . . . where the air is calm and pure; nature in her wildest mood has fashioned a narrow, winding glen." The writer lauded it as a place where a person could "drown for a while his vexations in a bath, and gratitude is uppermost in his mind for the rest of the day." (Terry Hill collection.)

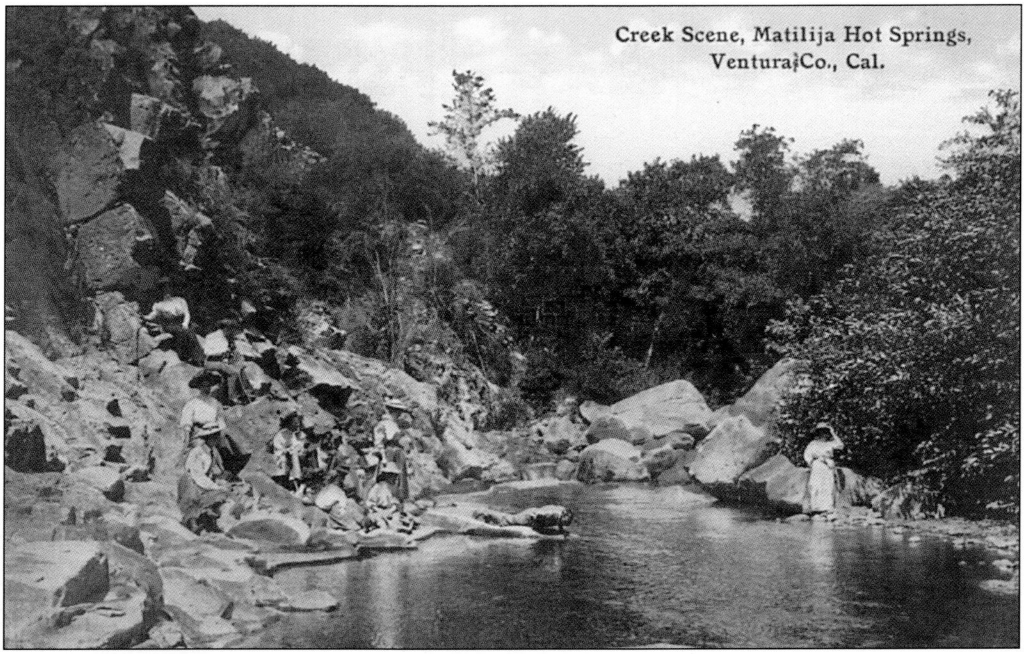

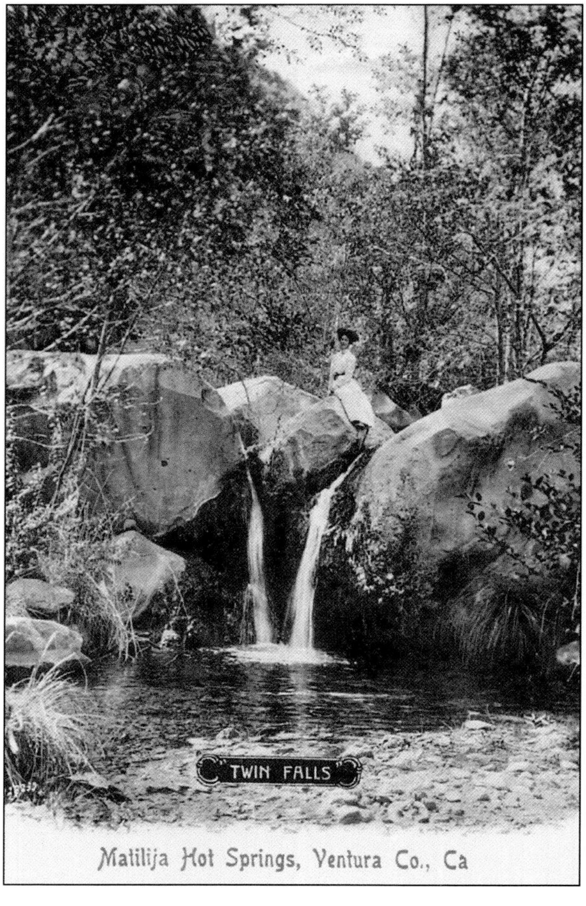

WOMEN GATHERING ALONG MATILIJA CREEK. What's a man to do in the company of nine women? The women enjoy the sun and the pleasure of the environment. He is flat on his stomach staring into the water! Does he see a trout? Is he looking for a lost ring? The women appear comfortable with his implied obeisance. (Brian and Connie Aikens collection.)

THE BEAUTY OF TWIN FALLS. A young woman sits atop the rocks that form Twin Falls, one of the attractions at Matilija Hot Springs. Her full-length skirt and covered arms suggest that the photograph was taken about 1910. The *Ventura Daily Democrat* reported in August 1905 that "A. F. Slade, photographer and 'scenic view sketcher' has been at work in the Matilija Canyon." Perhaps he caught this view. (Richard Barnett collection.)

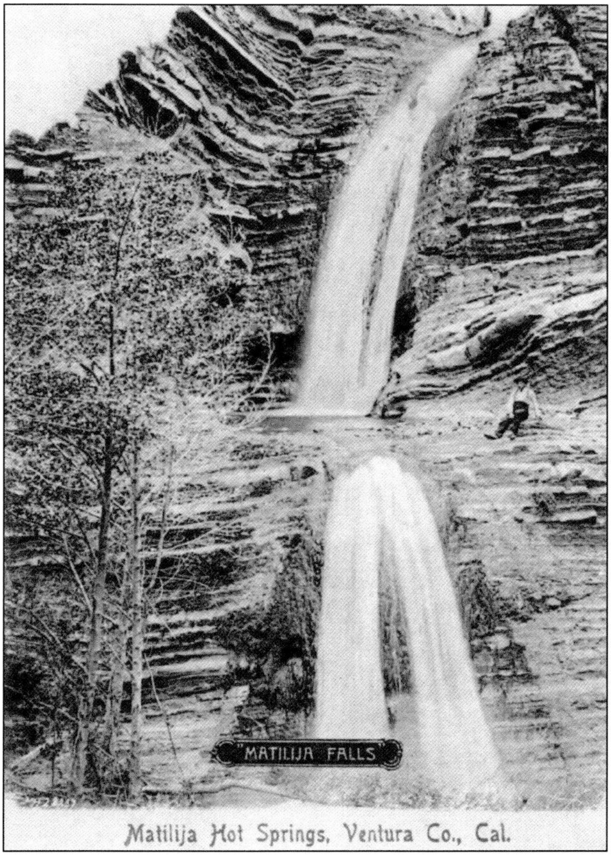

CLIMBERS AT MATILIJA FALLS. This postcard shows an image of the falls that were later lost with construction of Matilija Dam. Climbers have ascended the rugged outcrop of the Matilija Formation. The formation consists of sedimentary sandstone of such value that a mine was opened not far away from the falls. The mine has continued in operation to today. (OVM Collection.)

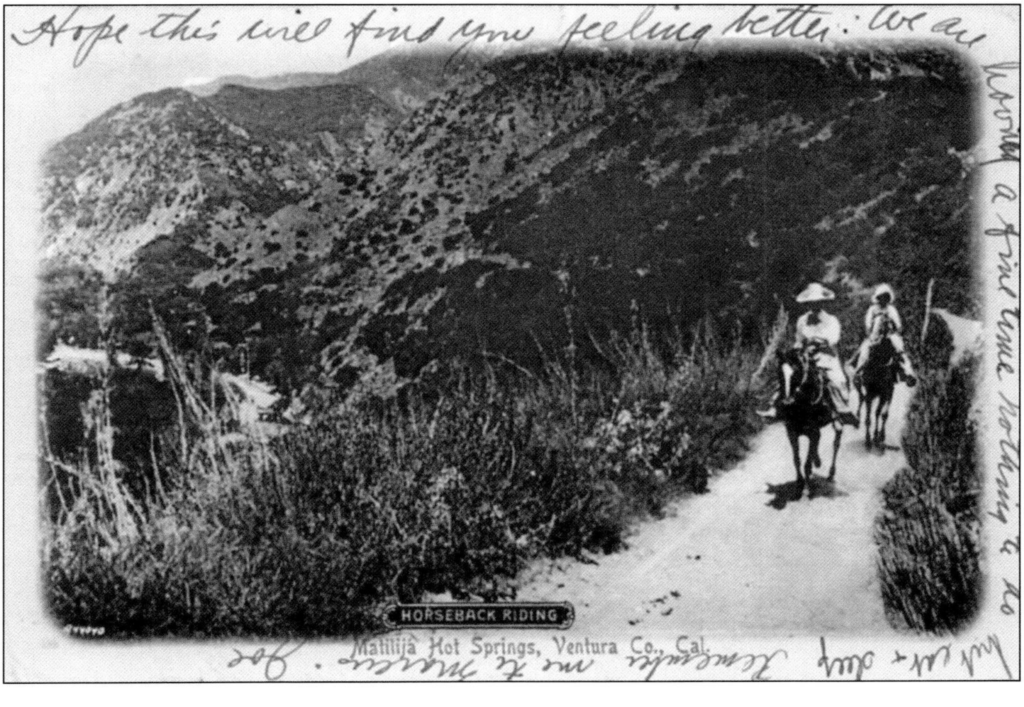

RIDING THE MOUNTAIN TRAILS. *The Ojai* newspaper reported in May 1892 that "Last Wednesday, Wheeler and Ward Blumberg piloted a party of Ventura people over to Cottonwood Camp on the Sespe, about 12 miles from the Matilija Springs." A system of mountain trails was constructed that connected the springs with locations such as Foothills Hotel in the Ojai Valley, Shepard's Inn at Carpinteria, and other mountain locations. (OVM Collection.)

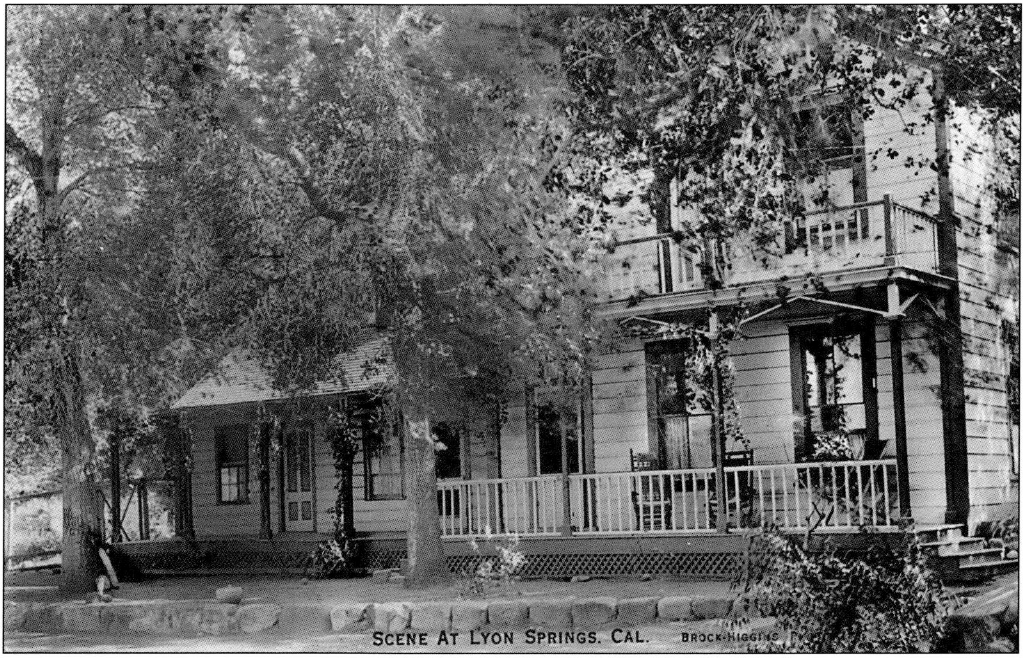

THE HOTEL AT LYON SPRINGS. Robert Lyon settled in Matilija Canyon in 1871 seeking restoration of his health. He established and maintained a productive ranch for 17 years, which he called Cliff Glen, before first welcoming guests in 1888. The hotel was ready for the opening day and was painted light gray with reddish-brown trim. (Terry Hill collection.)

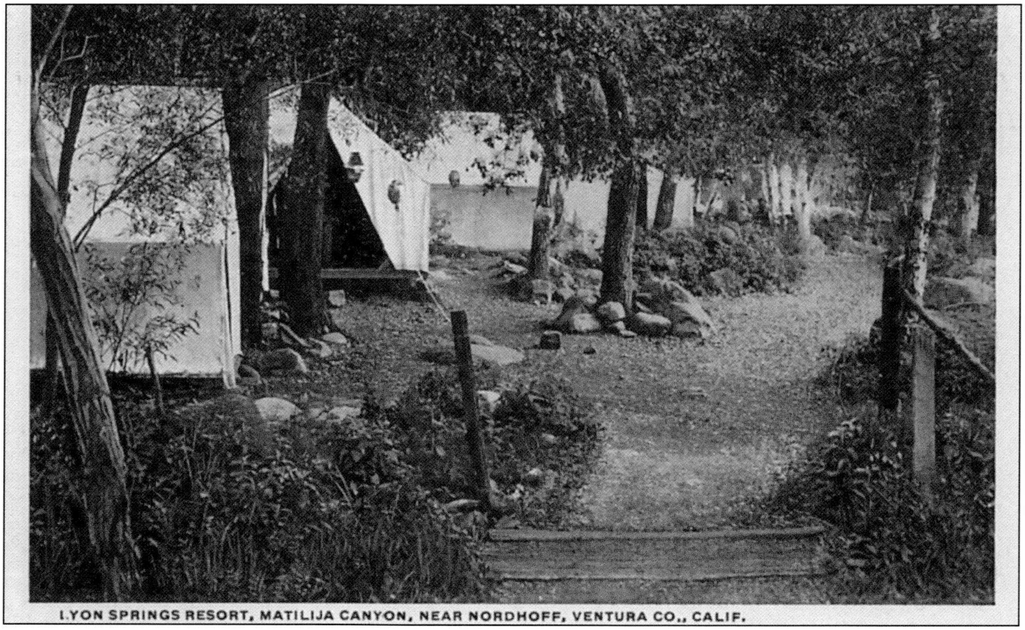

CAMPING AT LYON SPRINGS RESORT. Robert Lyon was reported to have 300 apple, 300 orange, 200 lemon, 50 lime, 500 walnut, 400 almond, and 150 peach trees, plus 600 grape vines. His campgrounds were established in a location that was still agricultural. A neighbor raised angora goats, and Lyon sued in 1877 to restrain his neighbor from allowing the goats to get into his fields and groves. (OVM Collection.)

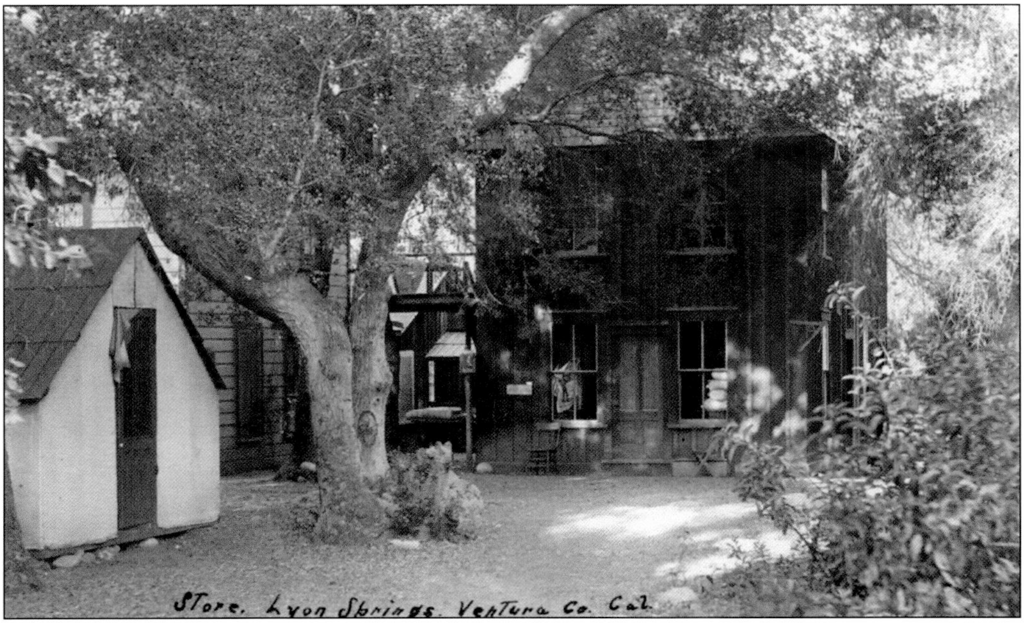

The Camp Store at Lyon Springs. Robert Lyon died in August 1889, the year following the opening of his camp. Nonetheless, his wife, Gertrude, and his daughter, Belle, carried on with the camp management for some 30 years thereafter. Cliff Glen was not called Lyon Springs until 1906, when a post office was opened at the camp, probably in the store shown in this picture. (John Fritsche collection.)

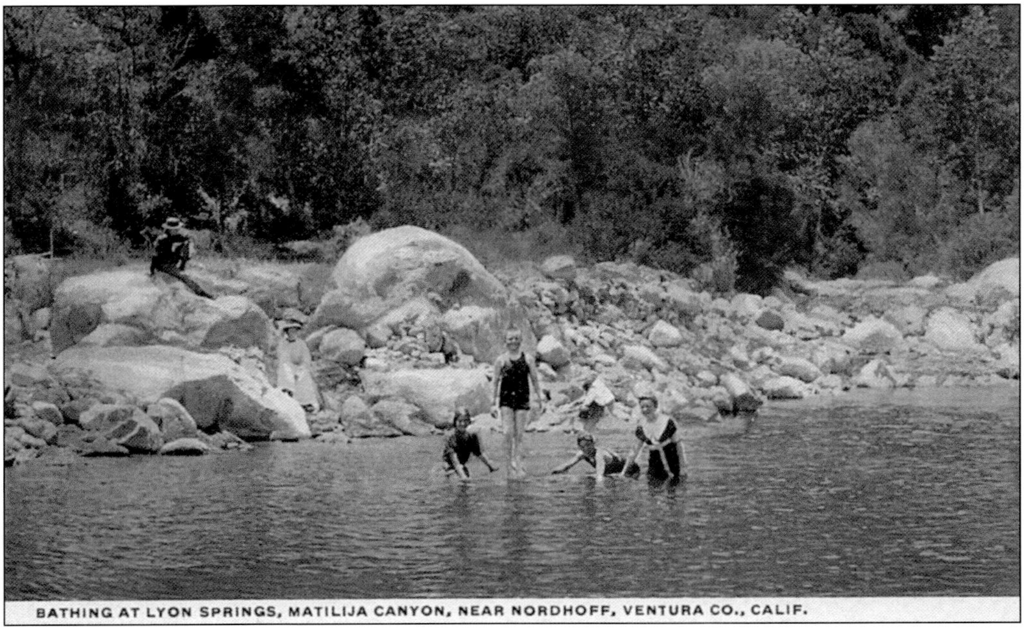

Bathers at Lyon Springs. The camp was situated on the north or left bank of Matilija Creek, several miles west of what is now Maricopa Highway. The creek, of course, was one of its major attractions. The camp was cut off by flooding in 1884, which largely destroyed Matilija Hot Springs. Lyon's served as a temporary refuge. The family's milk cows were marooned on the opposite side of the creek. (OVM Collection.)

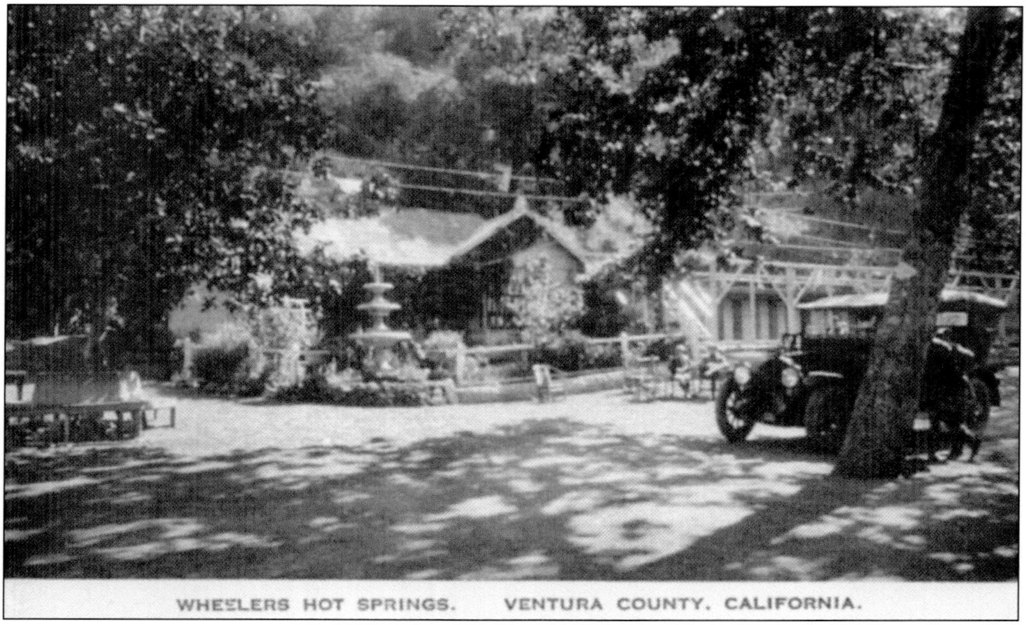

WHEELER'S HOT SPRINGS. Opened to the public by Wheeler Blumberg in 1891, Wheeler's Hot Springs were located in the north fork of Matilija Canyon. His father, Abram Blumberg, had constructed the first hotel in Nordhoff in 1874 and had also owned and managed the Ojai Hot Springs at the mouth of Matilija Canyon from 1887 to 1899 (afterwards known as Matilija Hot Springs). (John Fritsche collection.)

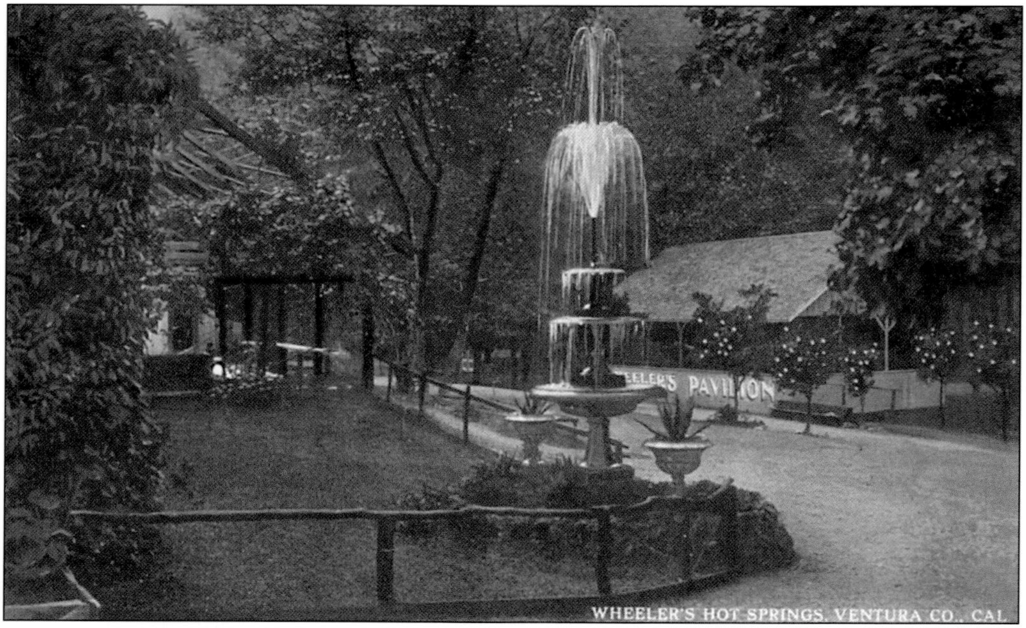

THE FOUNTAIN AT WHEELER'S SPRINGS. Wheeler's provided various amenities, a plunge, and a dancing pavilion, which can be seen at the right of this postcard. *The Ojai* newspaper reported in October 1899, "Dastarac and Shepherd, the Ventura scenic artists, have just completed some very fine scenic work on the ceiling of the great pavilion at Wheeler Hot Springs." Visitors to the springs were not necessarily expected to "rough it." (Brian and Connie Aikens collection.)

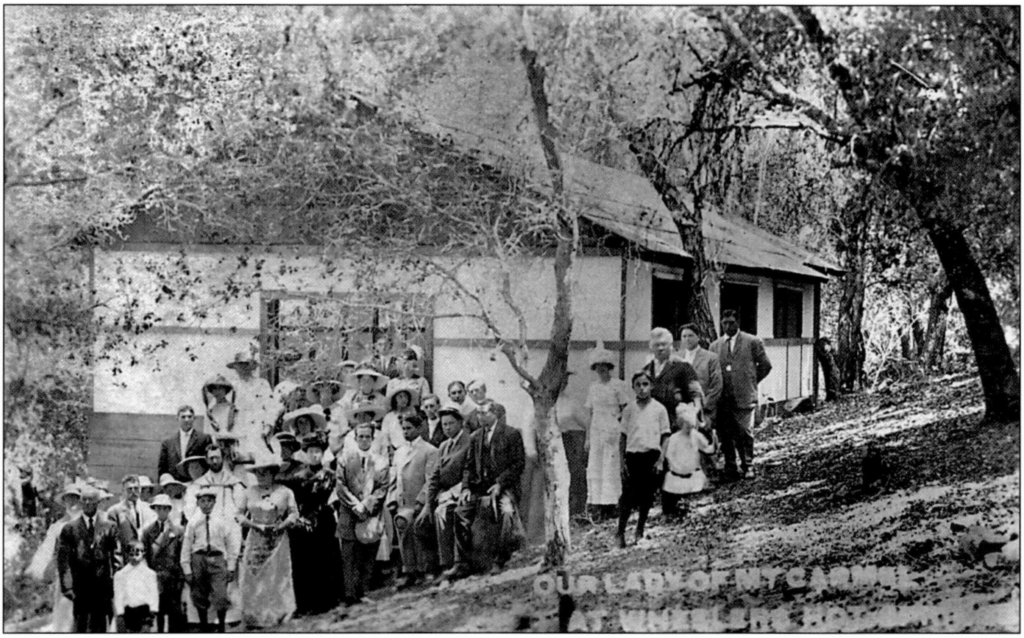

OUR LADY OF MOUNT CARMEL. This is a Catholic chapel that was dedicated at Wheeler's Hot Springs with a solemn high mass on July 14, 1912. This was a couple of years before the St. Thomas Parish was established at Nordhoff, so it was a mission chapel, probably served by the energetic founding priest, Fr. Emilio Ylla. (George Finn collection.)

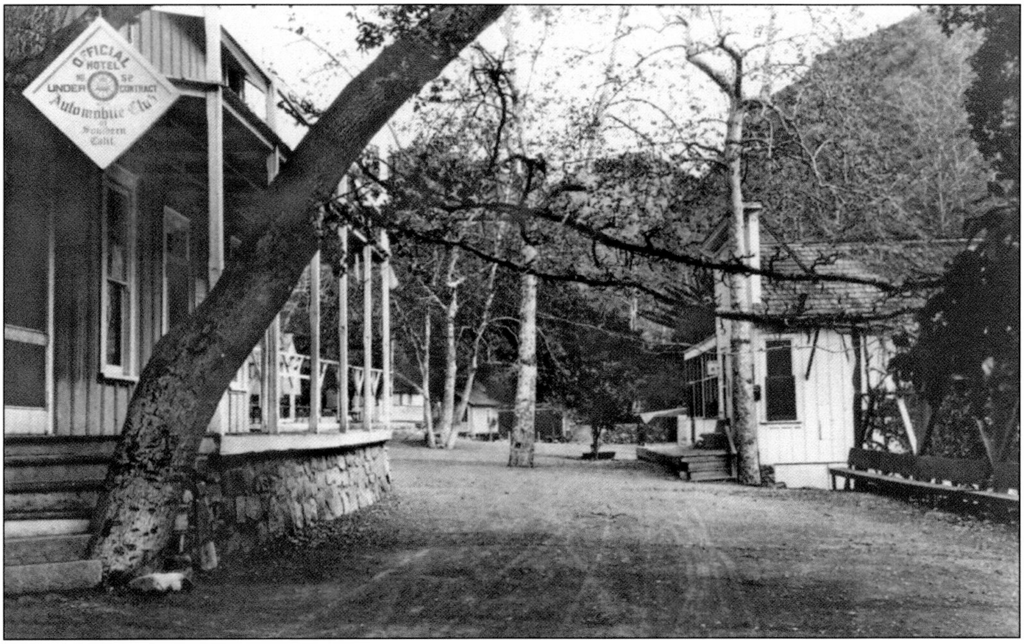

AN OFFICIAL AAA HOTEL. The camp was AAA-approved, but now and then, it fell on bad times. A great fire raged through the canyon in June 1917. Heavy flooding damaged the springs in February 1938 and February 1969. A second fire burned through the canyon in September 1948 and a third in 1985. The owners went bankrupt in 1997, and the life of the springs was pretty much ended. (OVM Collection.)

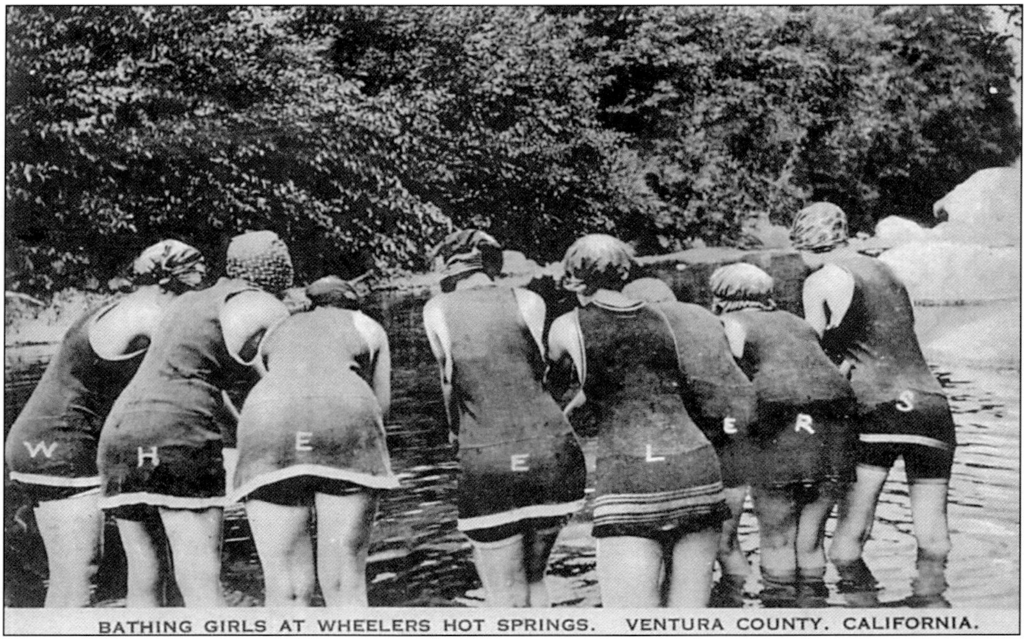

Bathing Girls at Wheeler's Hot Springs. There was no reason to be morose about the ultimate destiny of the springs. Here was one way of having fun. The women have arms and legs uncovered, so the photograph must be sometime during the 1920s. (Terry Hill collection.)

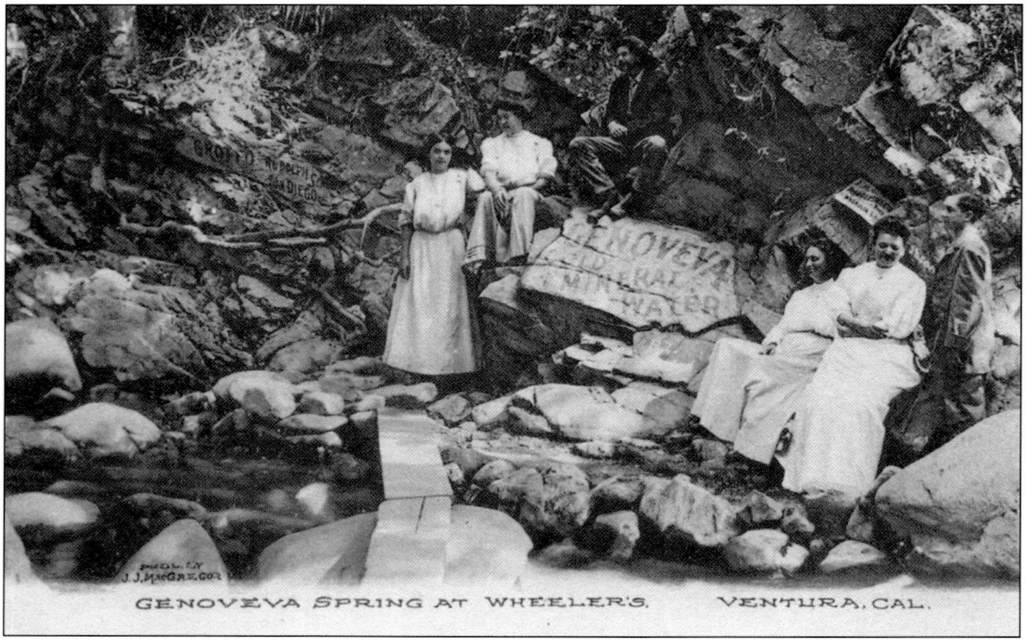

Genoveva Spring at Wheeler's. The types of natural springs at the different camps in Matilija Canyon varied. The springs at Wheeler's were hot springs. The ones at Matilija Hot Springs were hot, cold, and sulfur springs. Those at Lyon's camp were chemical springs only. The waters were used as tonics and for bathing. Predictably, miraculous cures were sometimes reported. (Terry Hill collection.)

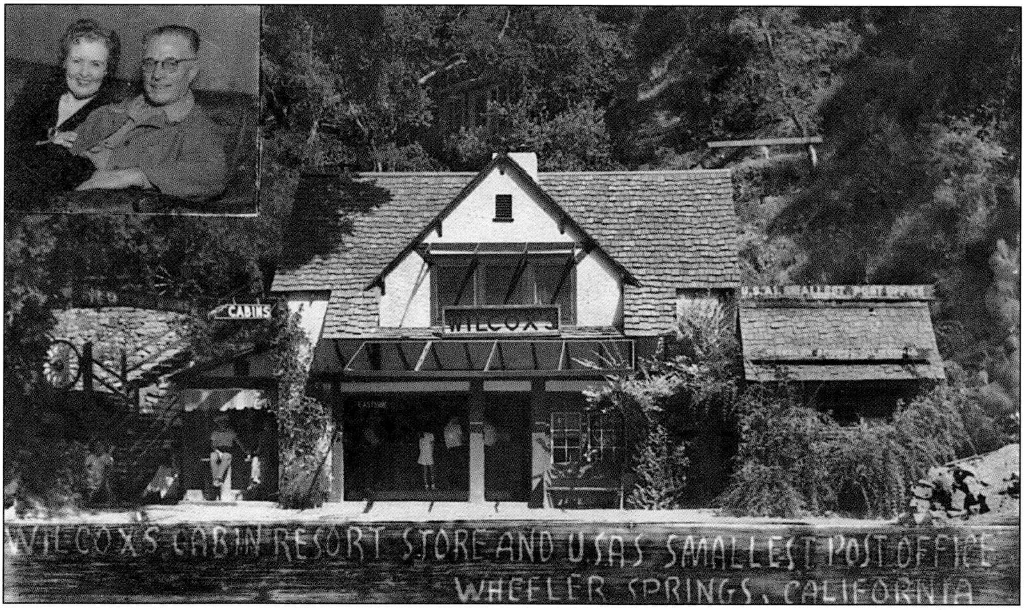

Webb Wilcox's Cabin Resort. Webb Wilcox managed Wheeler's Hot Springs for about three decades before retiring from that responsibility in 1935 and opening his own Wilcox Cabin Resort on the east side of Maricopa Highway, across from Wheeler's. His wife, shown on this postcard, was Etta Blumberg, Wheeler Blumberg's daughter. The main building included the Wagon Wheel Tavern, later known simply as "The Wheel." (George Finn collection.)

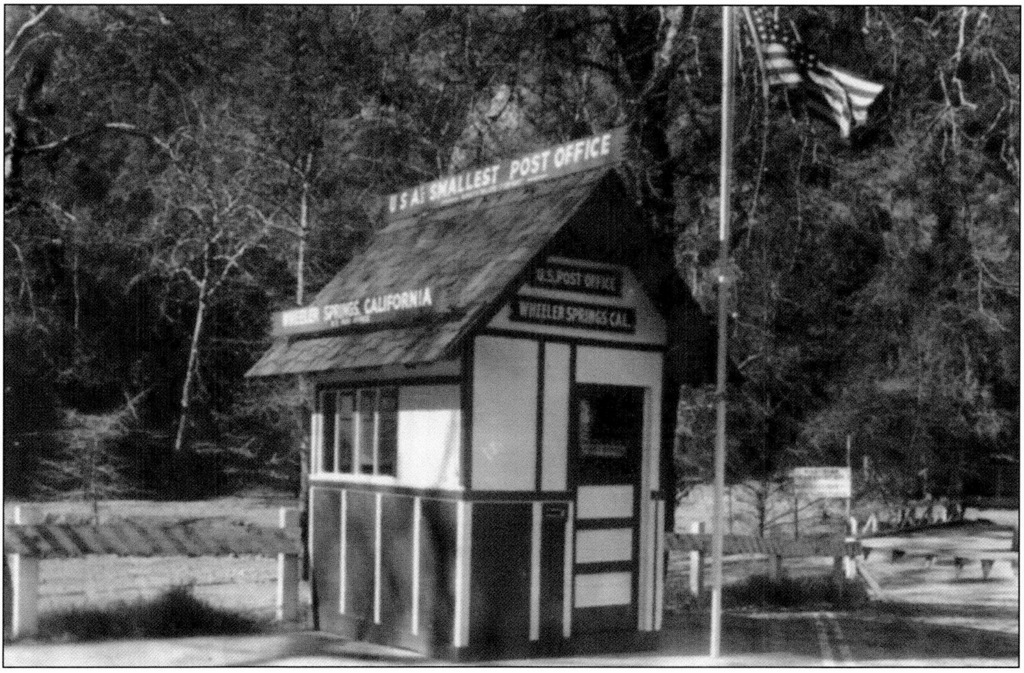

World's Smallest Post Office. This tiny post office (6 by 7 feet) is seen in both pictures on this page. It was dubbed "The World's Smallest Post Office" by *Ripley's Believe It Or Not* in 1948. The building was small enough that it could be moved about at the whim of the owner. Webb Wilcox served as postmaster at Wheeler's Springs for 33 years. (John Fritsche collection.)

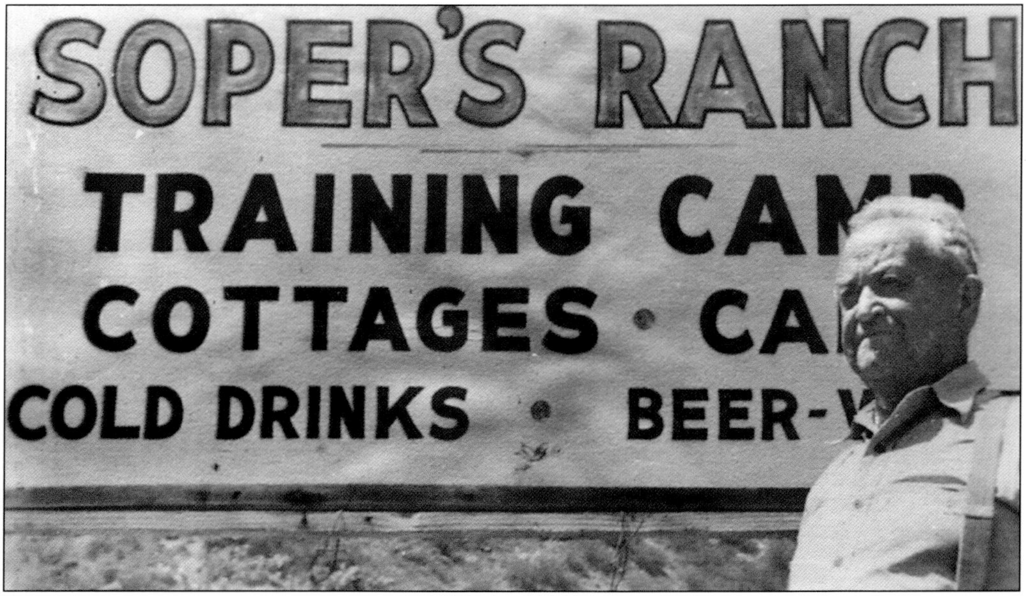

Pop Soper at His Camp. Clarence Anthony "Pop" Soper maintained a camp at the mouth of Matilija Canyon on property his father, Philander Wallace Soper, had purchased in 1895. Clarence died in 1957, and his obituary stated that he opened his camp to train boxers in 1927, after 20 years in railroading. Some records suggest that the camp was open as early as 1921. (George Finn collection.)

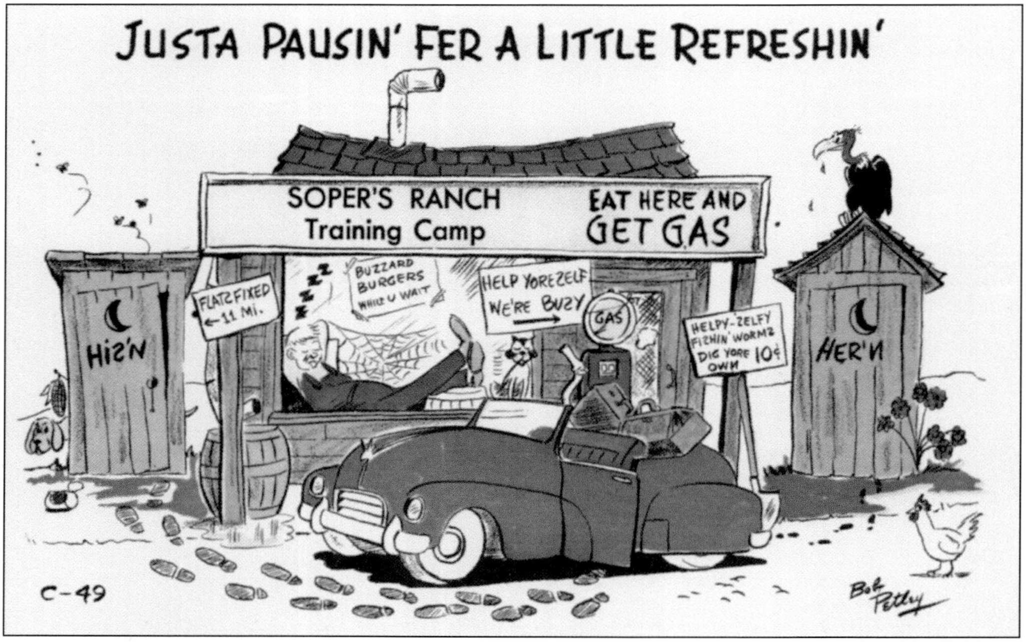

Soper's Ranch Training Camp. Despite the appearance of this card, there was a lot of hard work going on at Soper's Camp. Many boxers trained there, and by 1928, the camp had a ring with a gabled canvas roof. Abundant benches were provided for spectators beside the ring. Soper continued to train boxers for decades, except for the period during World War II. (George Finn collection.)

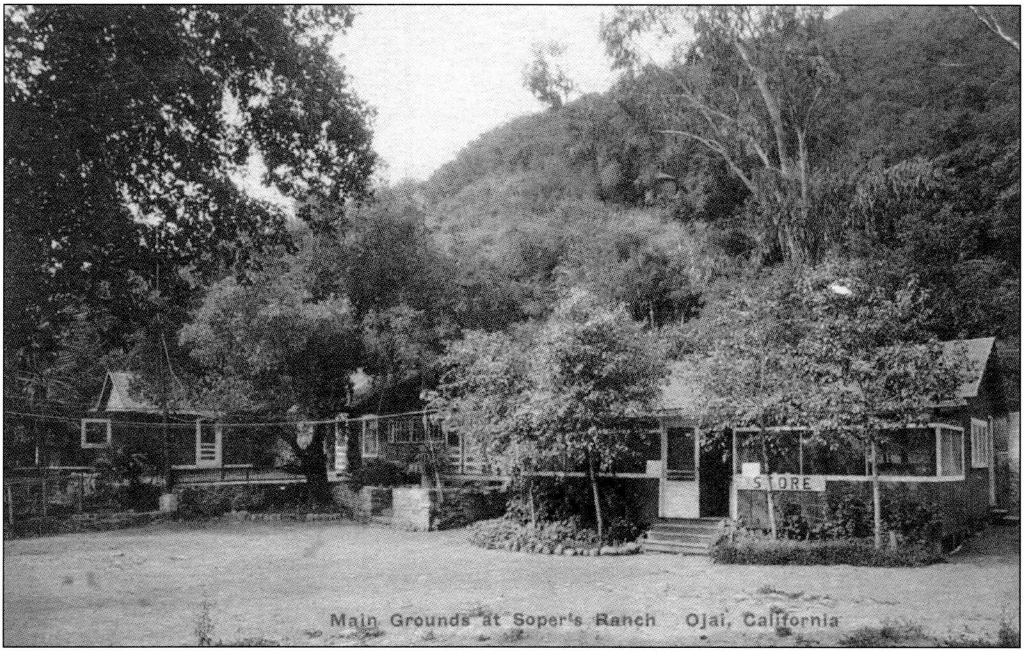

The Buildings at Soper's Camp. The most noted boxer who trained at Soper's Camp was Jack Dempsey. Dempsey had lost his title as World Heavyweight Champion to Gene Tunney in September 1926. He trained with Soper in 1927 for a return bout with Tunney, but Dempsey failed to regain his title in the September 1927 contest. (OVM Collection.)

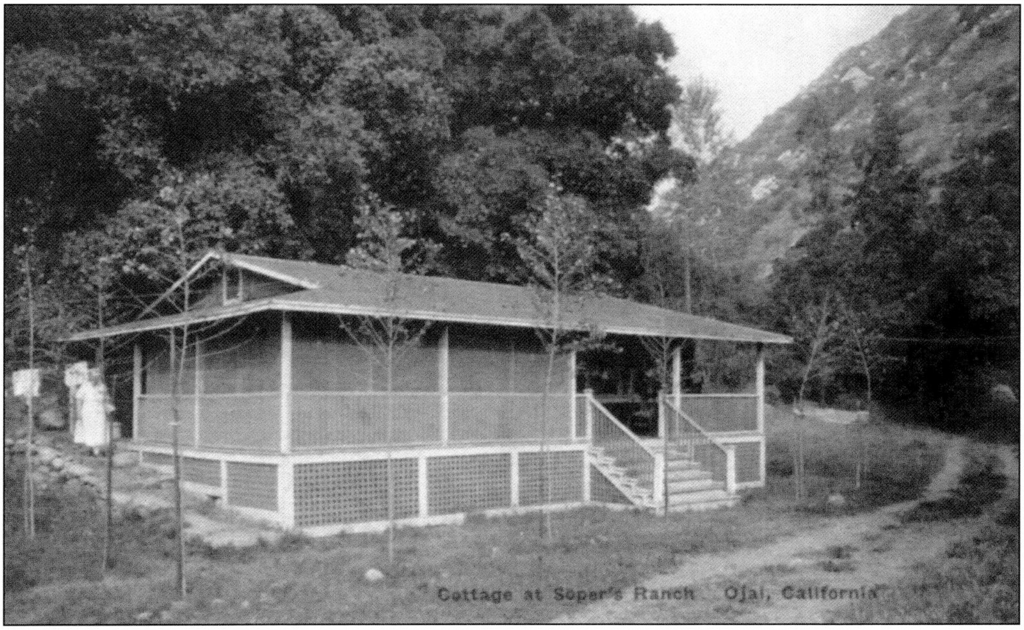

A Cabin at Soper's Camp. Pop Soper also used his land as a productive agricultural ranch, gaining a reputation as "the Matilija berry and fruit man" in 1921. He sold part of his land in 1929 to Rich and Eugenia Everett, who then established a nearby art colony called Ojala. Upon Pop Soper's death in 1957, the principal buildings of the camp were declared safety hazards, and most were removed. (John Fritsche collection.)

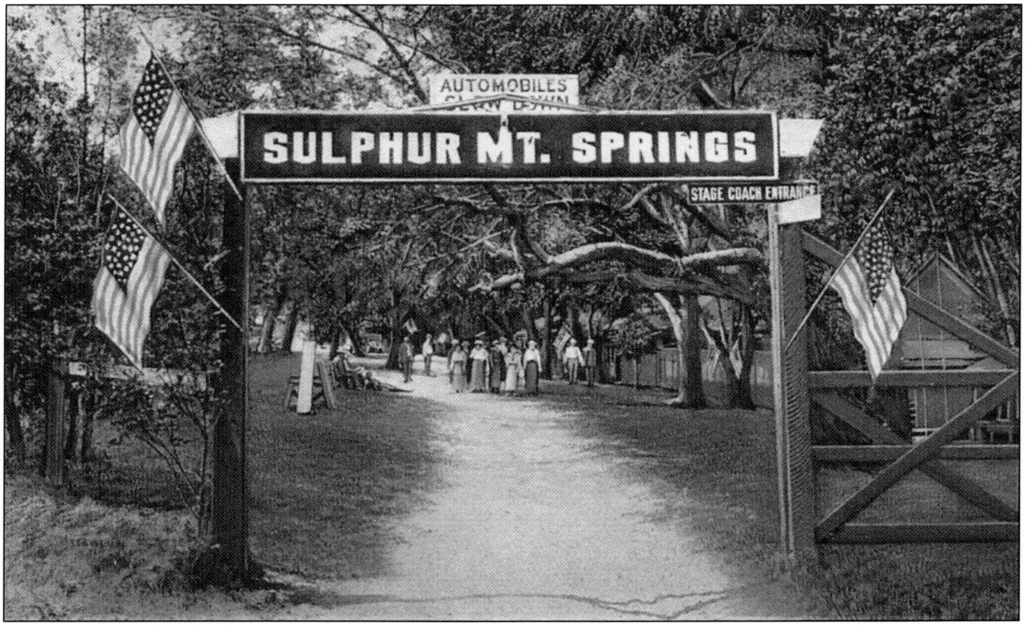

THE ENTRANCE OF SULPHUR HOT SPRINGS. In contrast to the other mountain resorts, Sulphur Hot Springs was not located in Matilija Canyon. Instead, it was located beyond the east end of the Upper Valley (but still within the area of Rancho Ojai). It was on the Ojai–to–Santa Paula Road and was a favorite stop for motorists who traveled "the Triangle" from Ventura to Santa Paula and over the mountain to the Ojai Valley. (John Fritsche collection.)

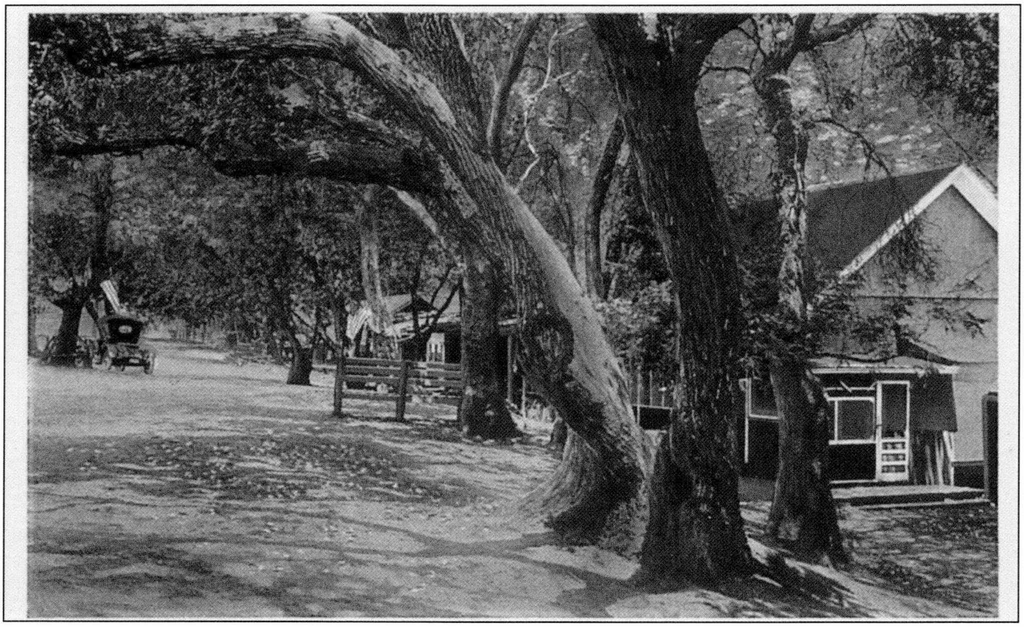

CABINS AT SULPHUR HOT SPRINGS. The camp was opened in June 1898 with a celebration that included games and contests. The swimming pool, however, was filled with only about a foot of water ("a very bum condition of affairs and a most disappointing one," according to a writer for *The Ojai* newspaper). The Sulphur Hot Springs were sometimes advertised as Santa Paula Hot Springs. (Brian and Connie Aikens collection.)

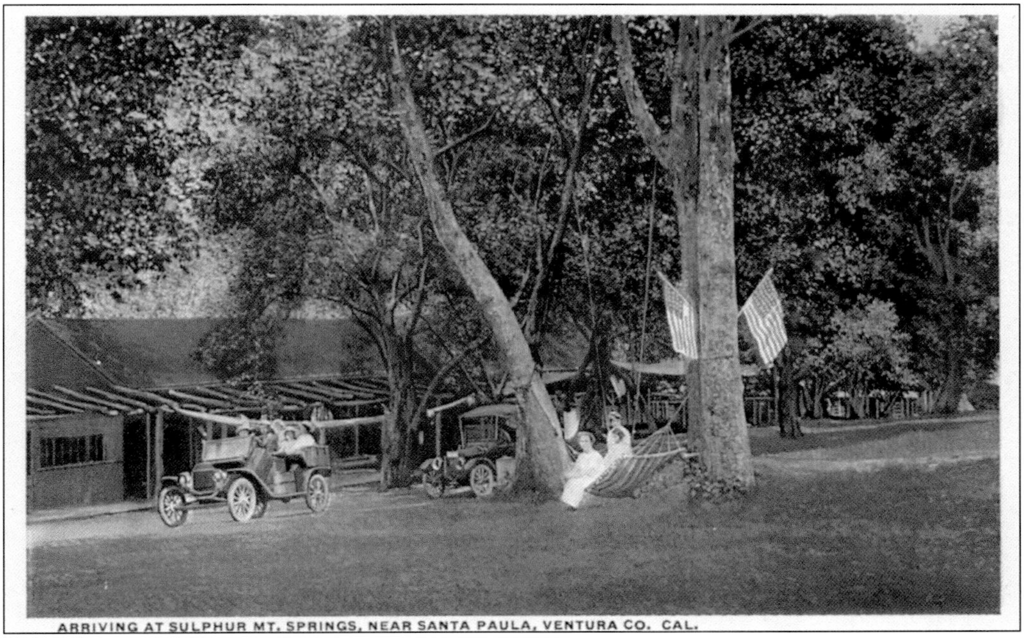

The Grounds at Sulphur Hot Springs. The hot springs gained special notice in May 1911, when the motion picture director Gaston Melies established a working film camp on the grounds. The company filmed *The Ghost of Sulphur Mountain* at the camp in 1912. During holidays, the actors would put on shows, with hooting and hollering and guns blazing, for delighted visitors. (Brian and Connie Aikens collection.)

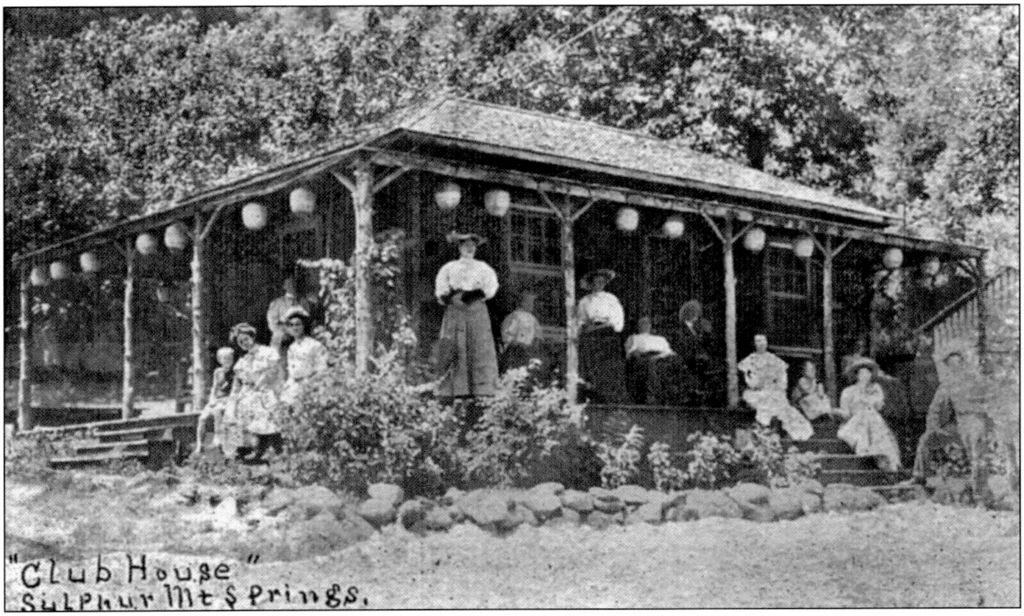

The Clubhouse at Sulphur Hot Springs. The camp was organized with stockholders "on the Chautauqua Plan" in 1902. This festively decorated clubhouse suggests how it must have functioned as a membership camp. Improvements were made at the springs in 1912 to accommodate people viewing the Melies film crew at work: a new pavilion and a reception room. (John Fritsche collection.)

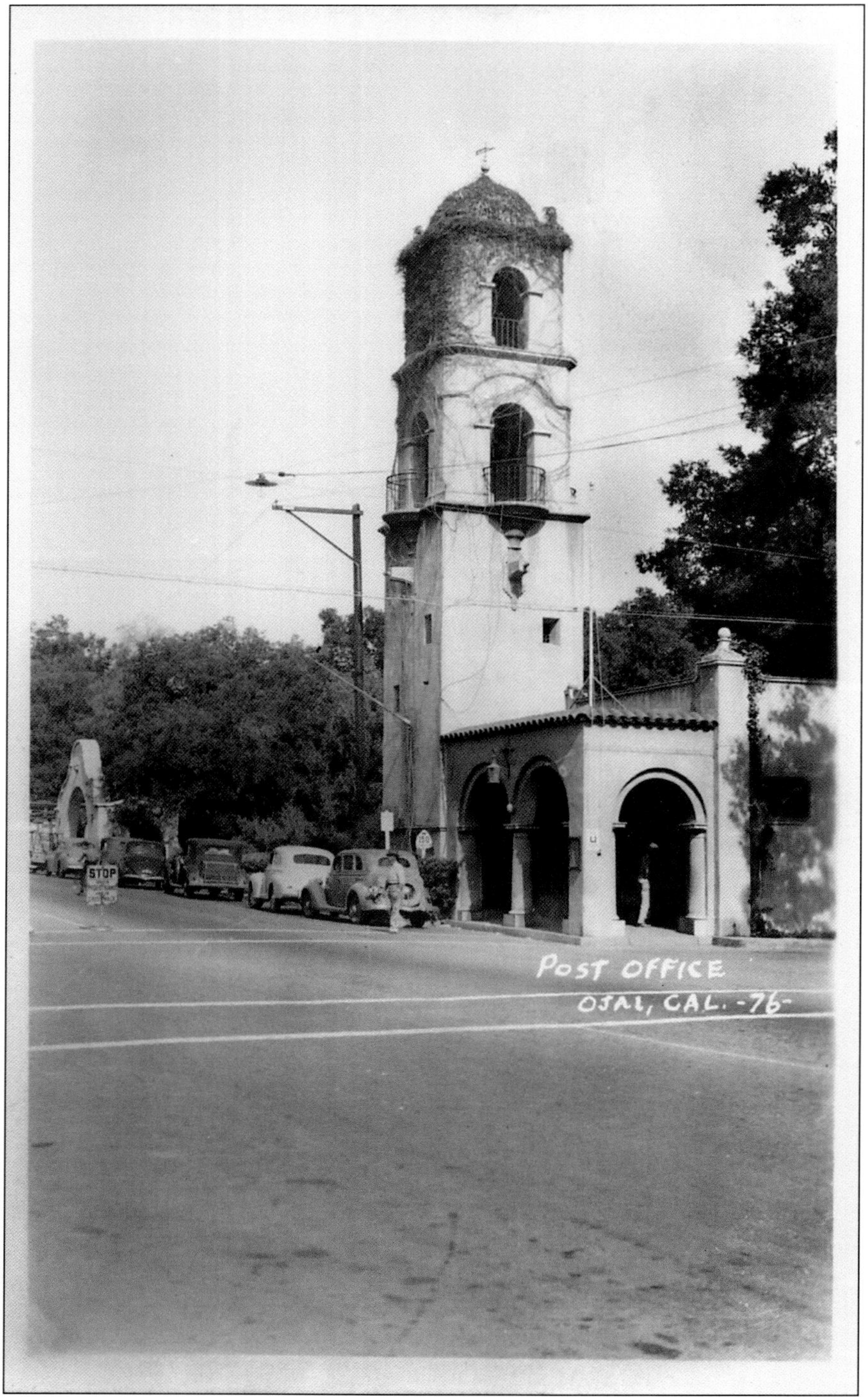

OJAI POST OFFICE TOWER. In 1914, Edward Drummond Libbey was inspired by the beauty of the Ojai Valley to renovate the town's nondescript, aging business district. "There has been too little attention paid to things aesthetic in our communities and in our homes," Libbey told *The Ojai*. "The time has come when we should encourage in ourselves, thoughts of things beautiful, and the higher ideals which art encourages and promotes." (OVM Collection.)

Six

The Libbey Legacy

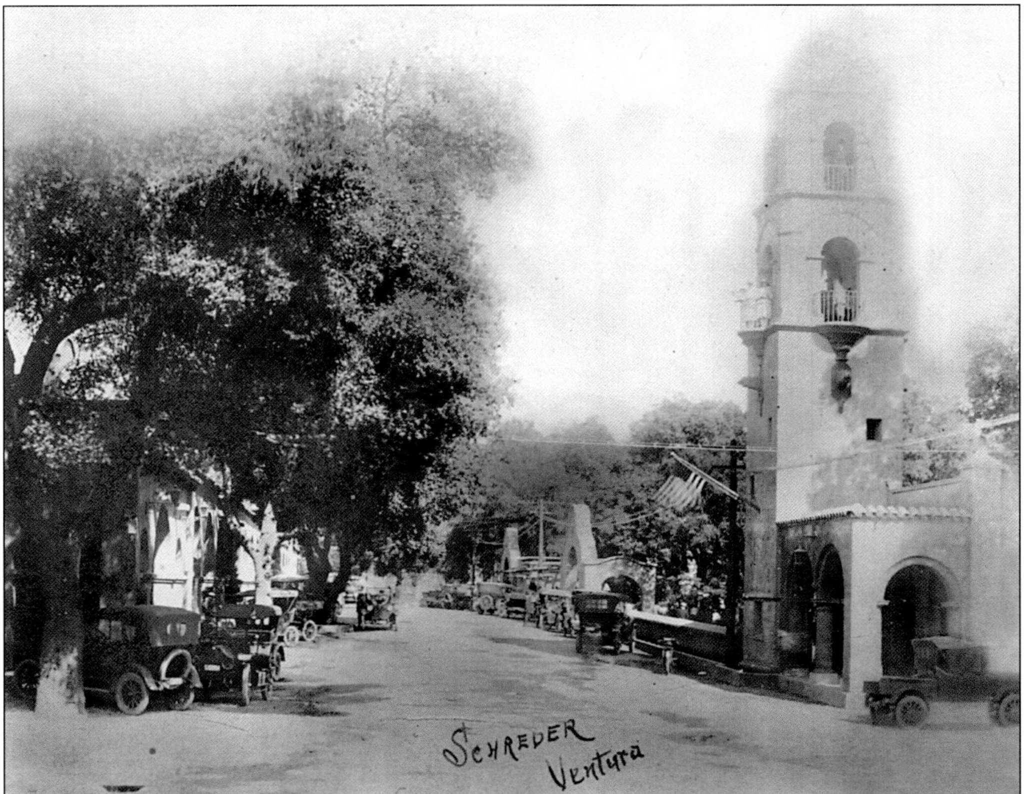

Libbey's Mission Revival Makeover. The 1915–1916 Panama-California Exposition in San Diego's Balboa Park showcased the new Mission Revival architectural style, which reflected a highly romanticized tradition of Old California missions and Spanish ranchos. This new style captured the imagination of many Californians, including Edward Libbey. In 1916, he commissioned the San Diego firm of Mead and Requa to apply the style to his planned renovation of downtown Nordhoff. (David Mason collection.)

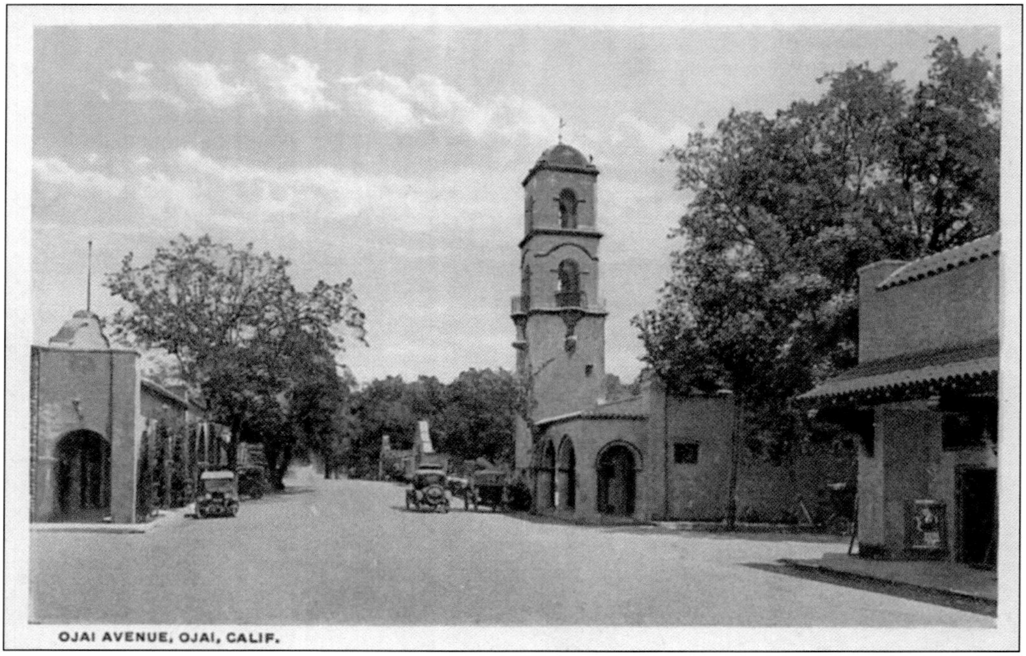

An Architectural Masterpiece. Libbey's transformation of downtown Nordhoff began with the attachment of a Mission-style arcade to the existing storefronts along the north side of Ojai Avenue. Libbey then purchased the properties across the street, which he demolished to make way for a new civic park. To separate the park from the street, architect Richard Requa constructed a traditional pergola, with two large arches framing the entrances to the park. As the centerpiece of his architectural plan, Requa erected a 65-foot Spanish bell tower over a new post office building. The gleaming new structures were dedicated on the first Ojai Day in 1917, a celebration established by the community to honor Edward Libbey. Not long afterwards, the residents of Nordhoff changed the name of their town to Ojai. (Both, OVM Collection.)

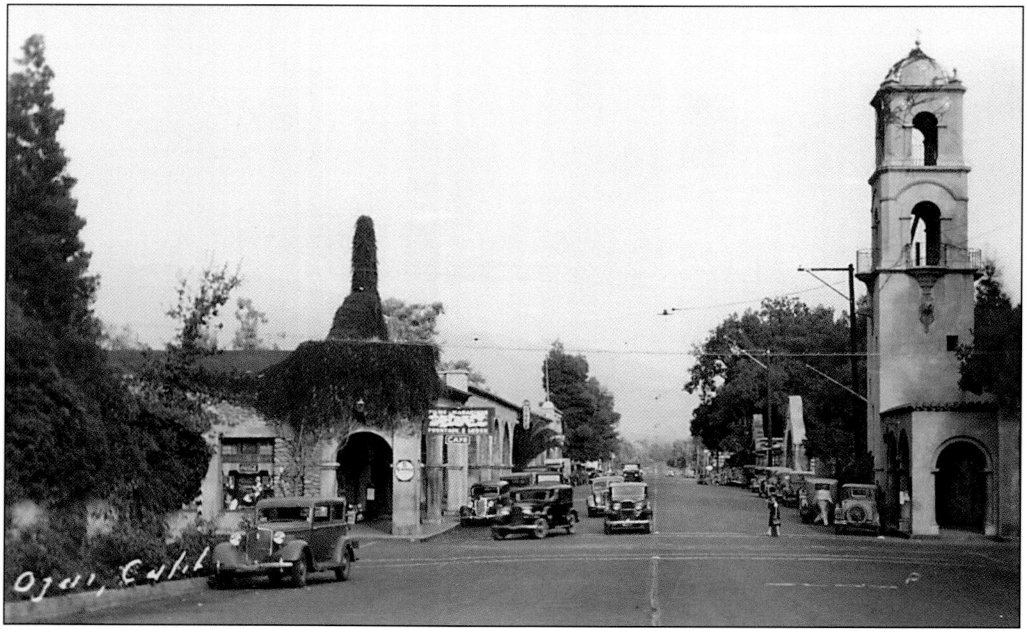

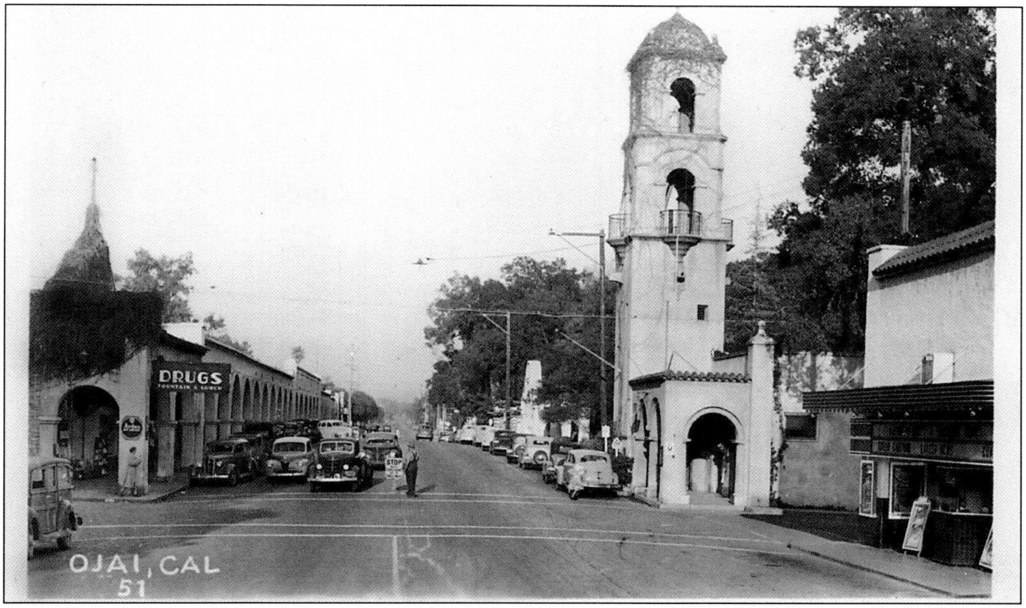

Renovation and Preservation Efforts. In 1917 the editor of *The Ojai* commented on Libbey's grand design for Ojai: "As citizens, it is now up to us to pull together for greater betterments, in full keeping with the plans of the man from Ohio, who has set the pace." Many new Mission Revival homes, stores, and public buildings were constructed between 1917 and 1945, but interest in the Mission look began to fade during the 1950s. By the 1960s, Libbey's structures—including the park—were neglected and deteriorating. Some on the city council wondered if they weren't standing in the way of progress. In 1971, the city demolished the pergola, and in the 1980s, it declared the arcade unsafe. Fortunately, a new interest in preservation took hold in the 1990s. The post office was renovated, the arcade restored, and the pergola rebuilt. (Both, OVM Collection.)

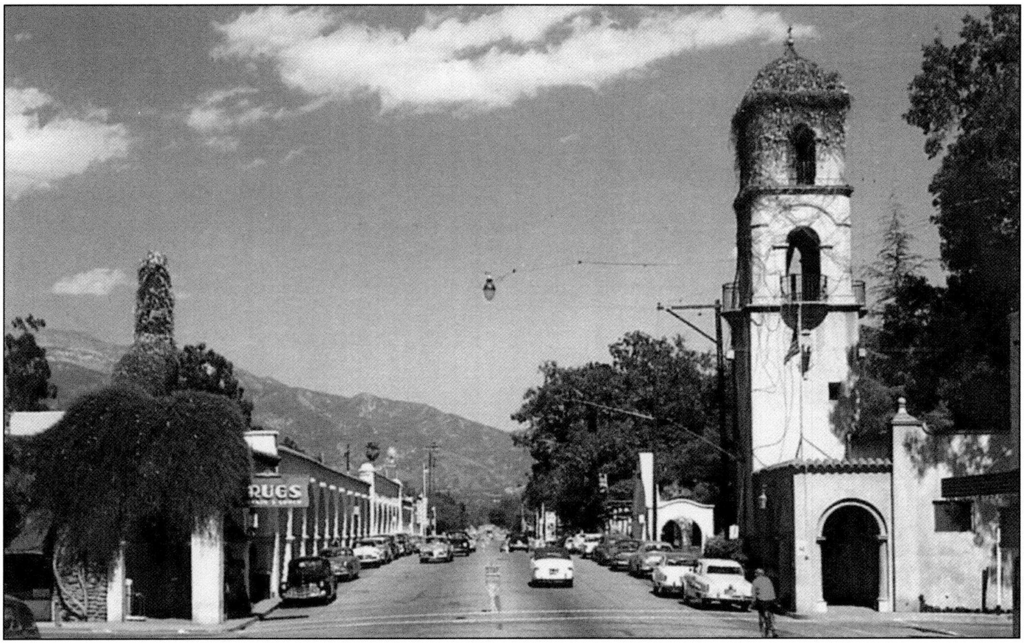

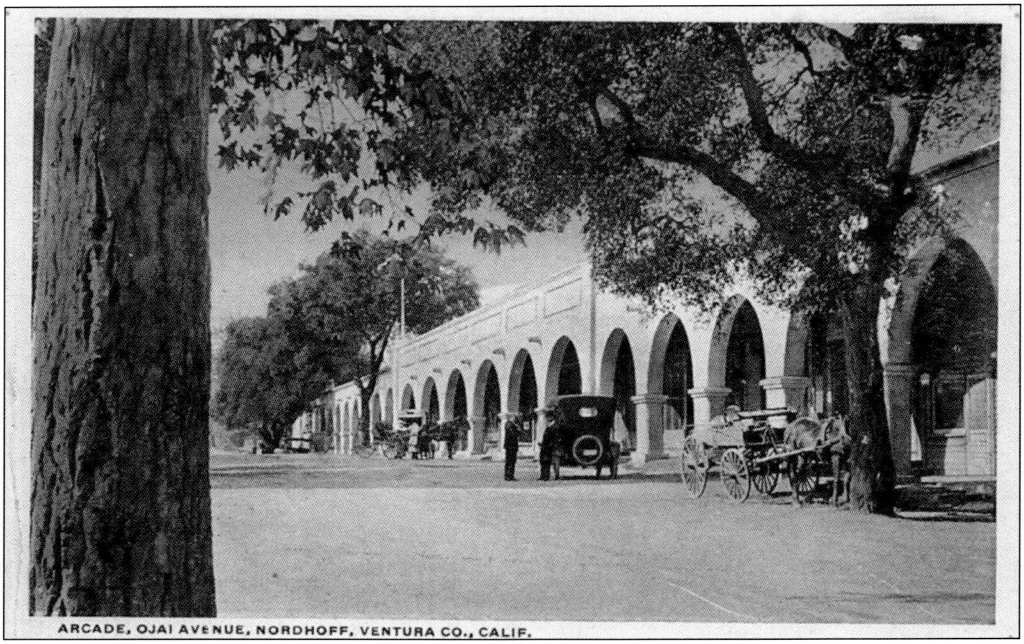

The Ojai Arcade. The Spanish never built towns in California in the style of the missions, so Requa turned to the missions themselves for inspiration. For the Ojai arcade, he used the arcade at the San Juan Capistrano Mission as his model. Requa also included some Moorish design elements, such as the large center section with spires at either end. The arcade is a freestanding structure attached to the front of the original stores, as shown in the postcard above. It was Libbey's wish that the oak trees remain in the street, but they were removed in 1926 for reasons of safety. The postcard below shows the post office tower under construction in the background. Originally, the arcade terminated where it does in this image. Ten years later, it was extended by four arches. (Both, David Mason collection.)

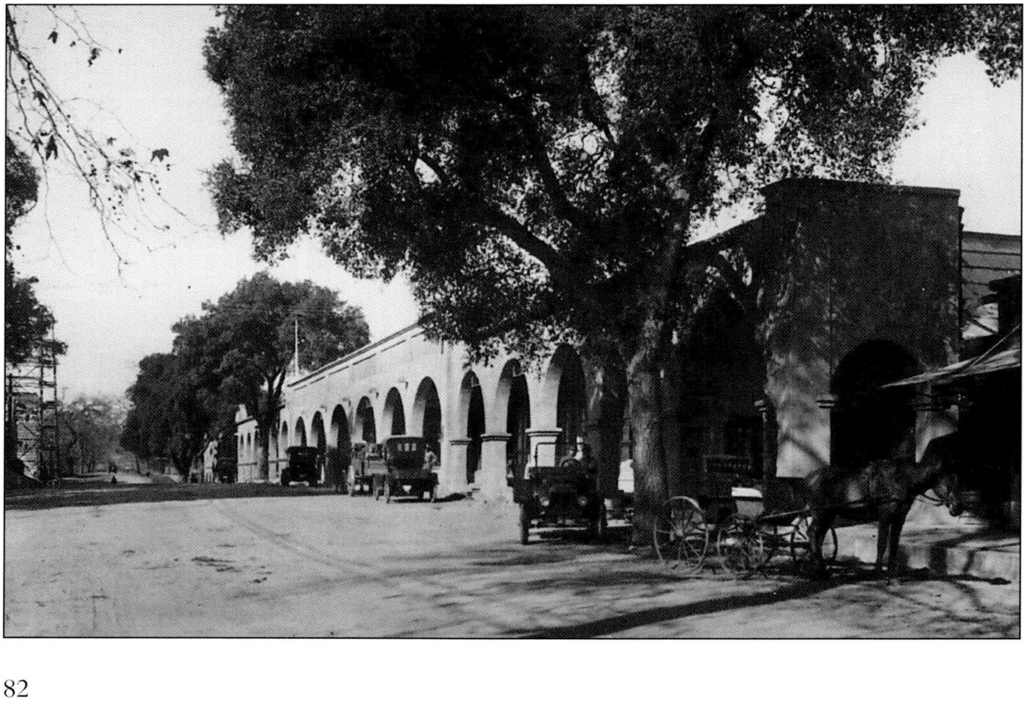

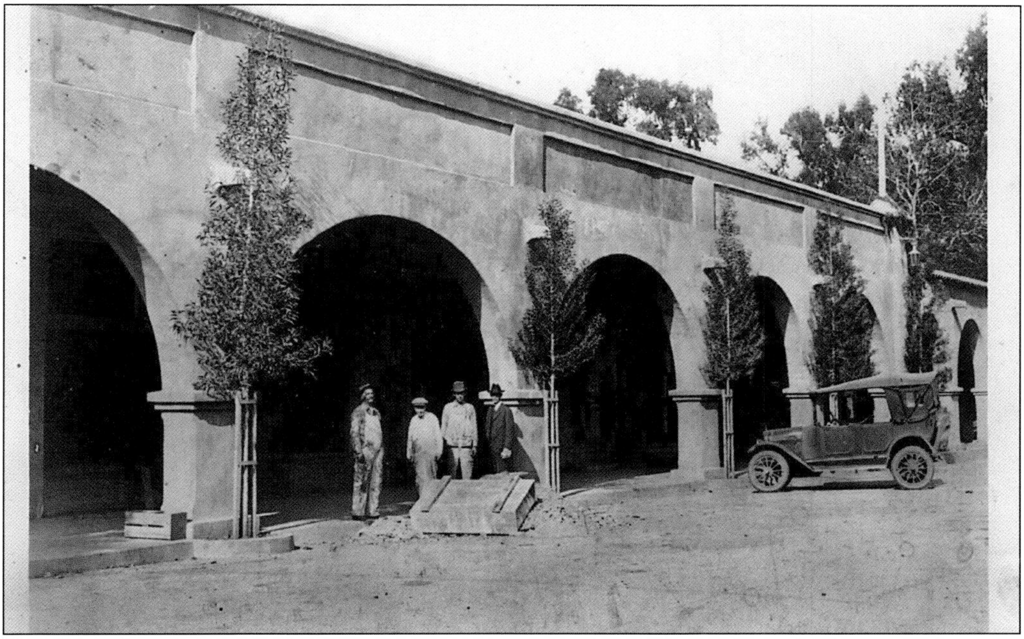

CONSTRUCTION AND RECONSTRUCTION. The card above shows the newly constructed arcade with J. J. Burke (right) and three workers. John J. Burke was a member of the Ojai Civic Association, formed in Libbey to take ownership of the new park and post office on behalf of the people of Ojai Valley. The card below shows the result of a 1917 fire that destroyed half of the businesses in the arcade. A gasoline stove in Elvie Peasley's shop ignited the fire, which quickly spread through the old wooden structures behind the new arcade. The stores on the west end of the arcade were completely destroyed. However, the buildings were quickly rebuilt and the arcade repaired. In another act of benevolence, Edward Libbey donated a new fire truck to help combat future fires. (Both, David Mason collection.)

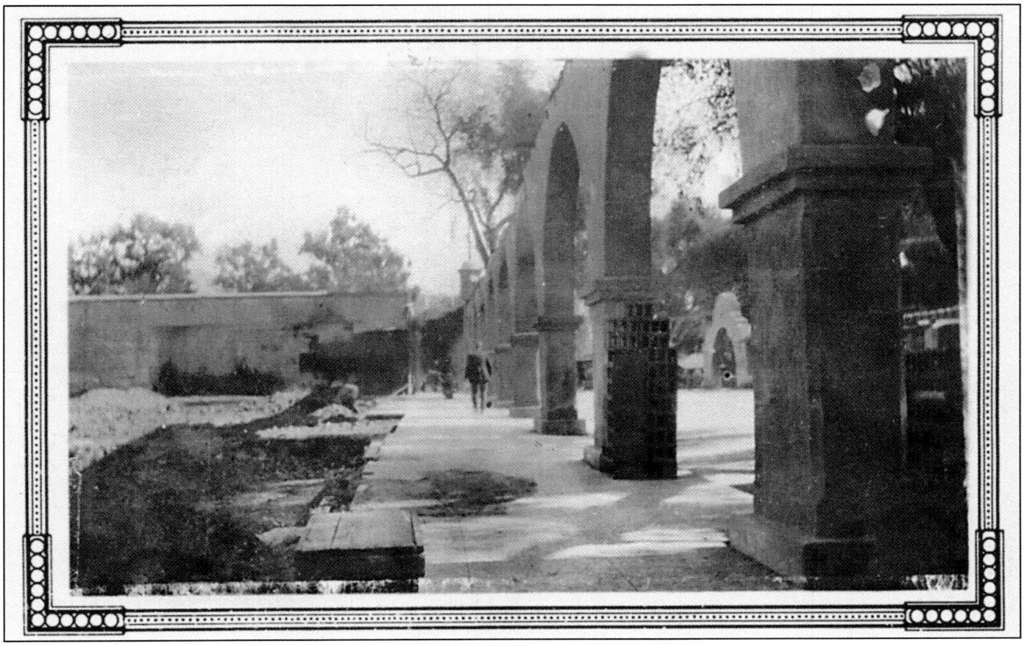

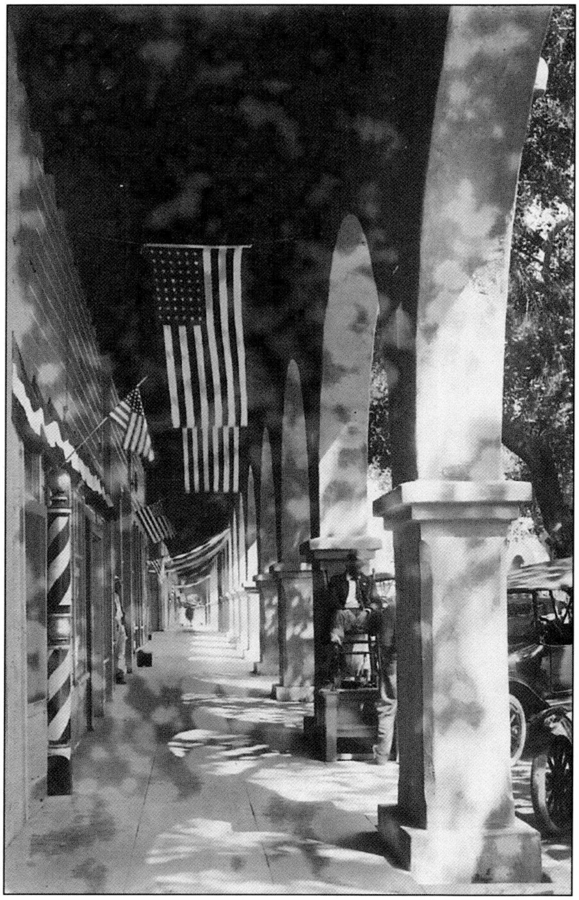

Ojai's Arcade Bootblack. With the display of so many American flags, this postcard undoubtedly shows the arcade on a national holiday. The barber pole on the left marks the location of the arcade barbershop. To the right is a bootblack stand. Records show that when the City of Ojai incorporated in 1921, one of the first acts of the town marshal was to remove the bootblack from the arcade. (David Mason collection.)

Arcade Extension. In 1927, local architect John Roine supervised the addition of four arches onto the arcade. One of the new arches is visible on the right. For many years, cars parked at an angle, but as traffic increased and automobiles grew in size, the city instituted parallel parking. To this day, Ojai has resisted installing parking meters. (OVM Collection.)

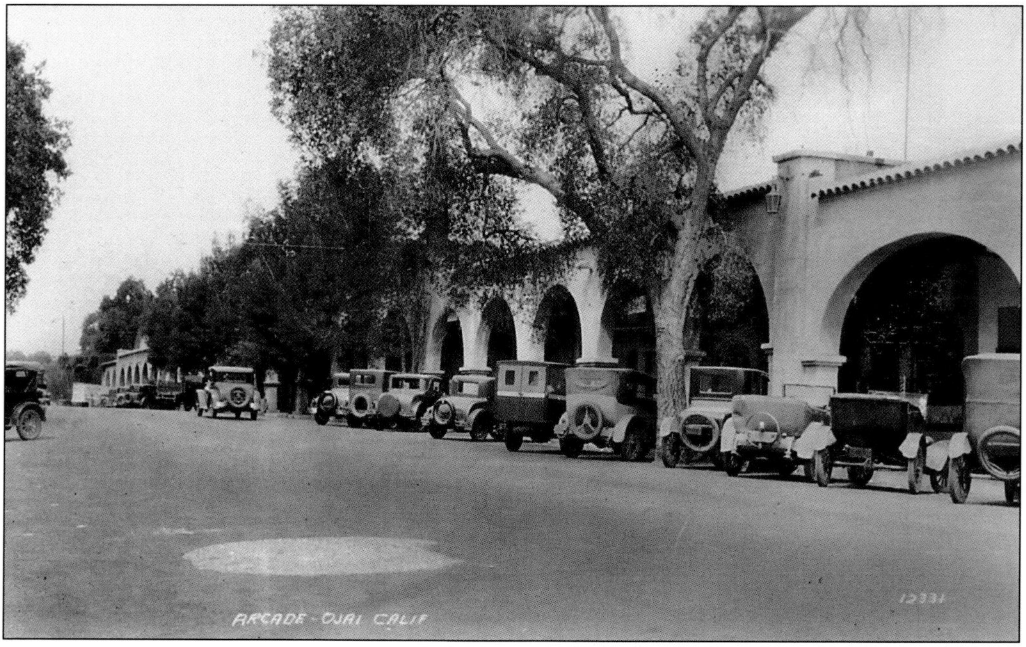

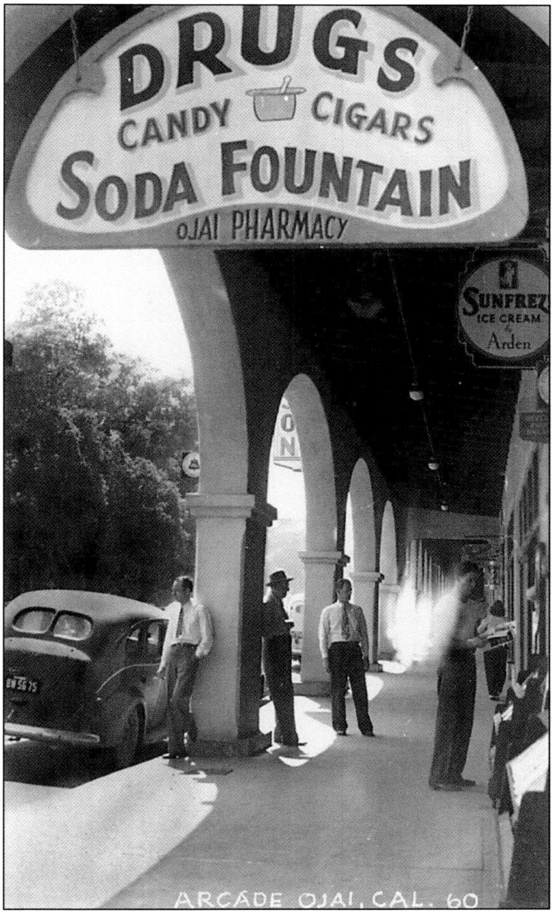

The Ojai Pharmacy. Until the 1960s, the arcade was Ojai's primary business district, catering to the everyday needs of local residents. One such business was the Ojai Pharmacy. In addition to filling prescriptions, it featured a full soda fountain and lunch counter. Howard Nelson Rockafellow, a colorful Ojai personality, started the business in 1927. Over the next 30 years, he helped organize the Ventura River Municipal Water District, served as president of the Lions Club and chamber of commerce, and sat on the Ojai City Council. Rockafellow single-handedly thwarted a move by the Ventura Chamber of Commerce to rename Lake Casitas "Lake Ventura." Ironically, while giving an autobiographical speech to the Retired Men's club at age 71, he ended with, "I expect to live the rest of my life in Ojai"—only to be struck dead by a heart attack at that very moment. (Both, OVM Collection.)

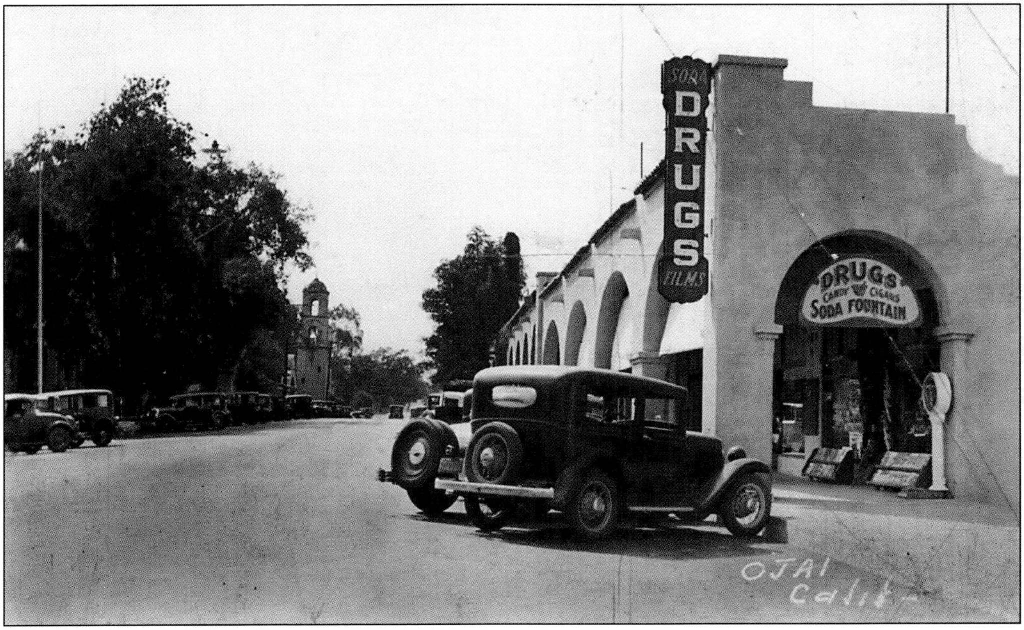

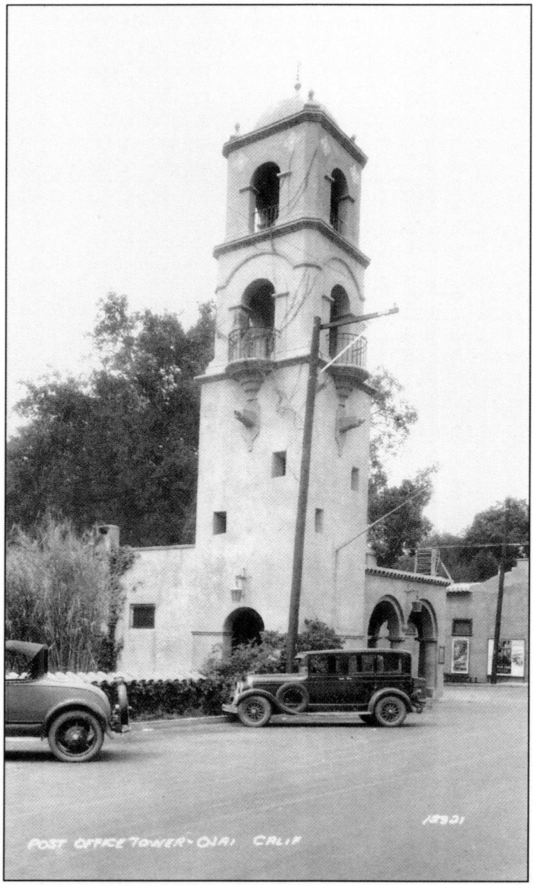

THE OJAI POST OFFICE. Richard Requa modeled the post office bell tower on the campanile of the Columbus Cathedral in Havana, Cuba. The portico and other architectural details were inspired by several colonial buildings in Mexico. Libbey deeded both his new Civic Center Park (now Libbey Park) and post office building to the Ojai Civic Association in 1917. In 1971, the civic association deeded the park to the City of Ojai but retained ownership of the post office building. Proceeds from rent on the building support Libbey Park maintenance, the construction of new parks, and funding for community programs. (Both, OVM Collection.)

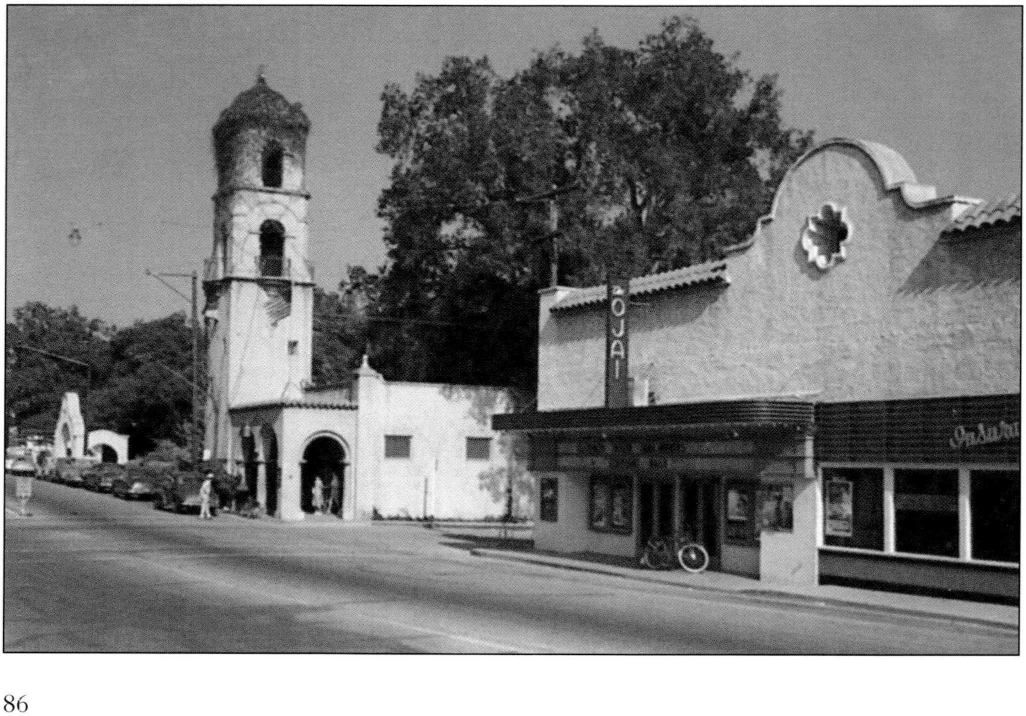

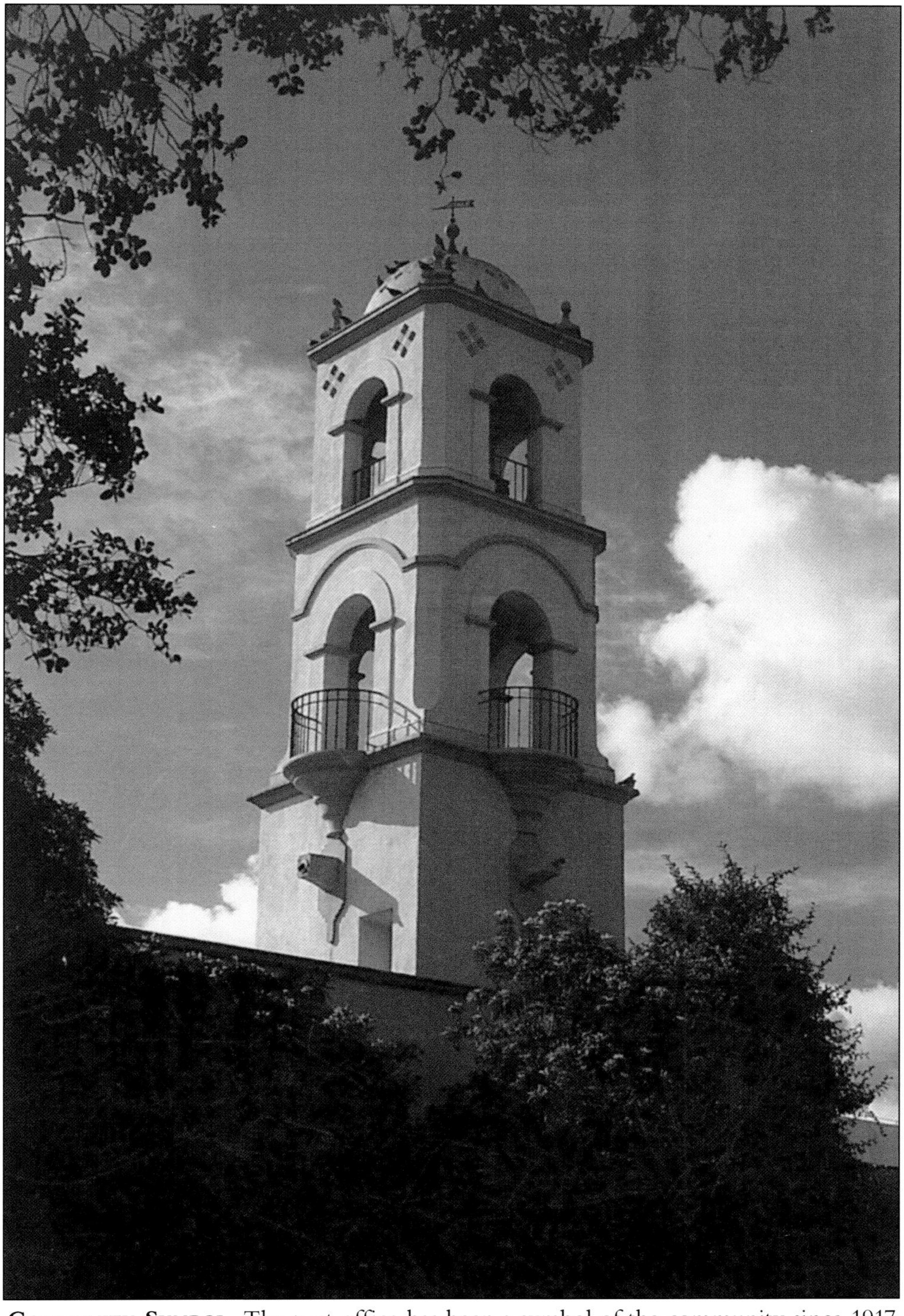

A Community Symbol. The post office has been a symbol of the community since 1917. It is a place where locals run into each other, exchanging news as they pick up their daily mail. More than once, the USPS has tried to move its operations to a larger facility, but each time, the community has rallied to prevent it—even expanding the building on three occasions to encourage the USPS to stay. (OVM Collection.)

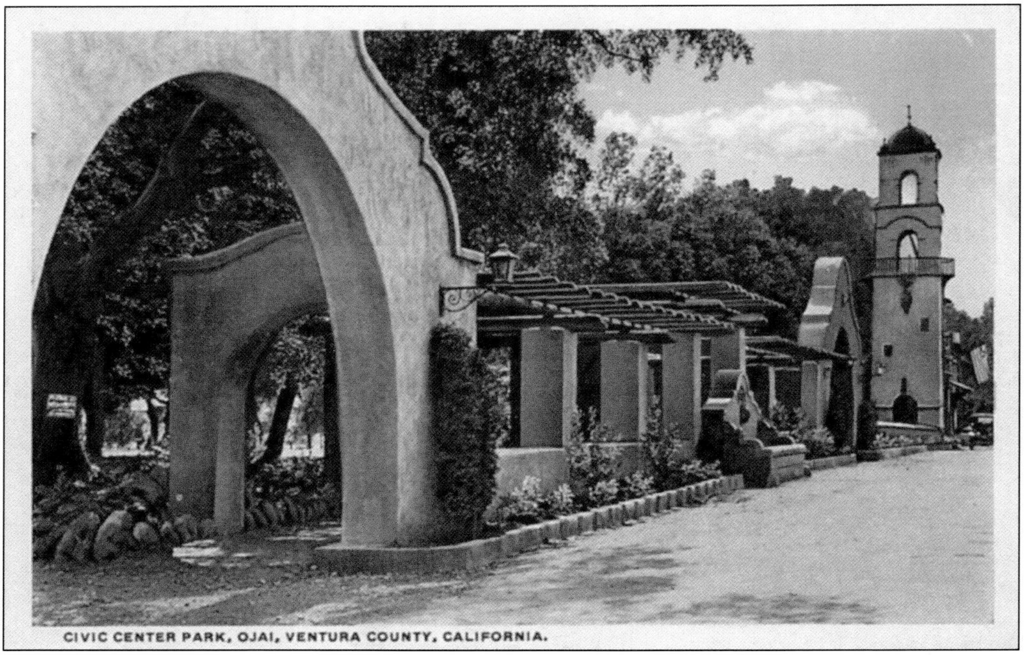

THE OJAI PERGOLA. The two large arches served as grand entryways into the park, through which cars drove into a courtyard and parking area. Requa based the design of these arches on the large east entryway to Mission San Luis Rey. A simple Spanish version of an Italian pergola connected the arches, providing charming, framed vistas into the park. Wisteria vines added color to the stuccoed pergola and shaded the walkway from the hot summer sun. The old Evelyn Nordhoff Memorial Fountain was moved back and incorporated into the pergola's design. When vandals damaged the west arch in 1968, the city claimed the pergola was unsafe and removed it. Twenty-one years later, a citizens' group headed by David Mason, Joan Kemper, and David Bury raised the funds and rebuilt it. (Above, David Mason collection; below, George Finn collection.)

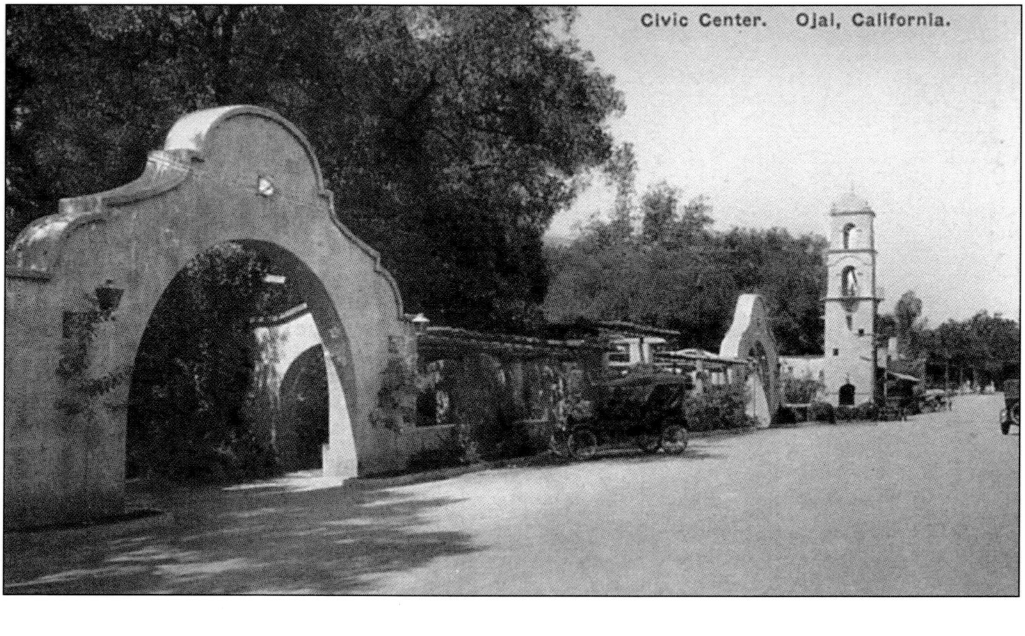

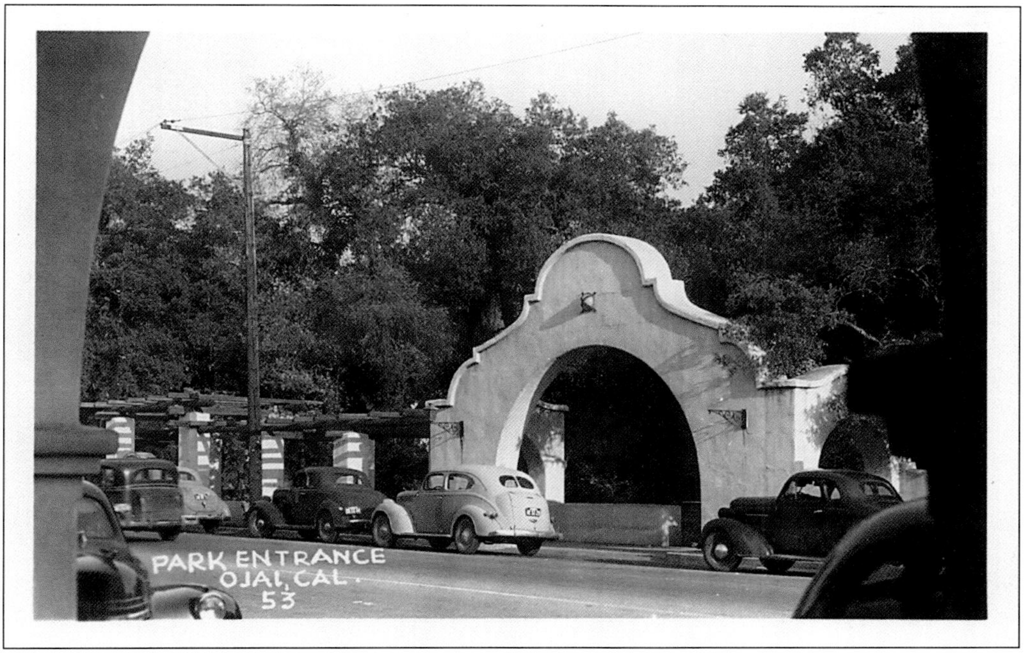

Civic Center Park. As part of his transformation of downtown Ojai, Edward Libbey bought up the dilapidated stores and inns opposite the new arcade. He tore them down to make room for a large community park fronted by the pergola. Requa incorporated the existing four tennis courts and clubhouse into the park design; by 1917, they had been the site of the Ojai Tennis Tournament for over 20 years. In 1954, architects Roy Wilson and Austen Pierpont added the Ojai Festivals Bowl to house the annual Ojai Music Festival. In 1969, Pierpont replaced the gravel courtyard inside the park with a paved courtyard, fountain, benches, new walls, and planters. On the City of Ojai's 50th anniversary in 1971, the park's name was changed to Libbey Park in honor of Ojai's greatest benefactor. (Both, David Mason collection.)

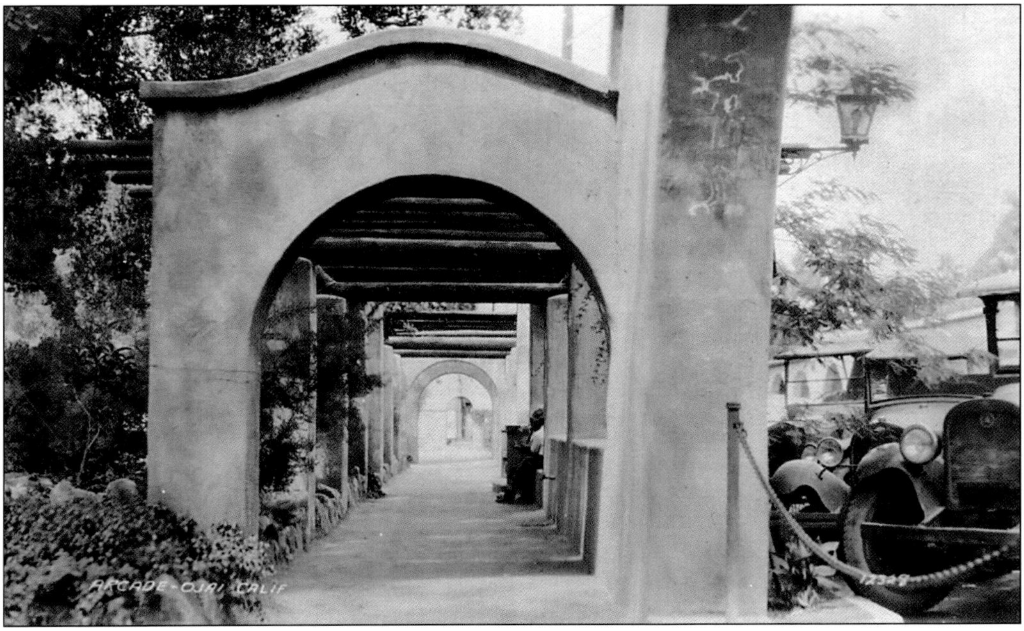

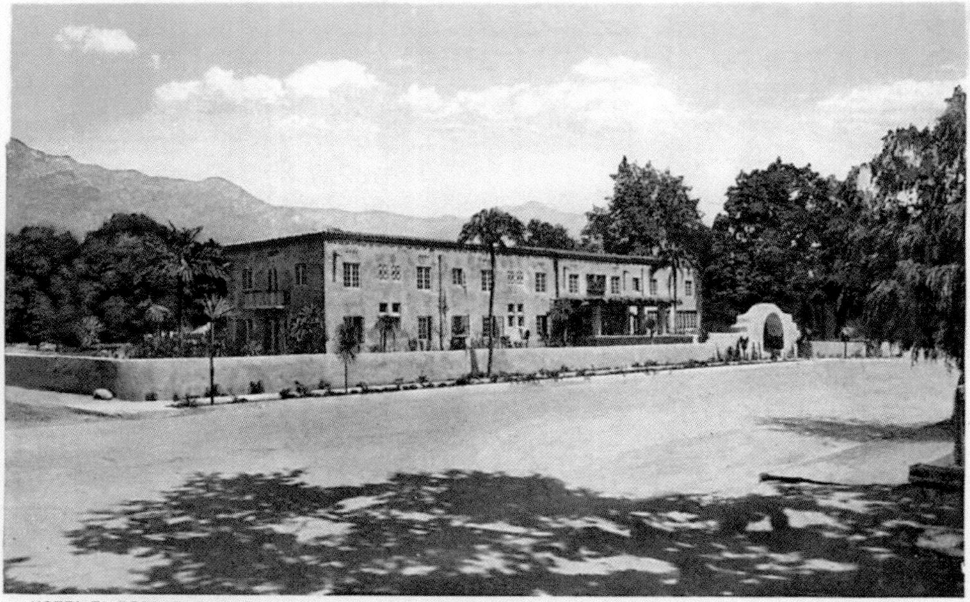

HOTEL EL ROBLAR, OJAI, CALIF.

El Roblar Hotel. Upon completion of the arcade, pergola, and post office, Libbey turned his attention toward building a downtown hotel that would remain open year-round. He organized the Ojai Hotel Company, which raised $30,000 in stock sales above the $10,000 he donated. Libbey then commissioned Richard Requa to serve as architect for the new hotel. Construction began in the summer of 1919, with the opening on January 29, 1920. The two-story hotel nicely complimented the new Mission style architecture of the downtown. That year, streetlights were added to Ojai Avenue. As reported in *The Ojai* (with a bit of hyperbole): "the street-lighting system that now adorns Ojai Avenue, the main street of the village, looms up by night in a class with Los Angeles's famous Broadway." (Both, OVM Collection.)

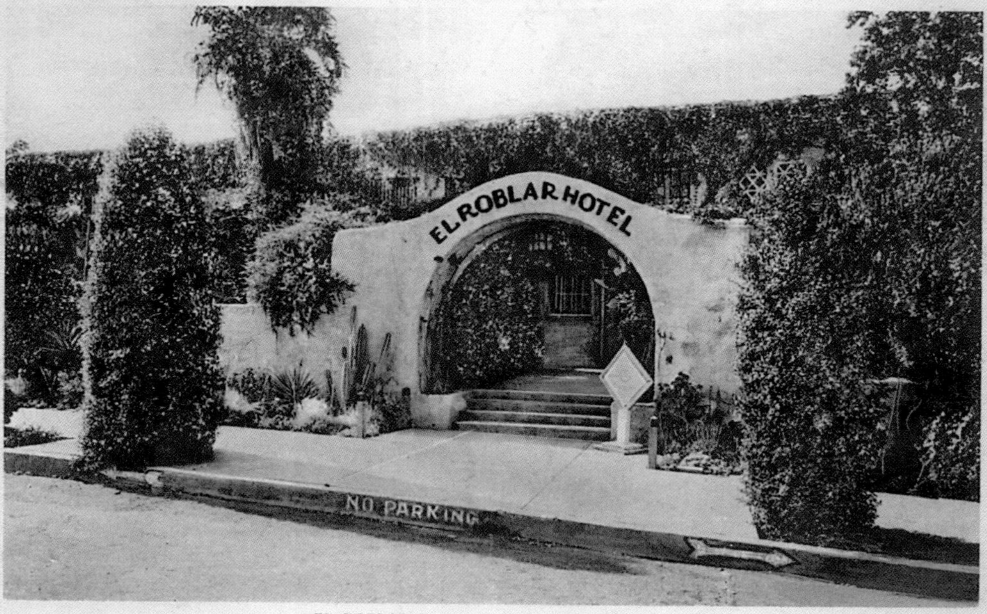

EL ROBLAR HOTEL OJAI, CALIFORNIA

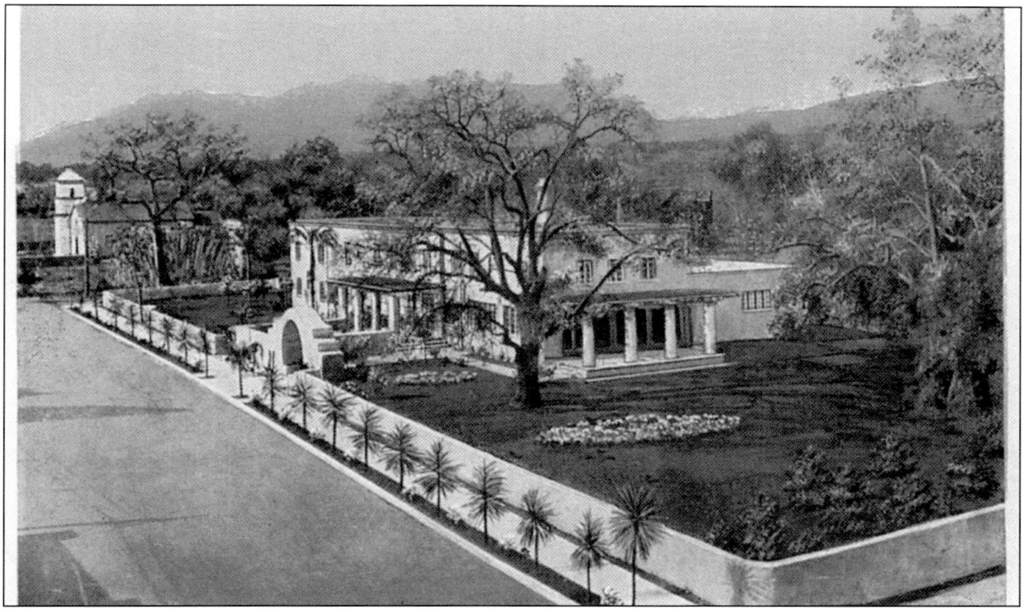

The Oaks Hotel. El Roblar Hotel was renamed the Oaks Hotel in 1953. The new owner, Frank Keenan, was reported to have mob connections back in Chicago. It was a colorful time for the Oaks, with many upgrades to the buildings and grounds and many well-known celebrities staying as guests. Even gangster Bugsy Siegel was sometimes seen lounging around the pool. Keenan applied to operate a casino on the property but was denied by the city. When Keenan was jailed for income tax evasion, the hotel fell on hard times. In 1966, the Oaks was bought by the El Roblar Corporation, a group of concerned residents led by Rodney Walker and Jerald Peterson. The hotel flourished under community ownership for 10 years. Today it is a health spa owned by fitness expert Sheila Cluff. (Above, Terry Hill collection; below, Carol Cohen collection.)

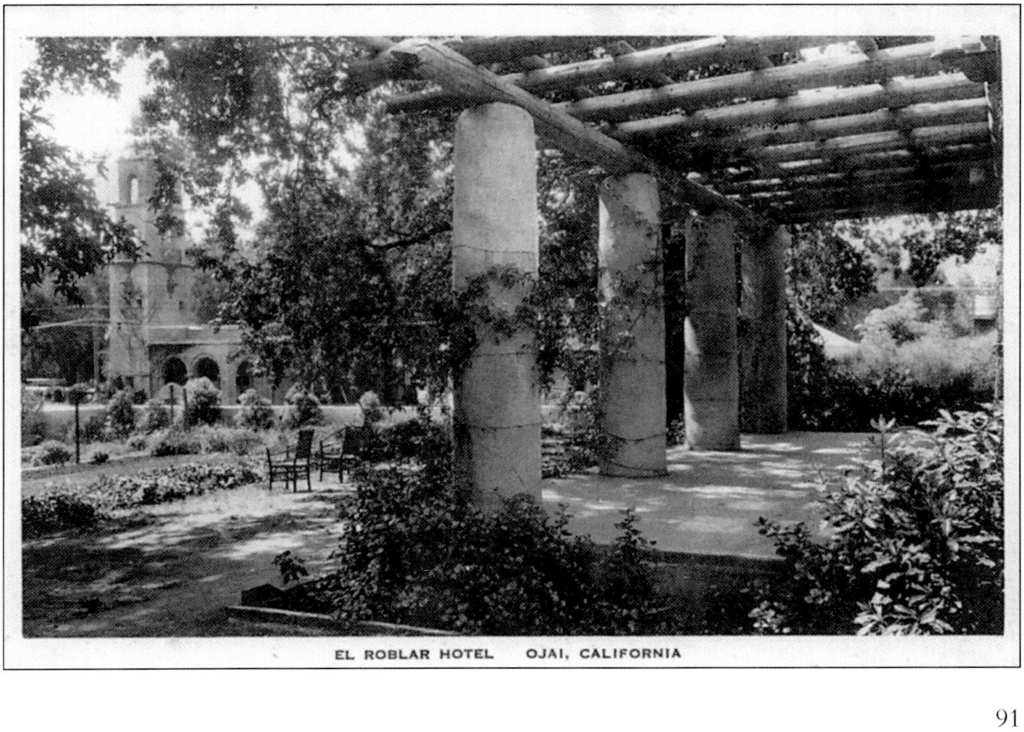

EL ROBLAR HOTEL OJAI, CALIFORNIA

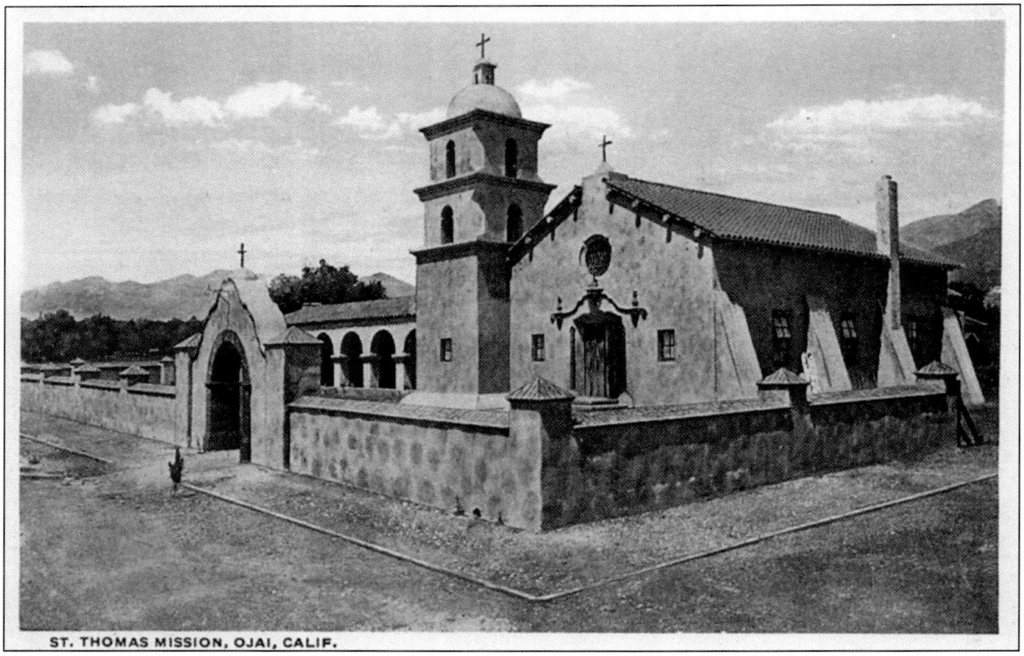

THE SECOND CATHOLIC CHURCH. The great Ojai fire of 1917 destroyed the original wooden Catholic church. The parishioners used the Isis Theater for worship while they pondered their next move. Fortunately, Edward Libbey was remaking the town and offered his help. He commissioned the firm of Mead and Requa to design a new building and donated $1,000 toward its construction, resulting in a beautiful example of Mission Revival architecture. When the church was completed in 1919, Libbey donated another $5,000 to build the entry arch and outside wall. The attached parish hall and rectory were added in 1923 and replaced in 1951. In 1993, the old Catholic church was sold to the City of Ojai; it now houses the Ojai Valley Museum. (Both, OVM Collection.)

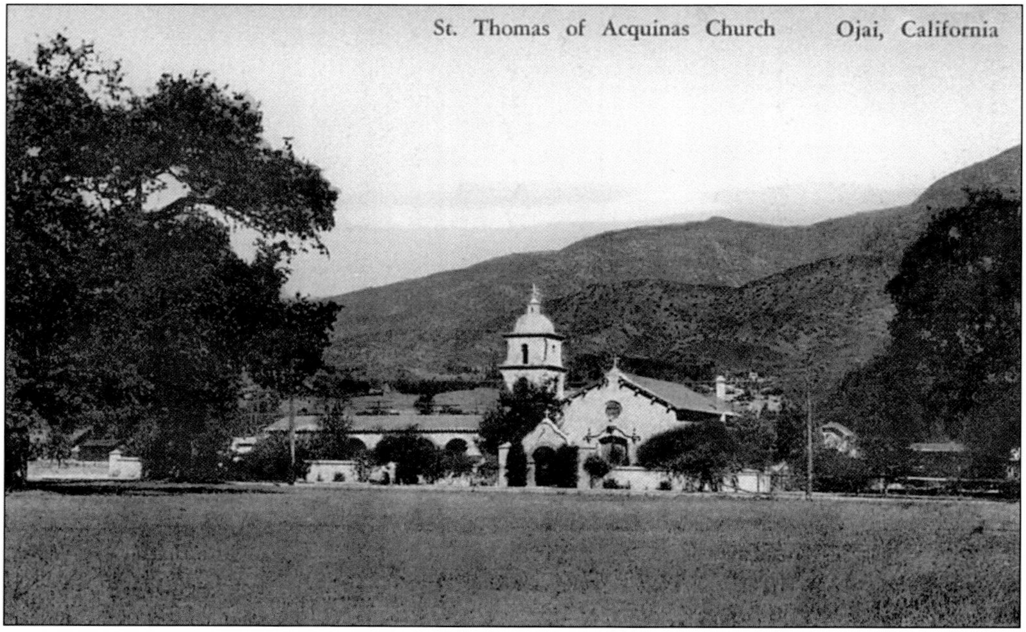

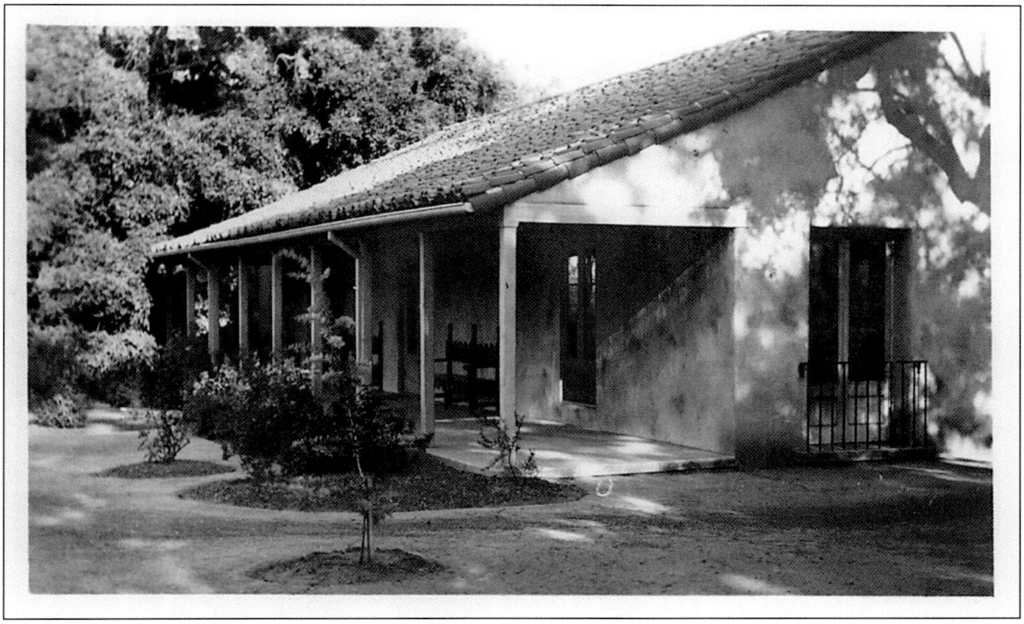

The Ojai Library. During Edward Libbey's transformation of the downtown between 1917 and 1920, there had been talk of constructing a new library building in keeping with Requa's Mission Revival architecture. Libbey favored the southeast corner of Ojai Avenue and Ventura Street, opposite El Roblar Hotel. The Ojai Improvement Company, using a $10,000 gift from the Libbey Estate and donations from the community, undertook the project in 1927. Carlton Winslow was commissioned as architect. The new library, with Zaidee Soule as librarian, opened to the public in 1928. In 1958, it became part of the Ventura County Free Library system. During the 1970s, it became apparent that the library had outgrown its capacity, and in 1981, a beautiful new wing was added, significantly increasing its size. (Both, OVM Collection.)

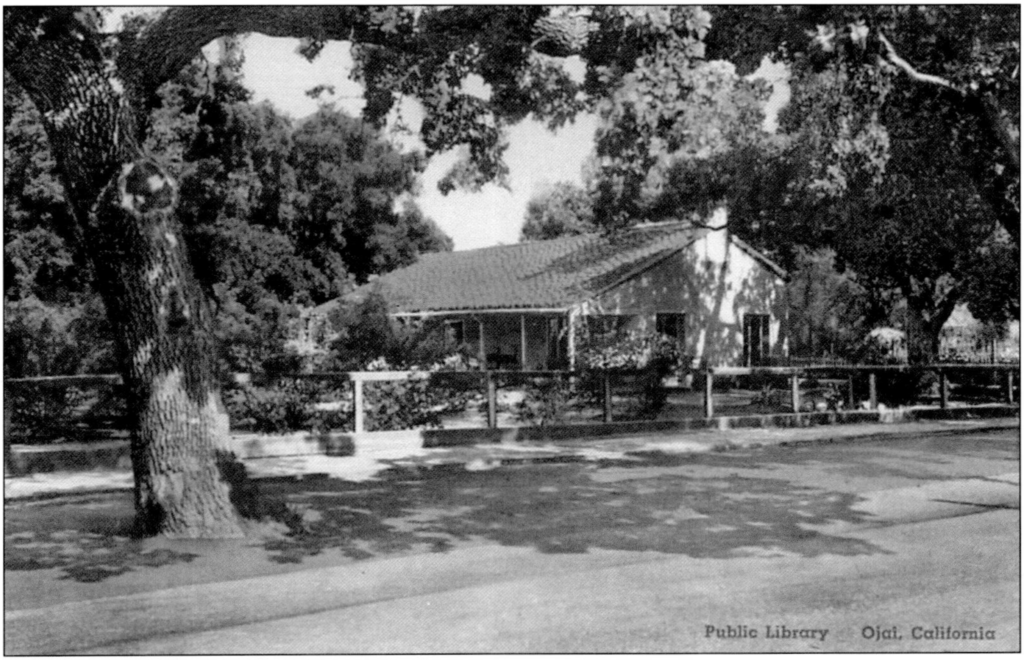

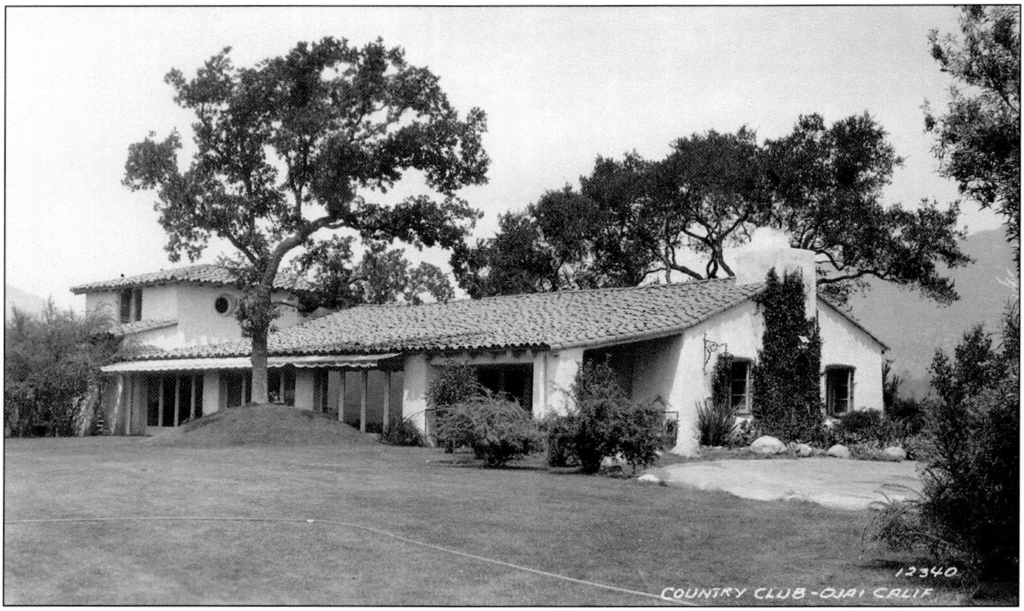

Ojai Valley Country Club. As part of his Ojai makeover, Edward Libbey envisioned a country club with an 18-hole golf course. He procured 170 acres across the street from his exclusive Arbolada residential development. Libbey hired Wallace Neff to design the clubhouse, which consisted of a large lounge, buffet-kitchen, a manager's office and apartment, and—on the sloping hillside—locker rooms and showers. The California Architectural Board awarded Neff a certificate of honor for "a structure in perfect harmony with its surroundings." Unfortunately, when Libbey's Arbolada lots didn't sell, membership at the country club lagged as well. In 1934, the Libbey Estate, operating as the Ojai Valley Company, added a 25-room hotel and opened the Ojai Valley Country Club to the general public. It was subsequently renamed the Ojai Valley Inn and Country Club. (Above, OVM Collection; below, Brian and Connie Aikens collection.)

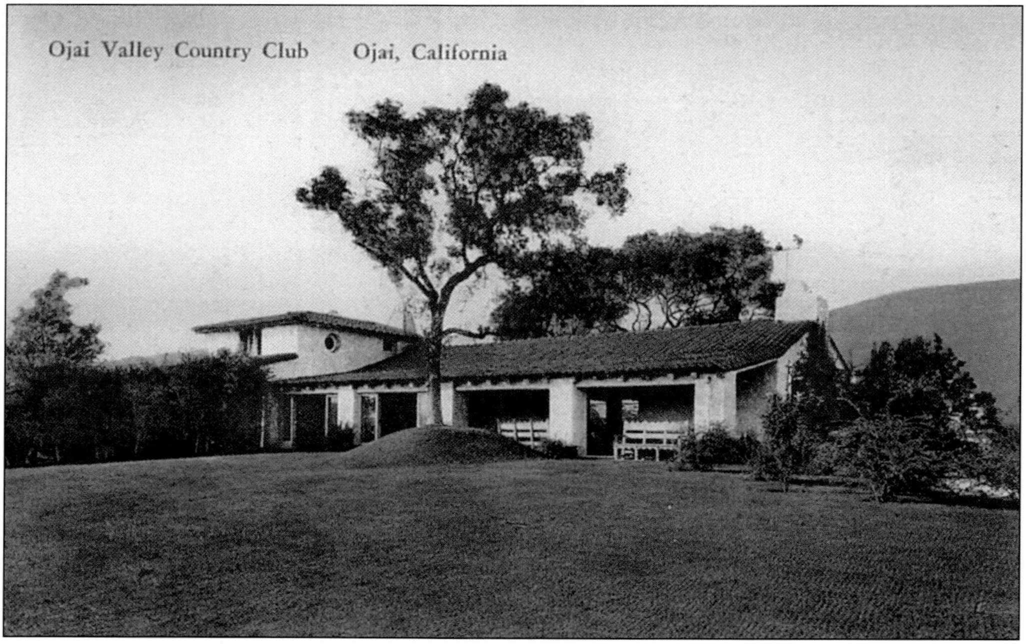

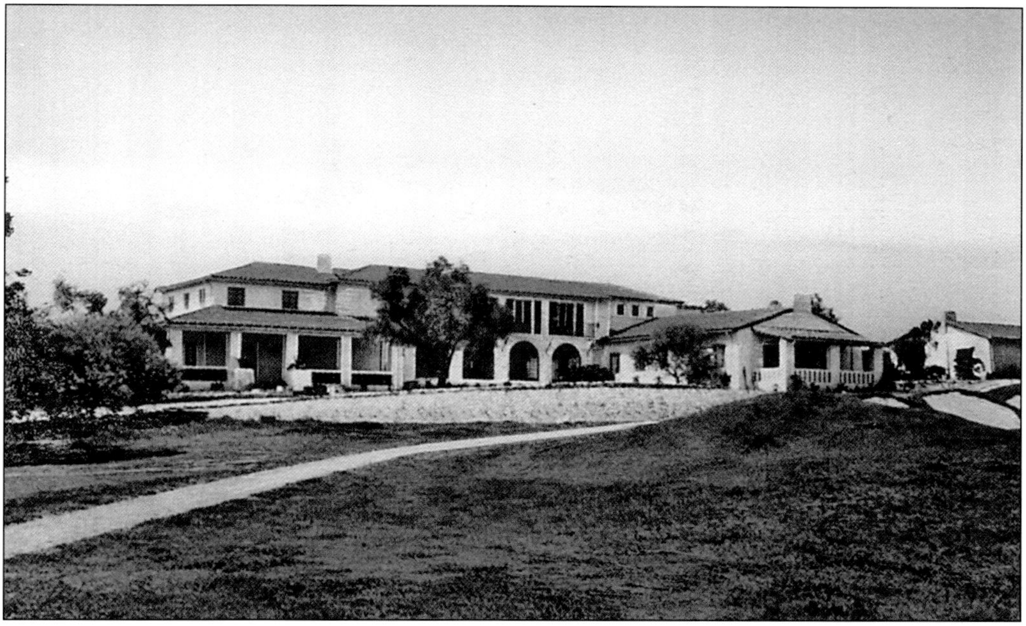

Ojai Valley Inn and Country Club. In 1934, the Ojai Valley Company hired Austen Pierpont to expand the country club to include an inn and larger dining facilities. Pierpont designed a large, two-story building (above) with suites of bedrooms and lavishly furnished interiors. He connected the new building to the original clubhouse by a glass passageway. A paved terrace (below) was added, with doors opening from the new, expanded dining room. The inn was taken over by the military during World War II. Over 1,000 men of the 134th Infantry Regiment were stationed there. Officers lived in the inn's rooms, and soldiers bunked in wooden barracks built on the golf course. In April 1945, Bing Crosby and Bob Hope performed at the country club in a benefit for the Navy Relief Welfare Fund. (Both, George Finn collection.)

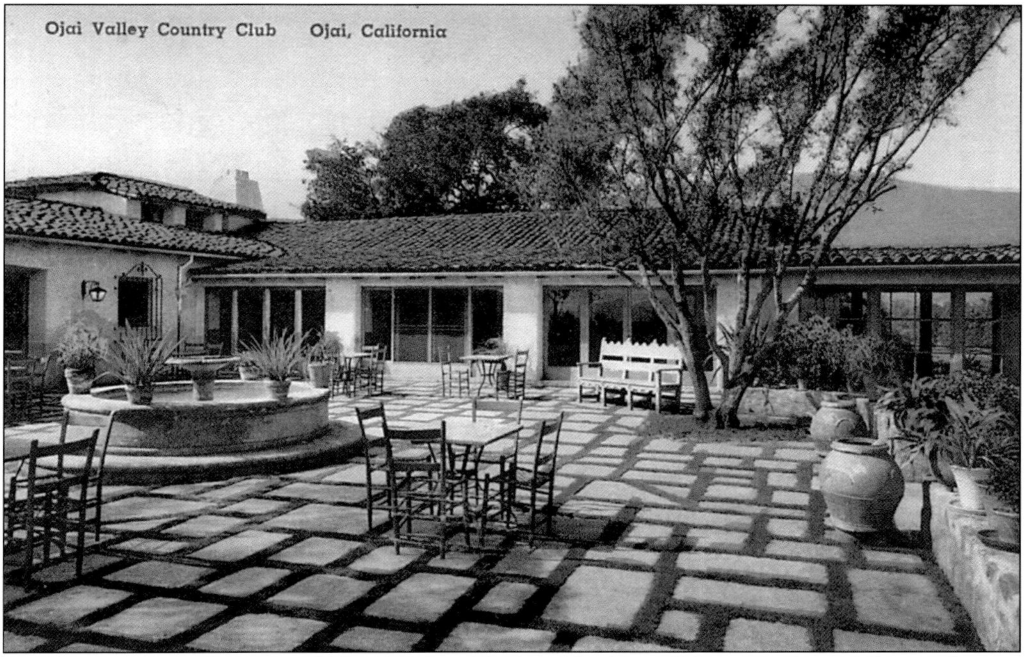

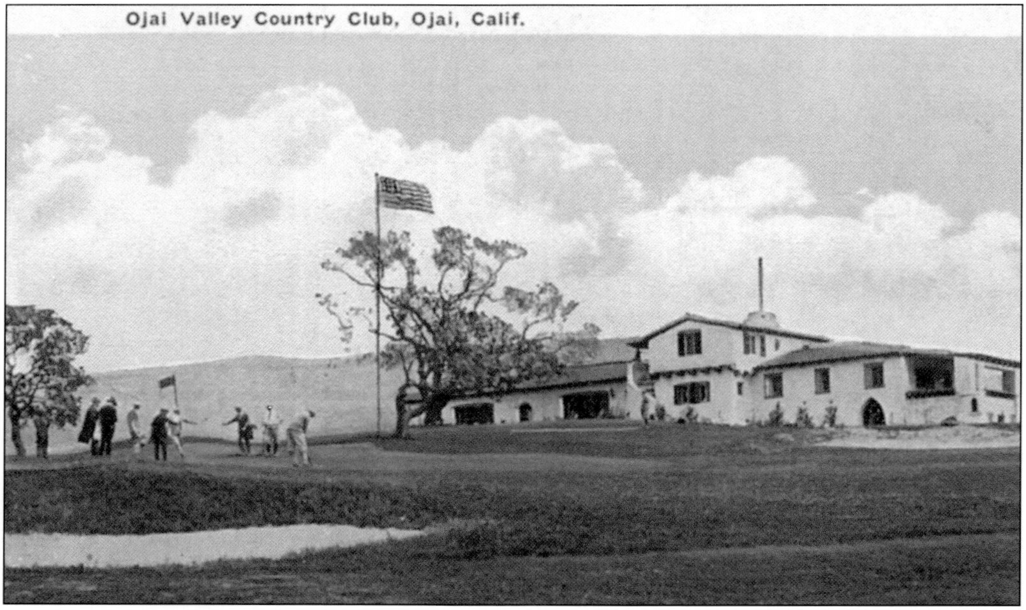

Ojai Valley Inn Golf Course. The Ojai Valley Country Club was one the first great golf courses in California. It was designed and built in 1923 under the direction of George C. Thomas Jr. and Billy Bell. According to Austen Pierpont, the new 18-hole golf course "brought raves and bravos from all the experts and players who played it, both for its skillful layout and for the beauty of the surroundings. It was opened with a gala exhibition match in which Edward Ray and Harry Vardon, the famous English players, participated." Over the years, many Hollywood stars played the course, including Bing Crosby, Bob Hope, Will Smith, Kevin Costner, Michael Douglas, and others. The course hosted several PGA senior tours, bringing such professionals as Arnold Palmer, Lee Trevino, Gary Player, Chi Chi Rodriguez, and Ben Crenshaw to challenge the historic course. (Both, Terry Hill collection.)

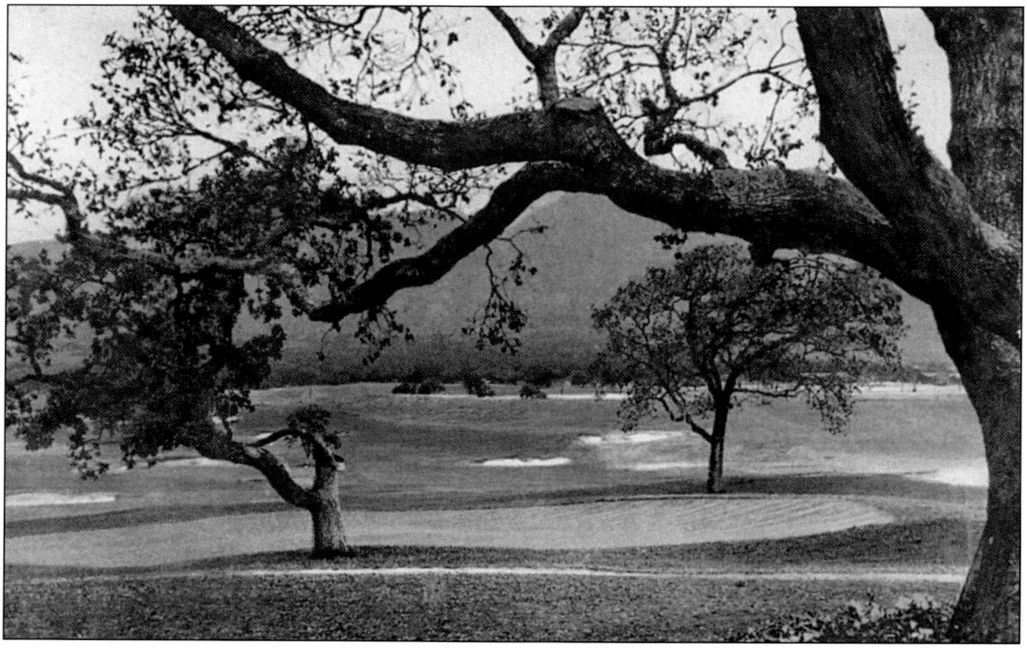

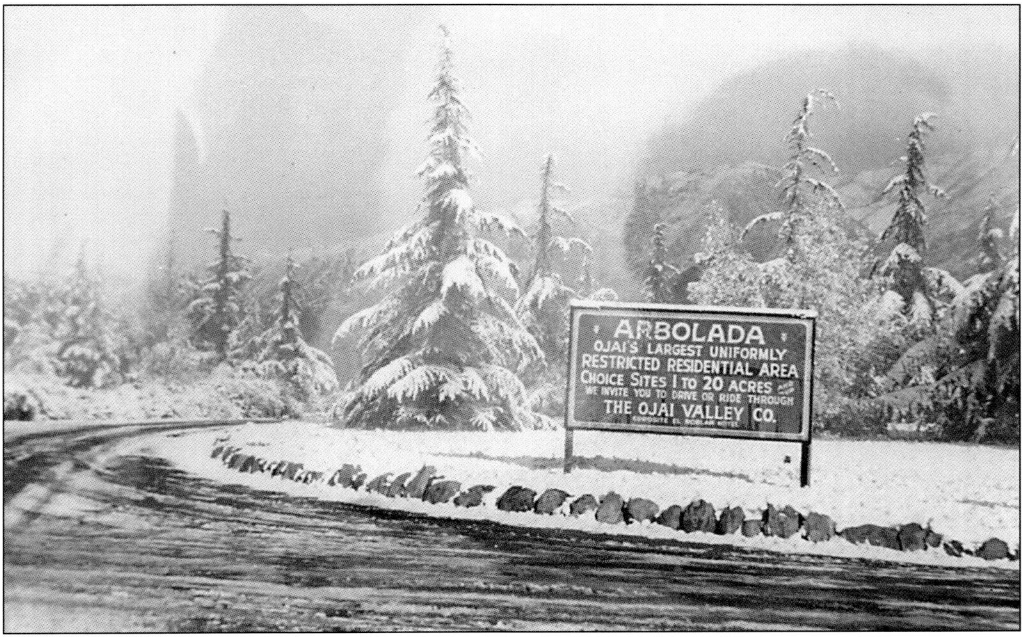

EDWARD LIBBEY'S ARBOLADA. This 360-acre, oak-studded woodland lay across Foothill Road from Libbey's home. When Libbey heard that someone intended to harvest the trees, he bought the acreage himself. Landscaper F. C. Fassel created winding roadways lined with rock. In 1917, six freightcar-loads of trees and plants, including the deodar cedars shown above, were planted throughout the park. Libbey hired George Washington Smith to design three Spanish-style model homes, built the Ojai Valley Country Club nearby, and advertised heavily in the east. None of this paid off. The last lot was not sold until 1958. (Both, David Mason collection.)

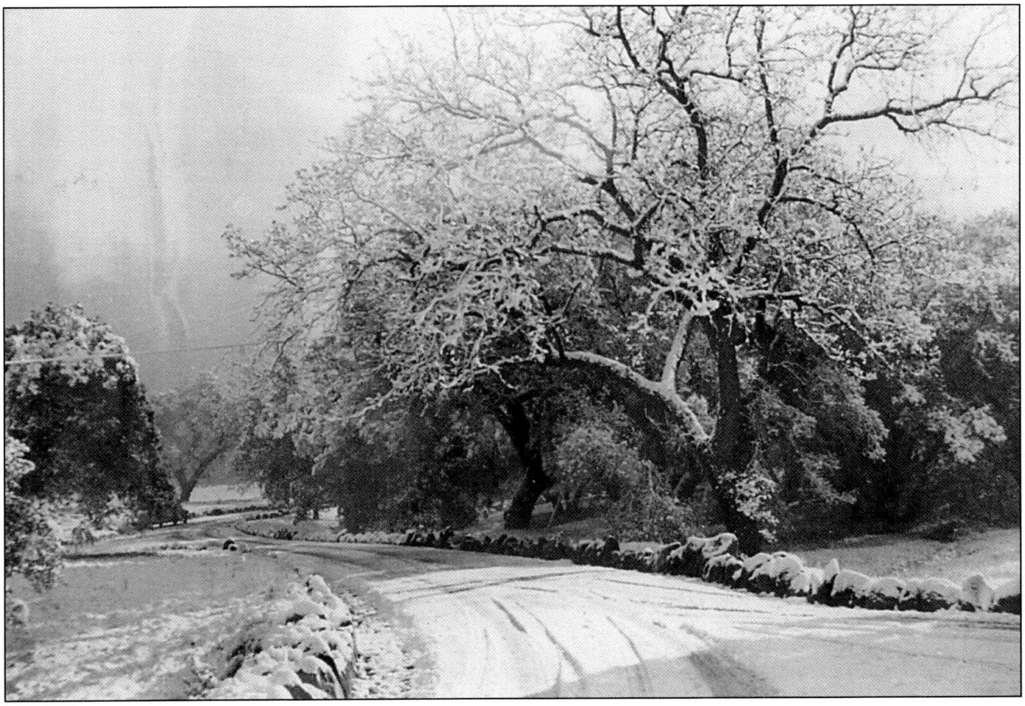

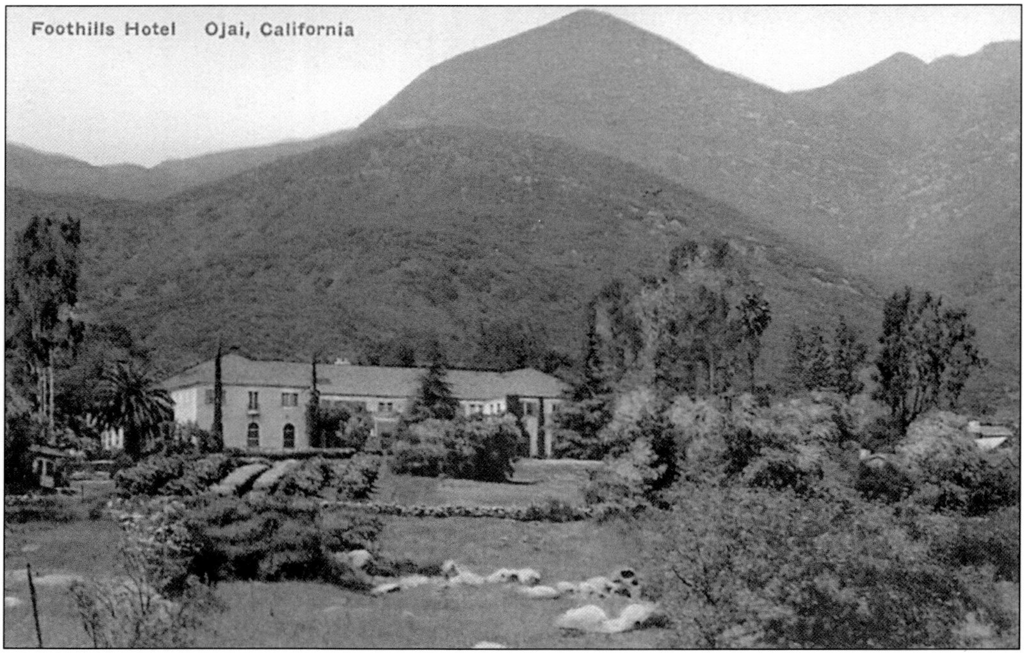

The Second Foothills Hotel. When the original craftsman-style Foothills Hotel burned to the ground in the great 1917 fire, the architectural firm of Mead and Requa designed a Colonial Revival replacement. This beautiful, elegant hotel captured the old-world charm of the new Ojai. Located near the top of Foothill Road, it afforded spectacular views of the Ojai Valley, with the new post office tower clearly visible through the oak trees below. The Foothills Hotel thrived during the 1920s but was hit hard by the Great Depression. In 1942, the buildings were sold to the California Preparatory School—a boys' military academy—and in 1955, it became the home of Camp Ramah, a Jewish summer camp. When Camp Ramah moved to a new facility, the old hotel was demolished, and its grounds became the new Del Oro housing development. (Above, OVM Collection; below, Terry Hill collection.)

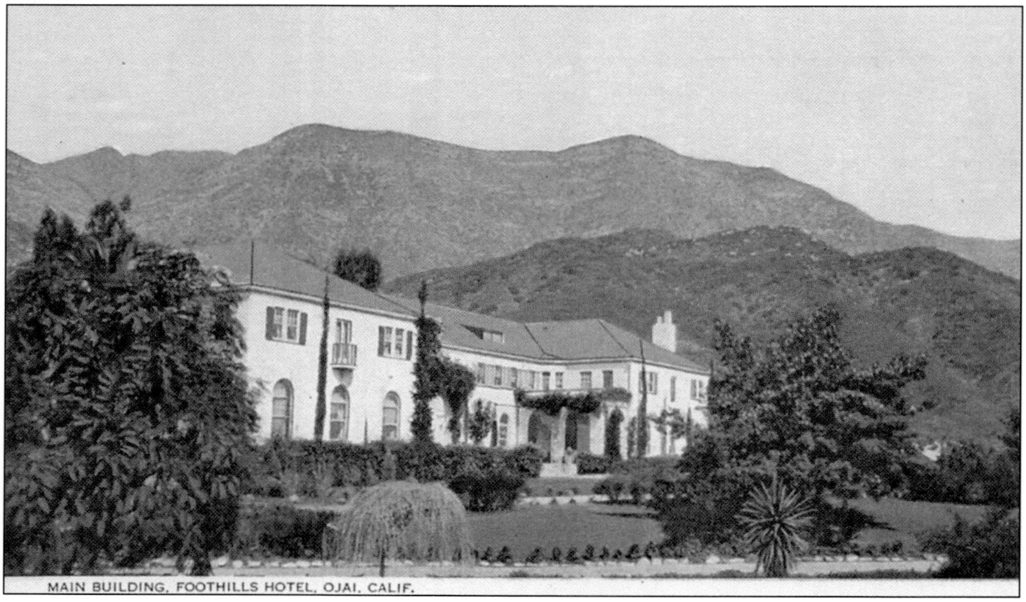

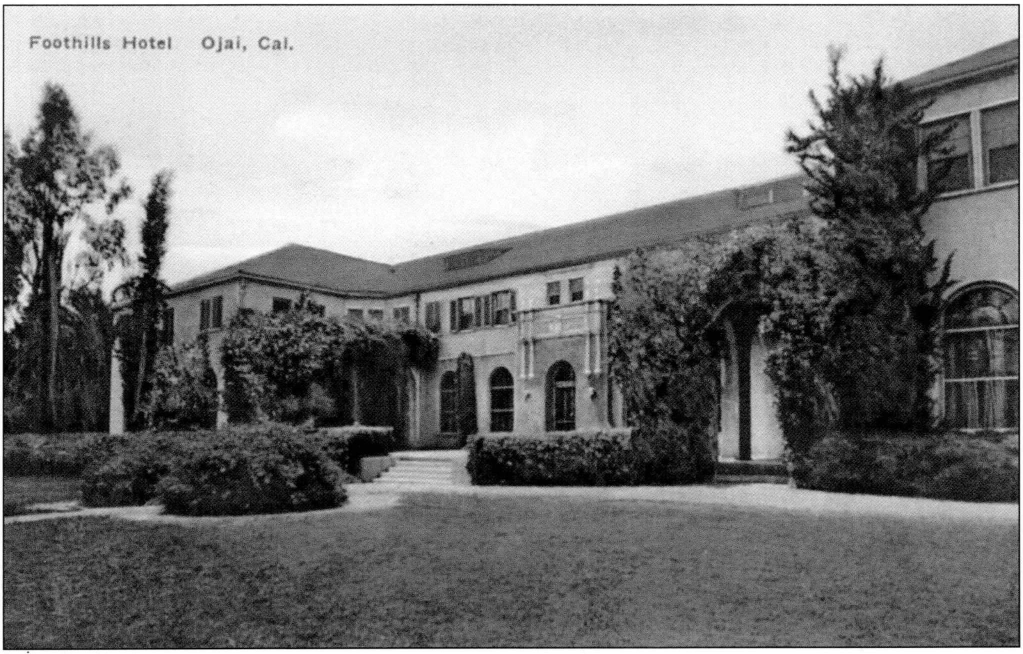

The Frost-Coolidge Music Festival. Although the Foothills Hotel catered to wealthy easterners, Ojai residents often benefitted from the cultural and social events held there. A good example was the Frost-Coolidge Music Festival of 1926. Elizabeth Sprague Coolidge, who had a winter home in Ojai, was one of America's foremost promoters of chamber music. She teamed up in 1926 with another Ojai resident, Frank Frost, to create a three-day chamber music festival at the Foothills Hotel. Two-thirds of the audience was Ojai residents. When the festival concluded, *The Ojai* proclaimed, "One of the greatest musical events that has ever taken place in America came to a close on Sunday evening with the final concert of the Ojai Musical Festival." Many consider the Frost-Coolidge Music Festival to be the forerunner of the current Ojai Music Festival. (Above, OVM Collection; right, David Mason collection.)

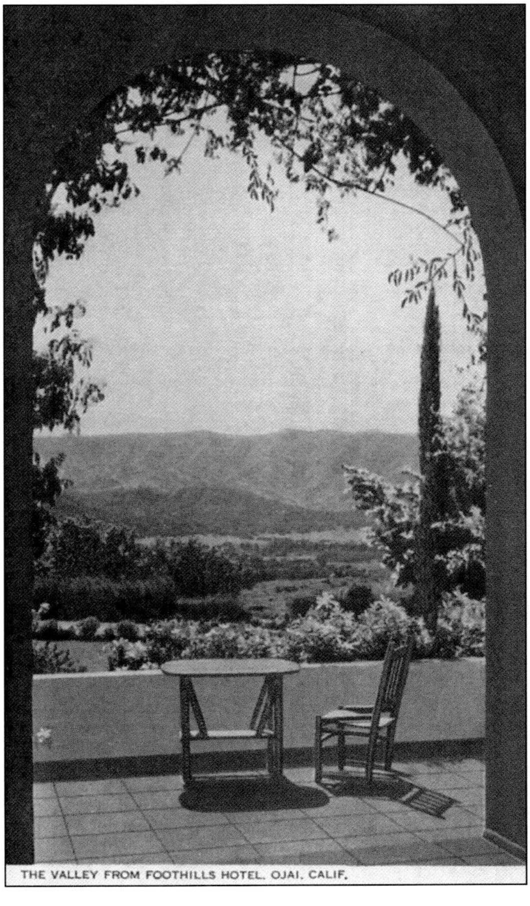

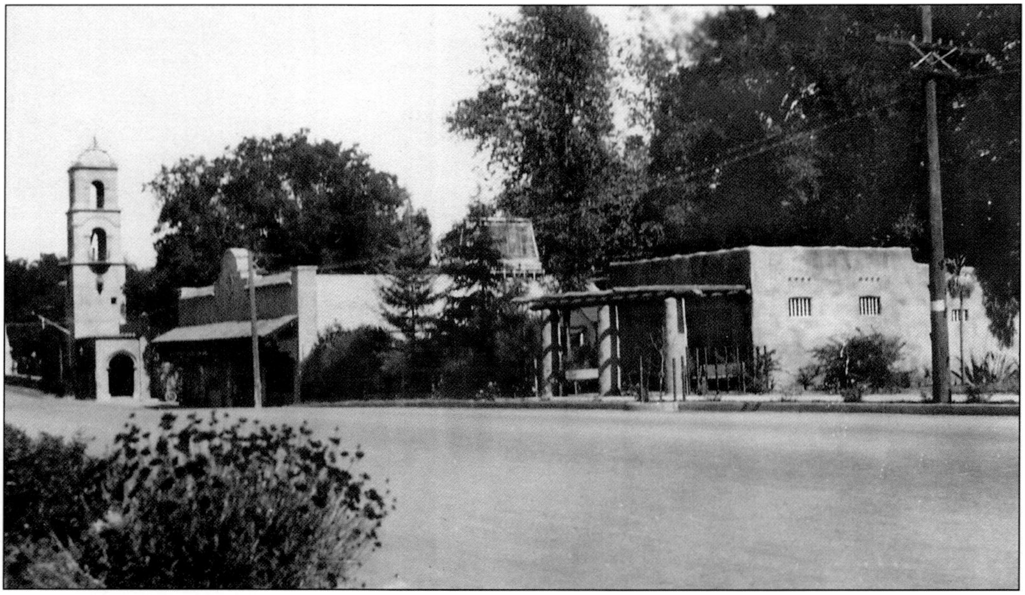

Ojai Theater and Maravilla Realty. Ojai's little movie theater opened in 1914 as the Isis Theater. The first film shown was Jack London's *Valley of the Moon*. In addition to screening films, the theater staged plays, vaudeville acts, and Saturday night dances. Talkies came to the Ojai Theater in 1930. To the right of the theater stood Maravilla Realty, the sales office for Libbey's Arbolada residential lots. (OVM Collection.)

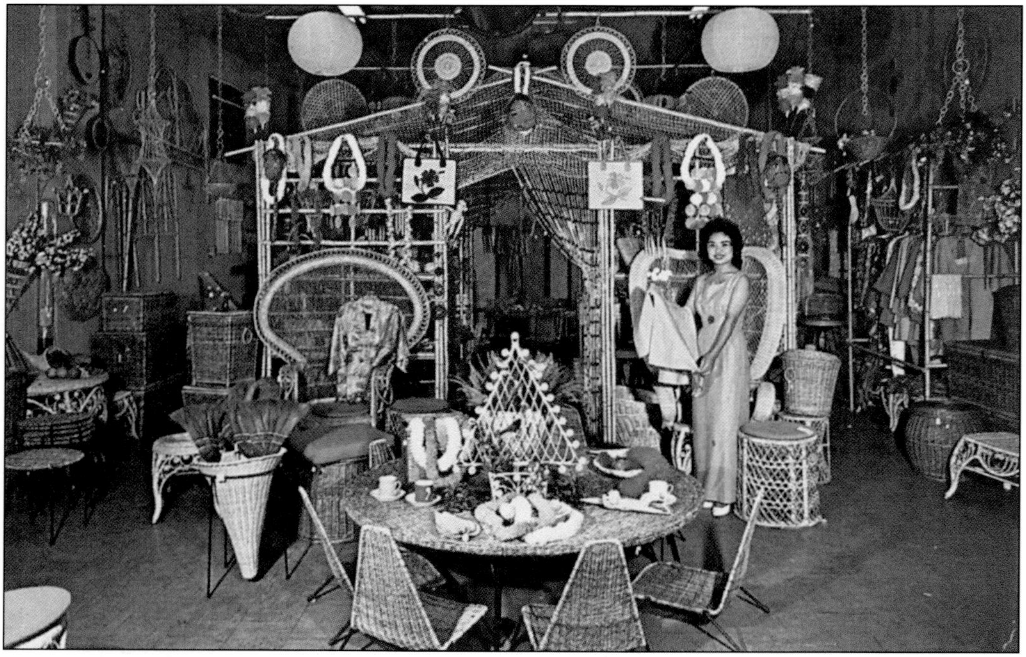

Polynesian Shop at the Arcade. From 1944 to 1960, Doug Jordan operated the Ojai Grocery from his small store in the arcade. When the Y Shopping Center opened, Doug could not compete with its new Safeway Market. He and his wife Claudia converted their business into a Polynesian store. This was the beginning of a trend leading to an arcade consisting mostly of specialty shops, restaurants, and boutiques. (George Finn collection.)

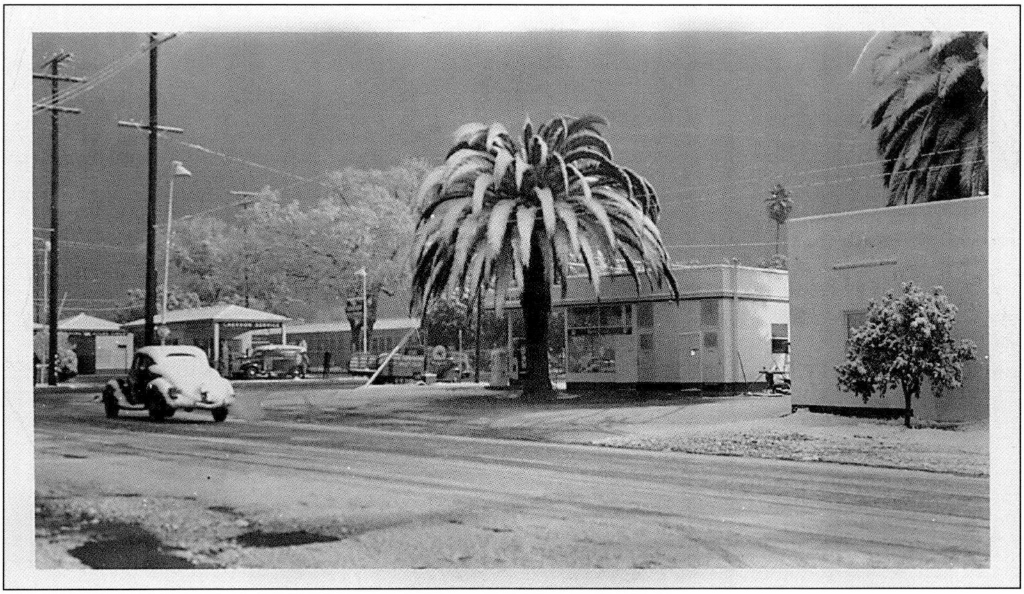

Downtown Ojai in the Snow. This 1930s postcard shows the corner of South Montgomery Street and Ojai Avenue after a rare snowfall. In the background are Ojai Elementary School and Watson's Chevron Station; in the foreground is another service station (now a restaurant). By the 1950s, nine gasoline stations operated in downtown Ojai. Today there are just two. (David Mason collection.)

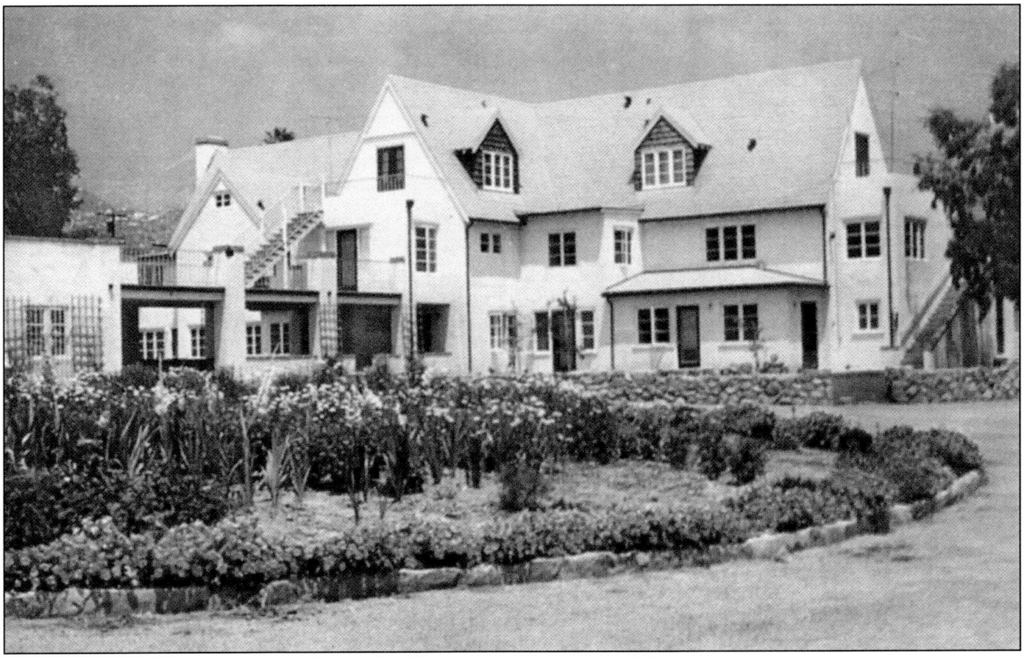

Ethel Andrus and Grey Gables. The National Retired Teachers Association (NRTA) established Grey Gables as a home for retired teachers in 1954. Ojai resident Ethel Andrus founded the NRTA in 1947. In 1958, she organized the American Association for Retired Persons (AARP), which she ran from her offices at Grey Gables until 1963. Today AARP is the largest nonprofit organization in the world, with over 35 million members. (George Finn collection.)

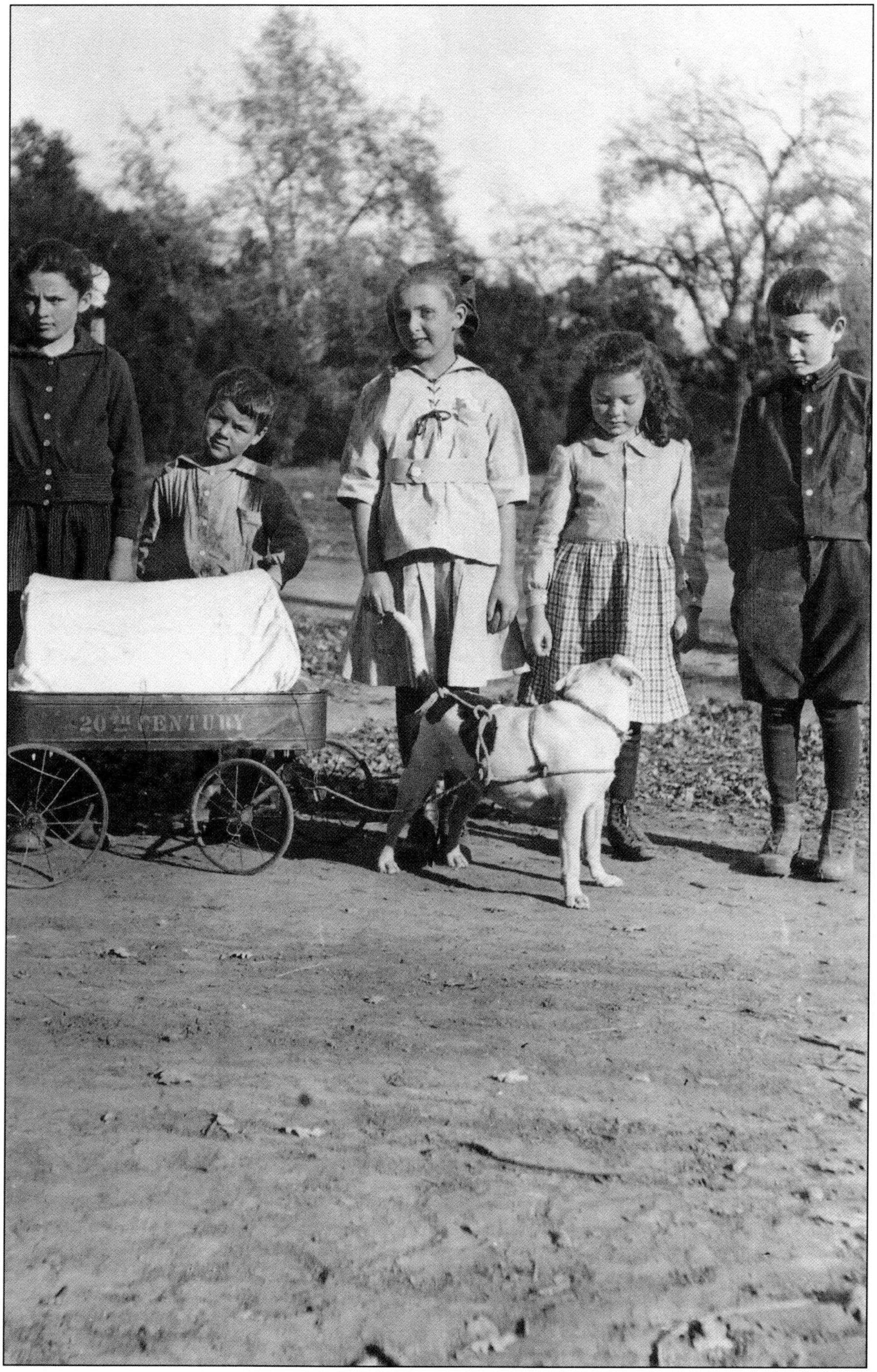

OJAI VALLEY SCHOOLCHILDREN. This 1919 postcard features young Dacy Linder (center) with her friends and pet dog. In addition to playing make-believe, popular children's games of the era included stickball, pum pum pull away, and marbles for keeps. Dacy was the daughter of Fred Linder, a plumbing contractor who was elected fire chief in 1921 and was Ojai's mayor from 1946 to 1954. (OVM Collection.)

Seven

Excellence in Education

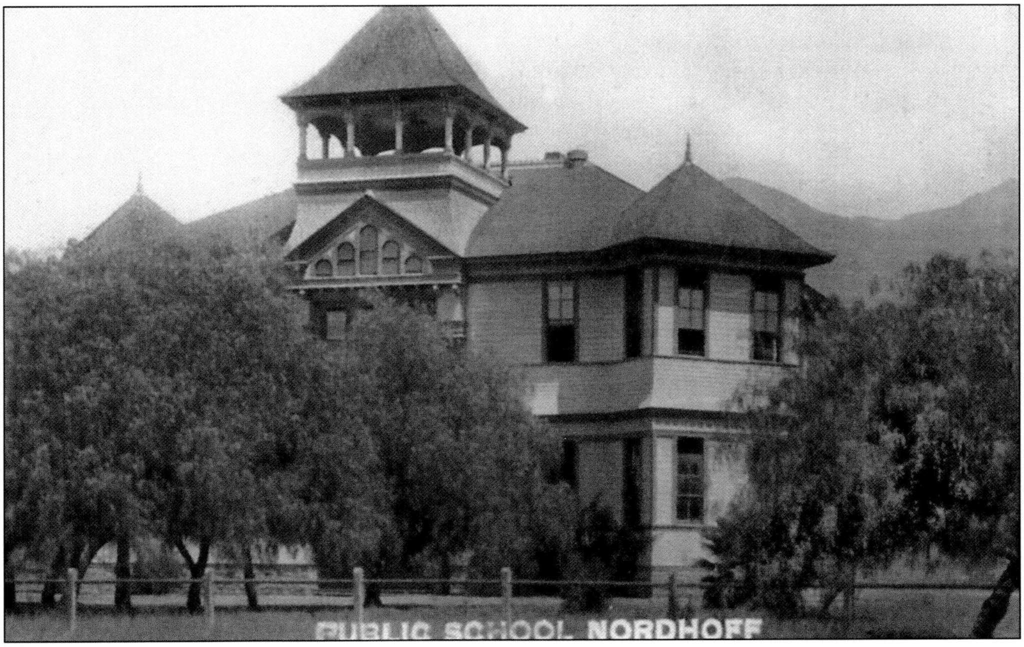

Nordhoff Grammar School. This large, wood-framed school was built in 1895 on the northeast corner of Ojai Avenue and Montgomery Street. Designed by Ventura architect F. P. Ward, it is a good example of Queen Anne schoolhouse architecture. The building served the needs of the community as well as its children; the assembly hall doubled as a community auditorium, and the school bell alerted the bucket brigade when fires broke out. (David Mason collection.)

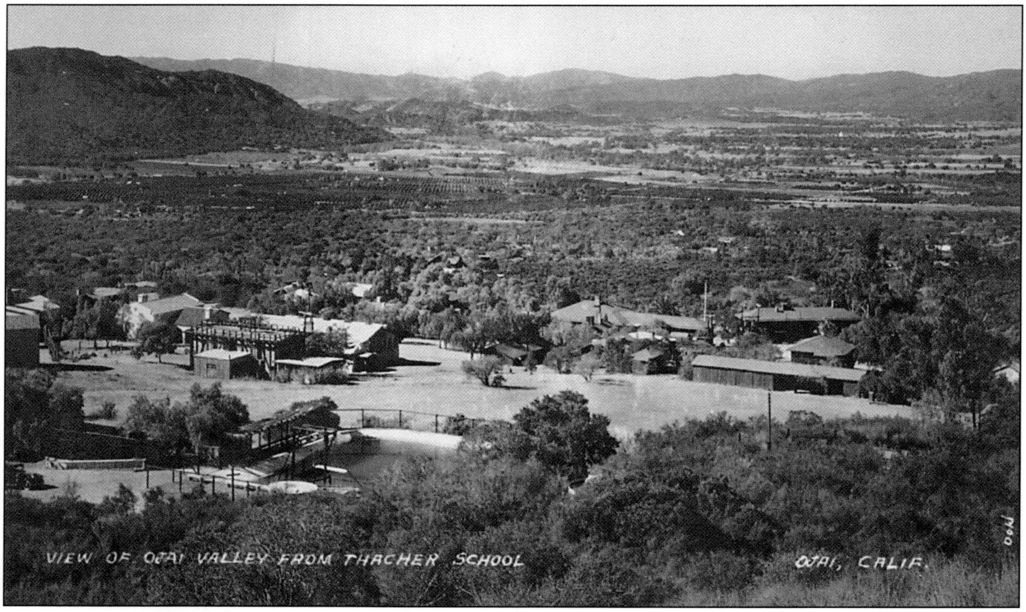

SPECTACULAR THACHER SCHOOL. Thacher School is located in the foothills of the Los Padres National Forest, where it overlooks the beautiful Ojai Valley and has ready access to numerous hiking and horse trails. Founded in 1889 by Sherman Thacher on his Casa de Piedra Ranch, the school describes its mission as one where the "challenges of academics are combined with those of mountains and horses." Sherman Thacher made horseback riding and camping an essential feature of the school's educational program. He was fond of saying, "there's something about the outside of a horse that's good for the inside of a boy." The Thacher Pergola (below) still frames the quad between the dining commons and study hall. Over the years, the school has retained its low-profile California "ranch" look, allowing the mountain and valley vistas to dominate. (Above, David Mason collection; below, Terry Hill collection.)

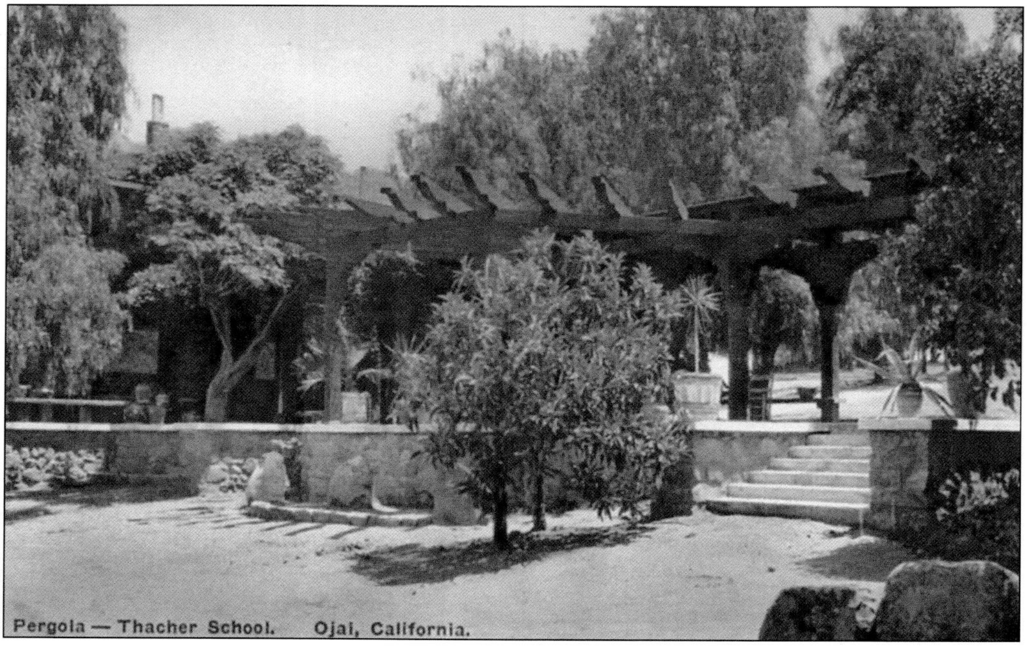

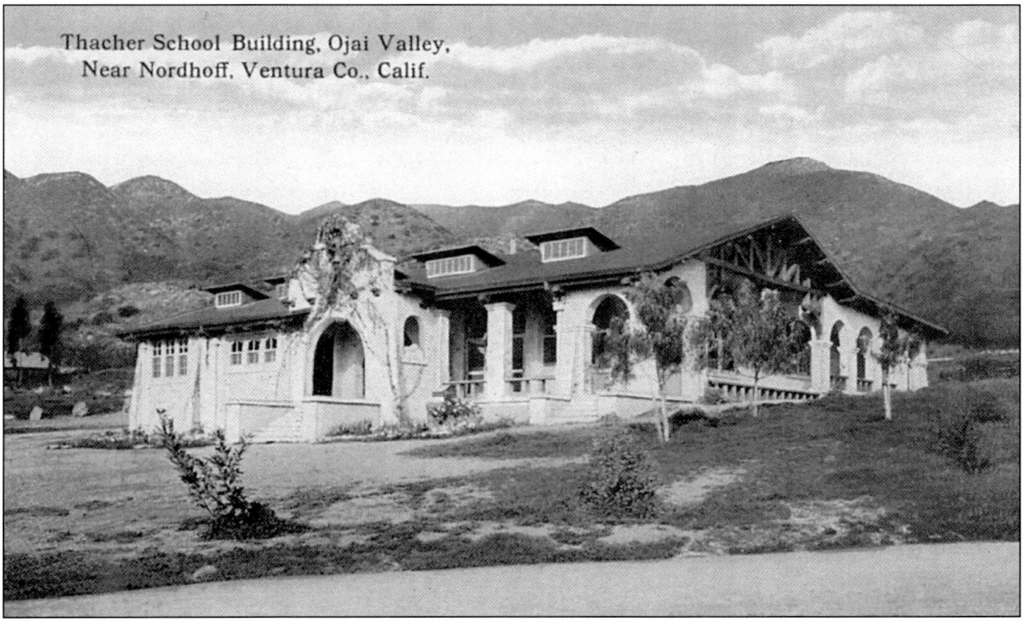

Thacher School Buildings. Several of the original school structures were destroyed in a 1910 fire. Sherman Thacher asked Arthur B. Benton, who was designing the first Nordhoff High School campus, to design the new Thacher schoolhouse and dormitory. Arthur Benton, best known for Riverside's Mission Inn, was one of the first proponents of Mission Revival architecture. Completed six years before Libbey's transformation of downtown Ojai, the Thacher schoolhouse (above) is probably Ojai's first Mission Revival building. Below, the Upper School Dorm—also designed by Benton—shows Mission Revival elements in the shape of the arches, pediment, and upper arcade. Among those who once boarded here were future author Thornton Wilder and capitalist Howard Hughes. (Above, Terry Hill collection; below, OVM Collection.)

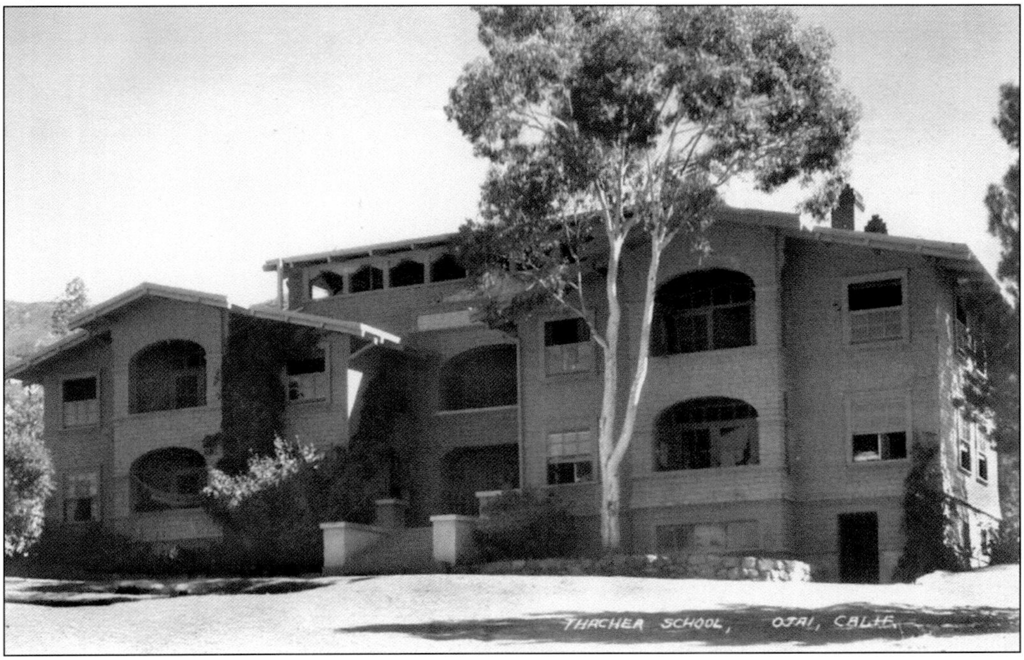

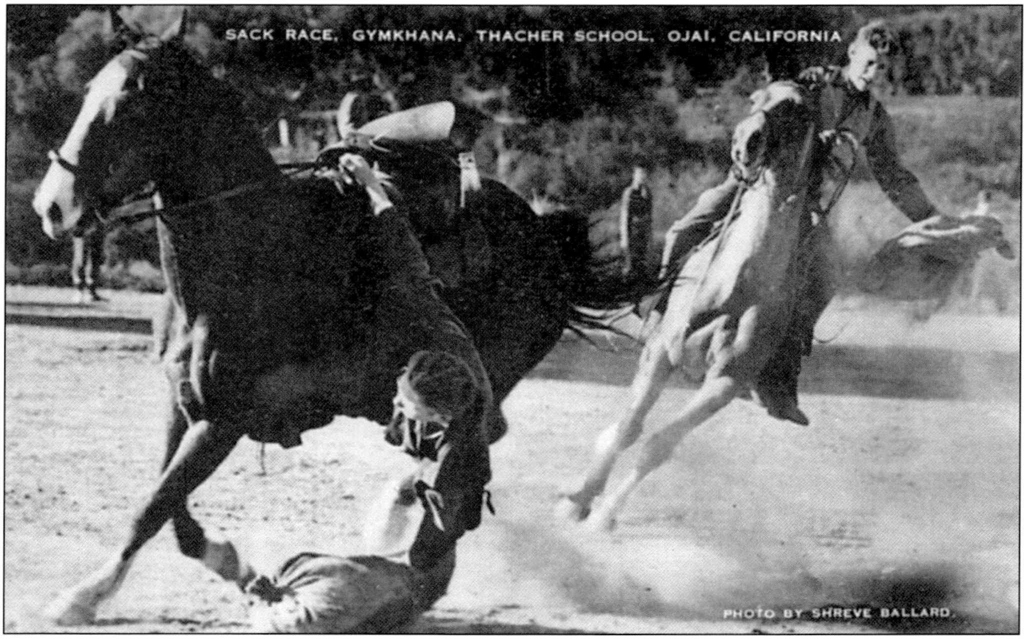

THACHER SCHOOL GYMKHANA. Begun in 1900, this Thacher School tradition is still a popular annual event at the school. In its early days, Thacher's gymkhana featured such events as tilting, in which the rider, armed with a lance, attempts to spear three rings in a row; bending, in which the horse and rider wind through five stakes, trying to keep from upsetting them; sack races; and broom polo. (George Finn collection.)

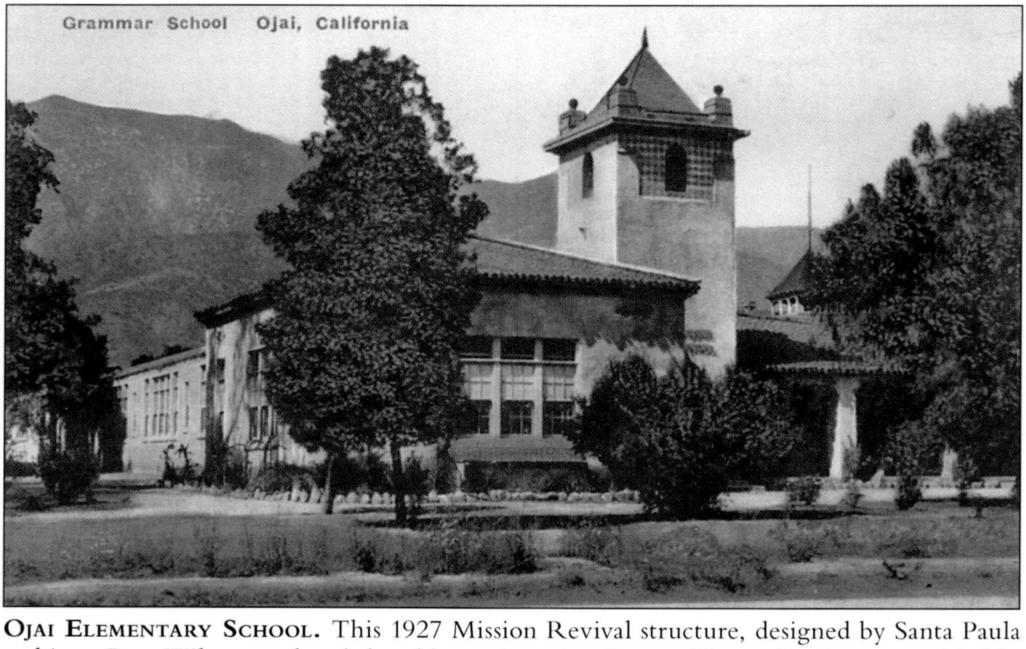

OJAI ELEMENTARY SCHOOL. This 1927 Mission Revival structure, designed by Santa Paula architect Roy Wilson, replaced the old wooden schoolhouse. The auditorium was added in 1937. In 1953, the school was renamed Ojai Elementary School. When the school was closed in 1976, the building was converted into the Ojai Unified School District offices. The bell from the original wooden schoolhouse is mounted on a pedestal in front. (Terry Hill collection.)

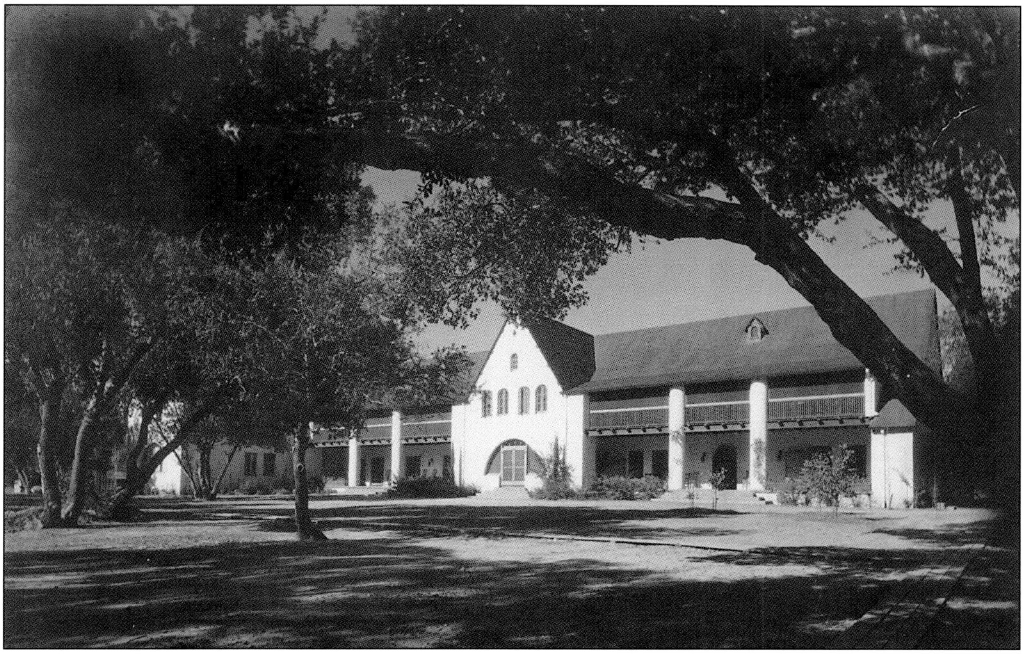

Frost Hall, Ojai Valley School. Progressive educator Edward Yeomans opened Ojai Valley School in 1923 on land donated by Edward Drummond Libbey. The private school began with 45 students in grades three through nine. A high school in Ojai's east end was added in 1962. Frost Hall was designed by Wallace Neff, who also designed the Ojai Valley Country Club and the Libbey stables. (Ojai Valley School collection.)

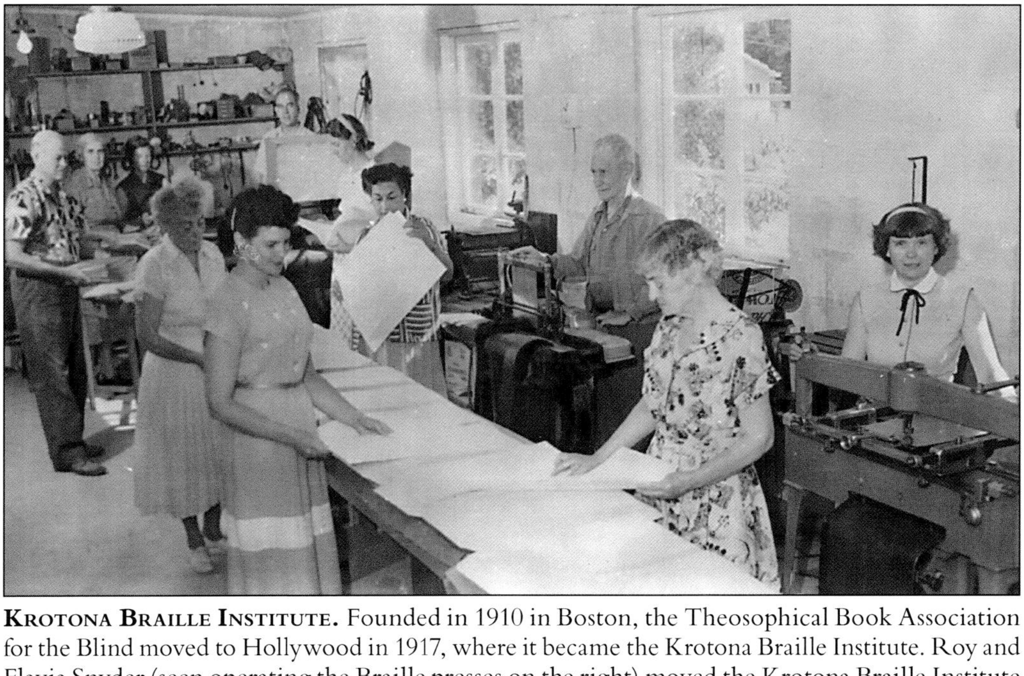

Krotona Braille Institute. Founded in 1910 in Boston, the Theosophical Book Association for the Blind moved to Hollywood in 1917, where it became the Krotona Braille Institute. Roy and Flavia Snyder (seen operating the Braille presses on the right) moved the Krotona Braille Institute to Ojai in 1947. The institute consisted of a Braille publishing house and the Baker Memorial Library, which loaned Braille books throughout the world. (George Finn collection.)

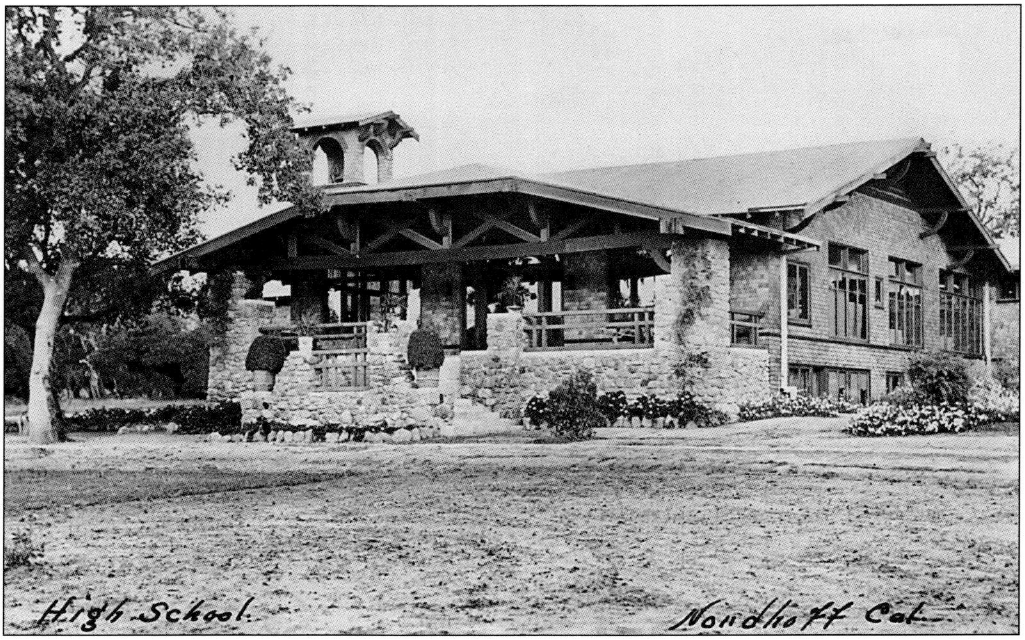

NORDHOFF UNION HIGH SCHOOL. In 1910, Arthur B. Benton designed this Arts and Crafts building (above) to house the new Nordhoff High School. Charles M. Pratt, a wealthy eastern oil tycoon who owned a home in Ojai, donated separate manual training and domestic arts buildings. When the high school was first organized in 1909, classes were held on the upper floor of the wood-framed grammar school downtown. The new high school campus opened in October 1911 with 40 students. In 1929, Santa Paula architect Roy Wilson designed a new Mission Revival building fronting El Paseo Drive (below). The auditorium was added in 1938. In 1967, Nordhoff High School switched campuses with Matilija Junior High School on Maricopa Highway. At that time, the original Arts and Crafts building was removed. (Above, Brian and Connie Aikens collection; below, George Finn collection.)

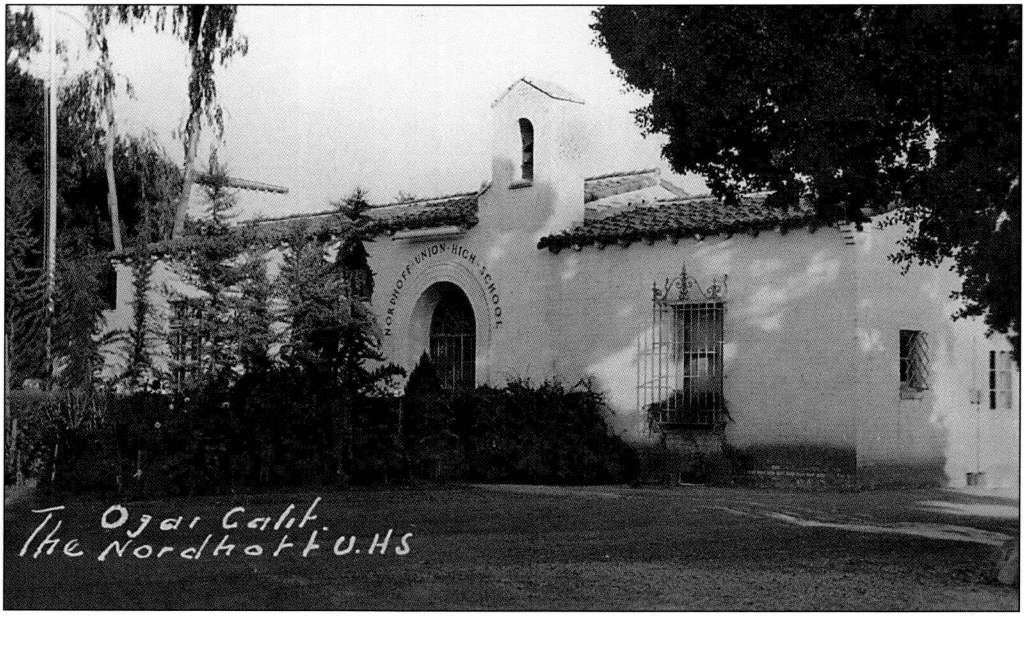

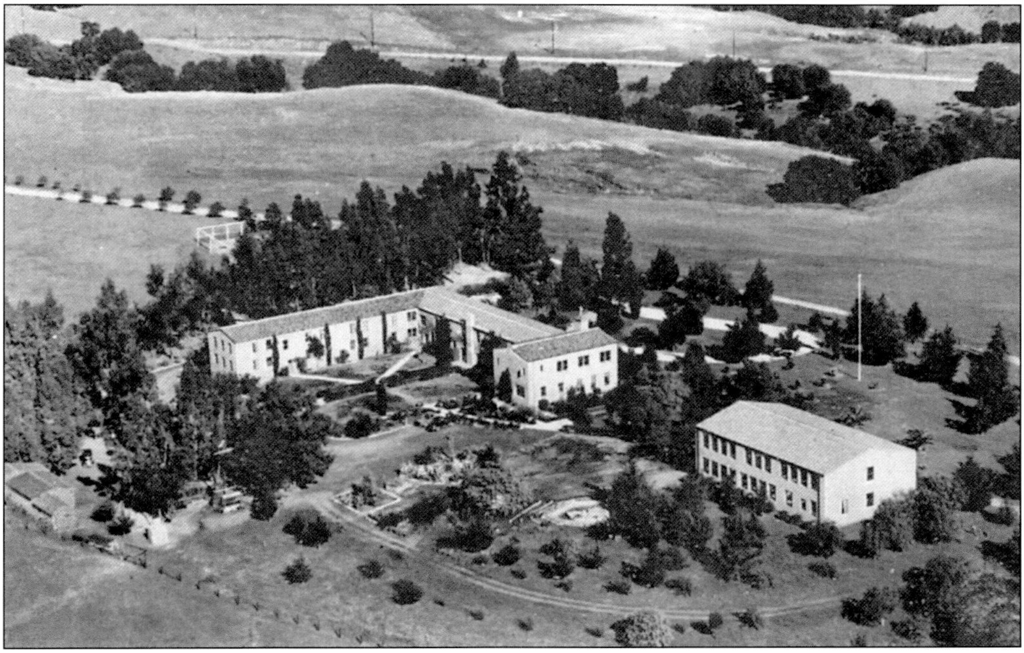

Villanova Preparatory School. Augustinian fathers founded Villanova in 1924 as an all-boys Catholic boarding school, "combining the ideals of a good Christian home and of a solid, sufficient education." The school is named after a Spanish saint of the Augustinian order, St. Thomas of Villanova. It sits on 131 acres at the entrance to the city of Ojai, across the highway from the Krotona Institute. Albert C. Martin Sr., a noted Los Angeles architect who designed the Ventura and Los Angeles city halls, designed the original buildings (above). Cantwell Hall (below) was named after John Cantwell, first archbishop of the Los Angeles archdiocese. Villanova remained an all-boys school until 1970. (Above, Terry Hill collection; below, George Finn collection.)

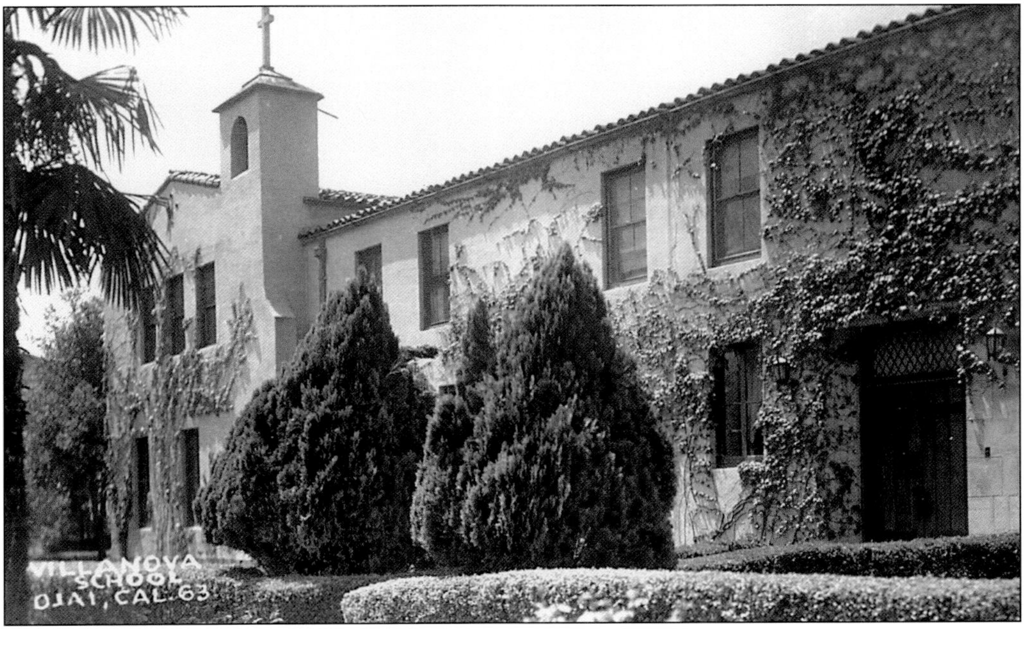

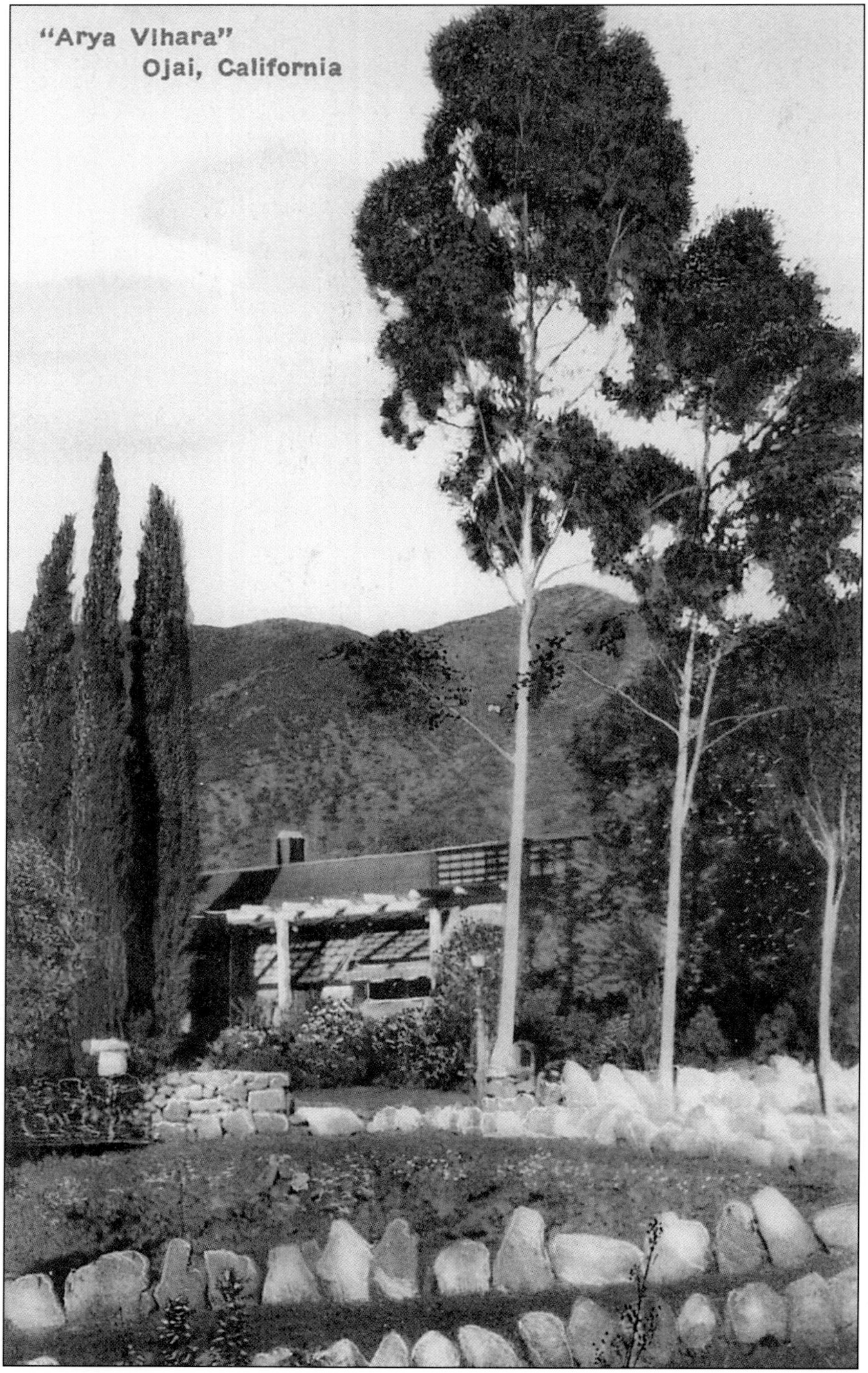

Krishnamurti's Ojai Home. The world-renowned spiritual teacher Jiddu Krishnamurti lived and taught in the Ojai Valley for over 60 years. Named one of five "Saints of the 20th Century" by *Time* magazine, Krishnamurti drew thousands of spiritual seekers to his annual Ojai talks. His very presence in Ojai attracted several New Age groups to the valley. (George Finn collection.)

Eight

A Spiritual Center

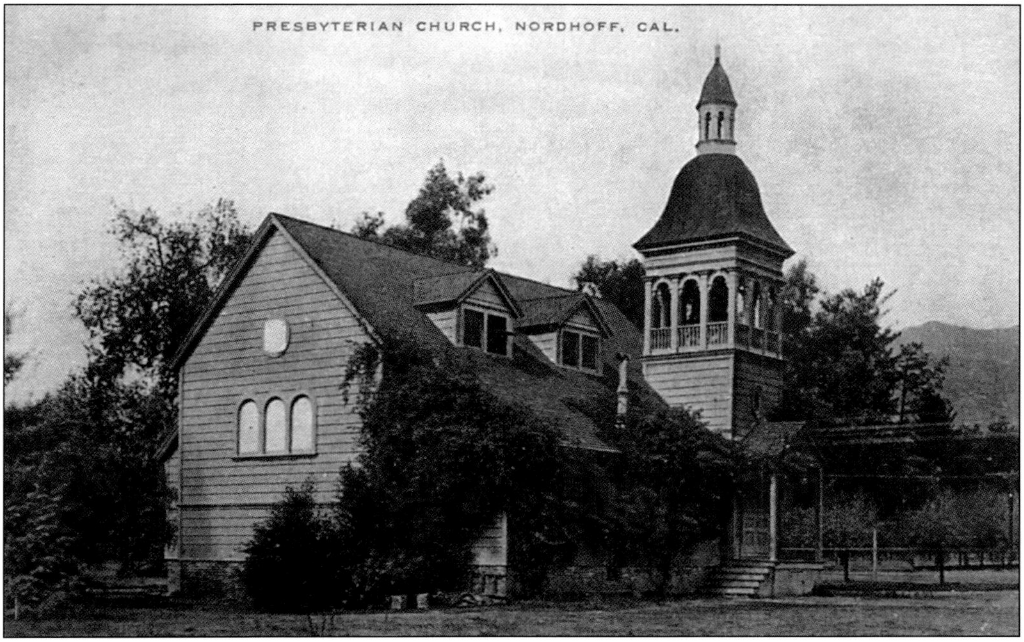

Presbyterian Church, East Ojai Location. The Presbyterians formed Ojai's first Protestant congregation in 1877. Their Queen Anne–Colonial Revival church, designed by J. Cleveland Cady, was completed in 1884. The location of the church, on the Soule Ranch a mile east of Nordhoff, upset some members of the congregation who lived in town. They left in 1888, building a Congregational church downtown where Ojai's library is now located. (OVM Collection.)

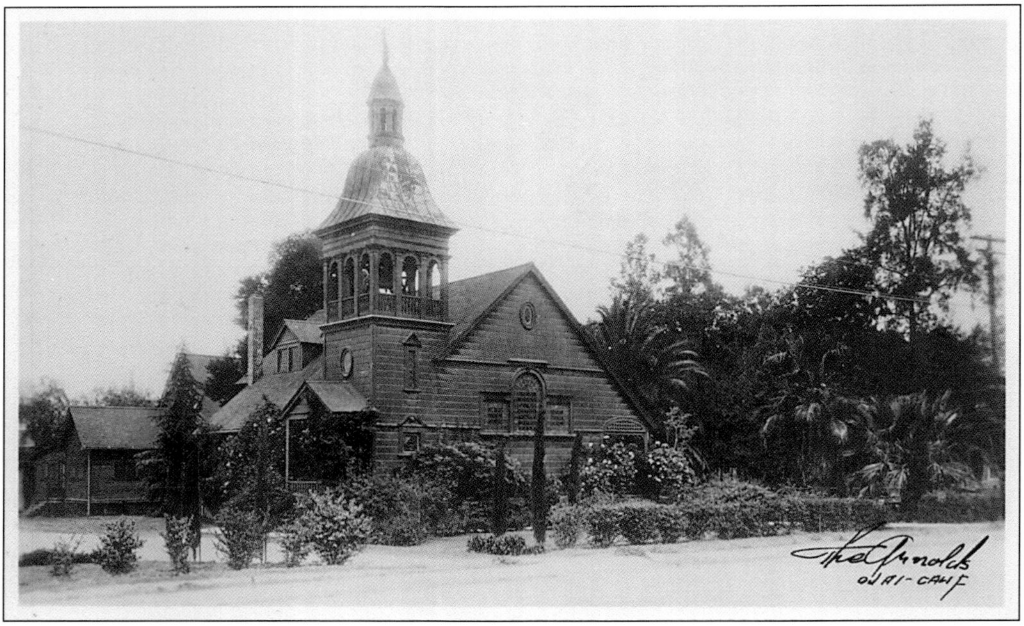

PRESBYTERIAN CHURCH, DOWNTOWN LOCATION. In 1900, the Presbyterian and Congregational churches united. The two churches were moved to a new site on the southeast corner of Ojai Avenue and Montgomery Street and combined, as shown above. When the Presbyterians built their current church (below,) the original church was moved again, to the southwest corner of Aliso and Montgomery Streets, where it became the Nazarene Church. (OVM Collection.)

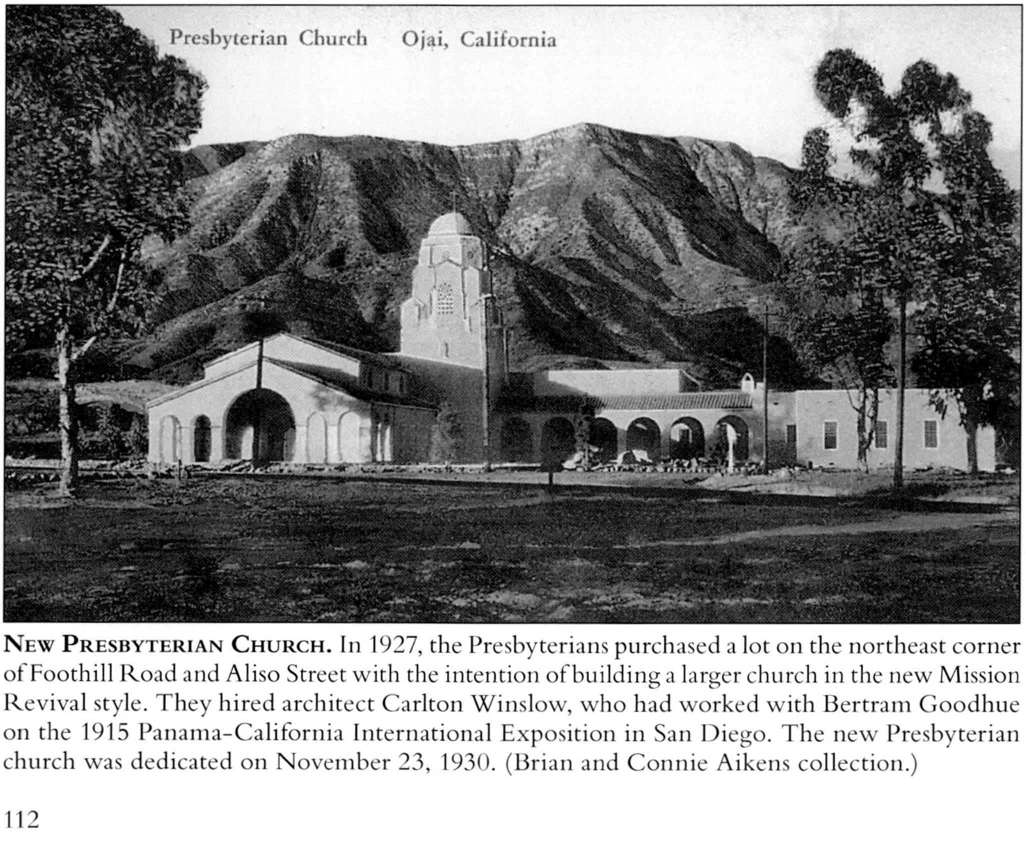

NEW PRESBYTERIAN CHURCH. In 1927, the Presbyterians purchased a lot on the northeast corner of Foothill Road and Aliso Street with the intention of building a larger church in the new Mission Revival style. They hired architect Carlton Winslow, who had worked with Bertram Goodhue on the 1915 Panama-California International Exposition in San Diego. The new Presbyterian church was dedicated on November 23, 1930. (Brian and Connie Aikens collection.)

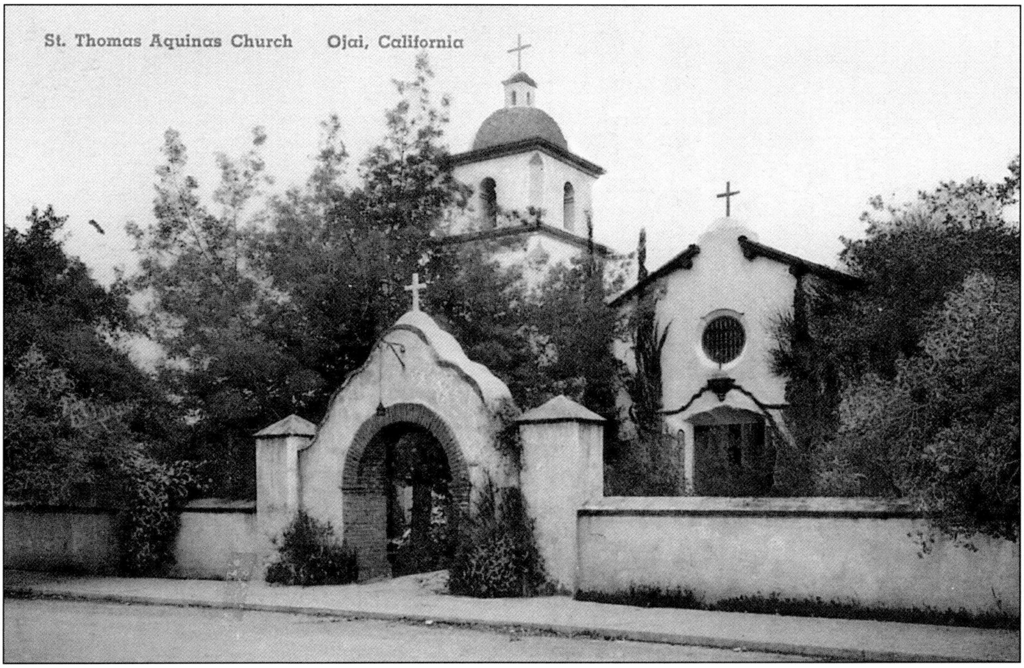

St. Thomas Aquinas Catholic Church. In 1903, Ojai Valley Catholics began worshiping in the assembly hall of the old Nordhoff Grammar School. In 1905, they built a small wood-framed chapel on the northeast corner of Ojai Avenue and Blanche Streets. When the 1917 Ojai fire destroyed this structure, Edward Libbey spearheaded the construction of a new church (above) in the Mission Revival style. The church, designed by Mead and Requa, was dedicated in 1919 as an independent Catholic parish. By 1963, the congregation had outgrown this church, and a larger, contemporary church was built in Meiners Oaks (below). In 1993, the downtown chapel was sold to the City of Ojai; it now houses the Ojai Valley Museum. (Above, OVM Collection; below, George Finn collection.)

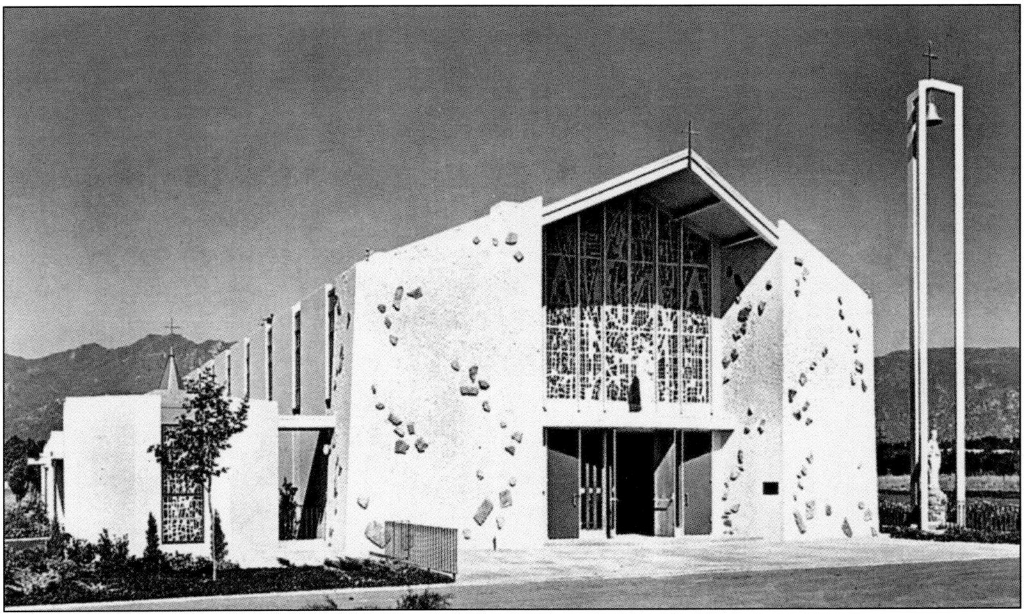

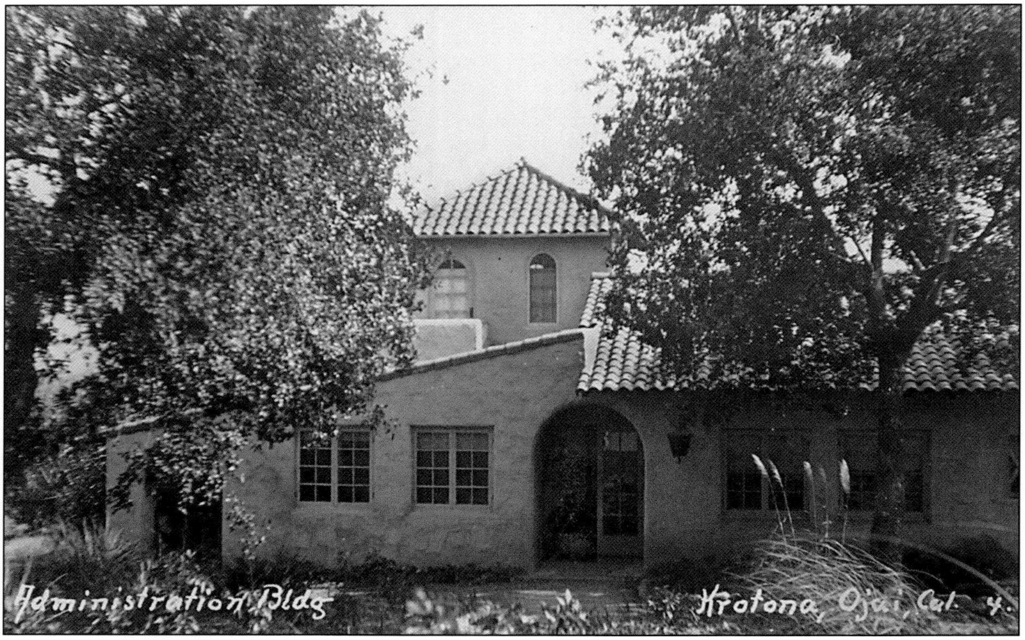

KROTONA INSTITUTE. The Krotona Institute of Theosophy moved from Hollywood to Ojai in 1924. Its founder, Albert P. Warrington, chose Ojai because of its serene beauty and because he believed the valley was "impregnated with occult and psychic influences." Warrington wanted Krotona to reflect Ojai's new Spanish architectural theme, initiated by Edward Libbey in 1916. He first interviewed Wallace Neff to serve as architect but eventually hired Robert Stacy-Judd. Krotona houses the American Division of the Esoteric School of Theosophy, the Krotona School of Theosophy, the Krotona Library, and the Krotona Bookshop. The library, shown below, is open to the general public several days a week. It has an extensive collection of occult and spiritual literature. (Both, George Finn collection.)

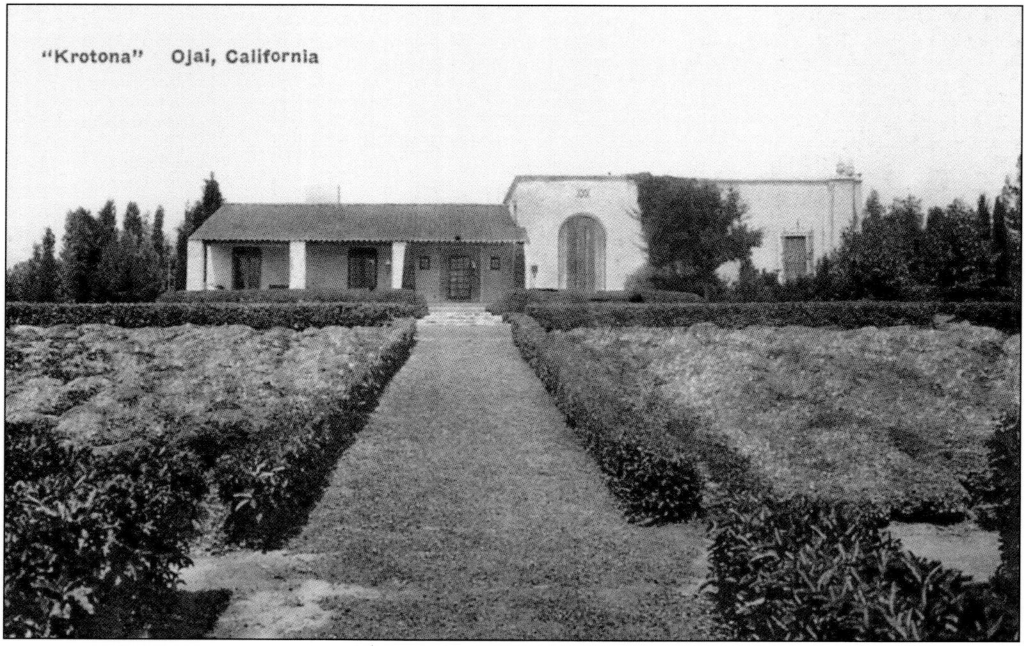

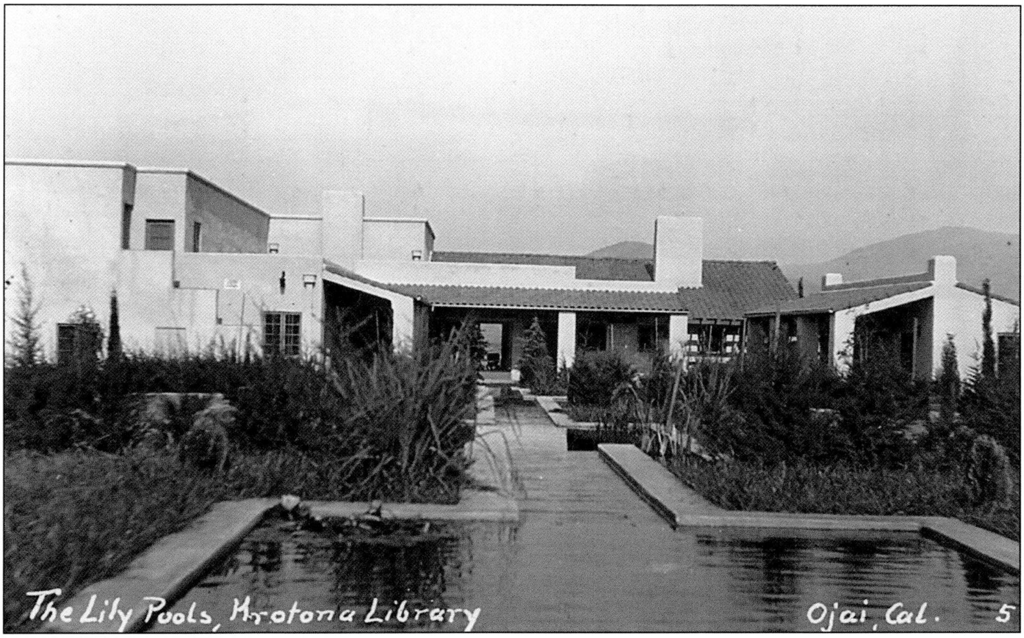

The Gardens of Krotona Institute. Krotona's formal gardens were patterned after the gardens surrounding the Taj Mahal in India. The water feature shown above is a series of reflective pools that connect the upper garden to the back of the library. The formal hedges shown below once straddled this elegant water feature. The postcard above looks east toward the back of the library; the one below looks west toward the mountains. The Krotona gardens welcome those of diverse worldviews to come to ponder the ancient wisdom or merely to enjoy the beauty of the Krotona estate with its Spanish architecture, lily ponds, and its magnificent views of the Ojai Valley. (Above, George Finn collection; below, Joseph Ross collection.)

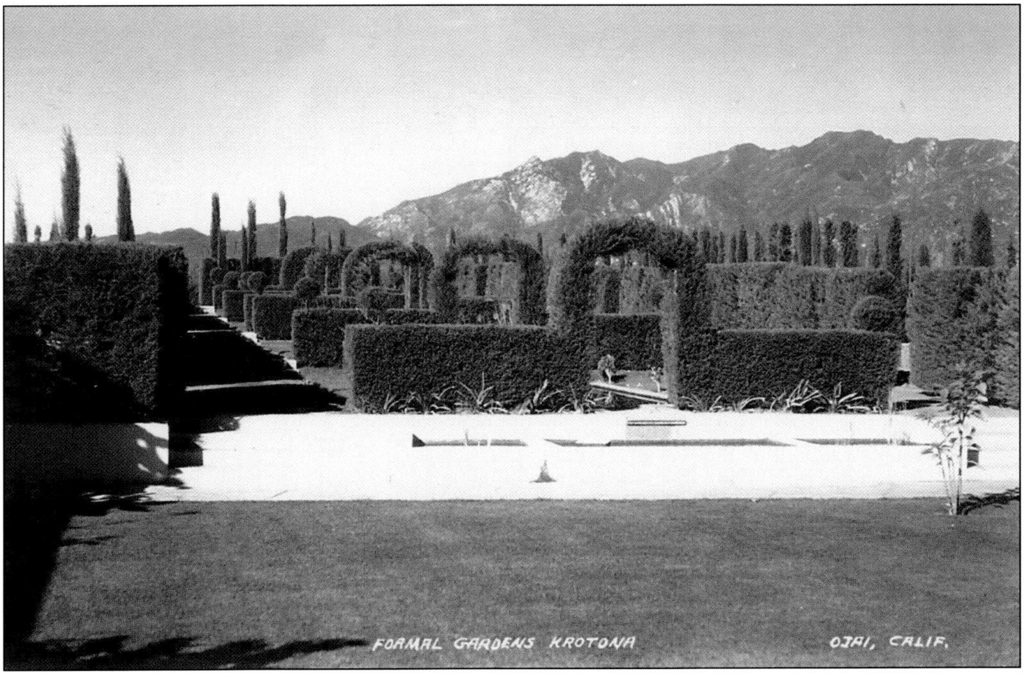

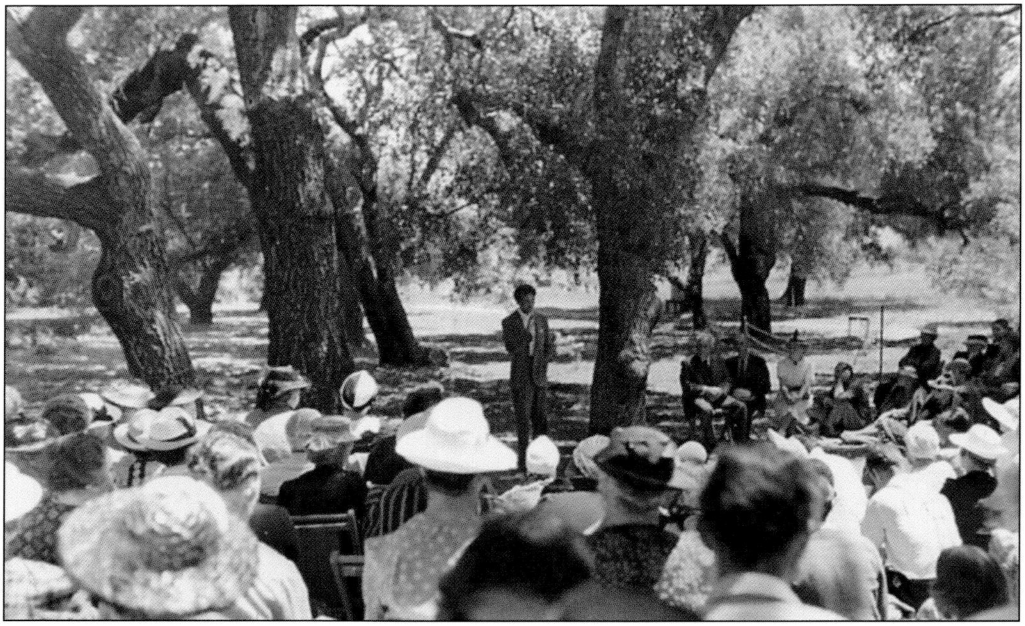

KRISHNAMURTI AT THE OAK GROVE. When Jiddu Krishnamurti first arrived in Ojai during the summer of 1922, he was already the leader of his own worldwide religious organization, the Order of the Star. During his 1922–1923 visit, he spoke at the Hollywood Bowl to an audience of over 16,000 followers. In 1924, he began giving talks in Ojai at the Oak Grove (above), which continued until his death in 1986. Krishnamurti established his Ojai home at Arya Vihara (below), making Ojai one of four worldwide centers for his teachings. He held many discussions and private interviews at Arya Vihara. Among those who visited Krishnamurti here were Annie Besant, Charlie Chaplin, Aldous Huxley, Jonas Salk, John Lennon, Greta Garbo, Igor Stravinsky, D. H. Lawrence, and David Bohm. (Above, Krishnamurti Foundation of America collection; below, David Mason collection.)

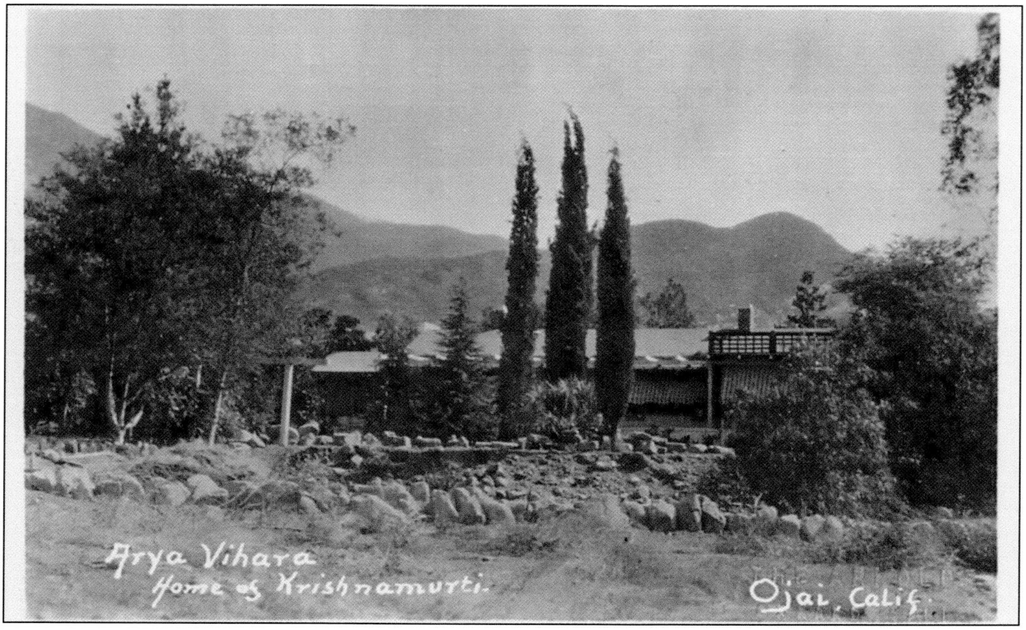

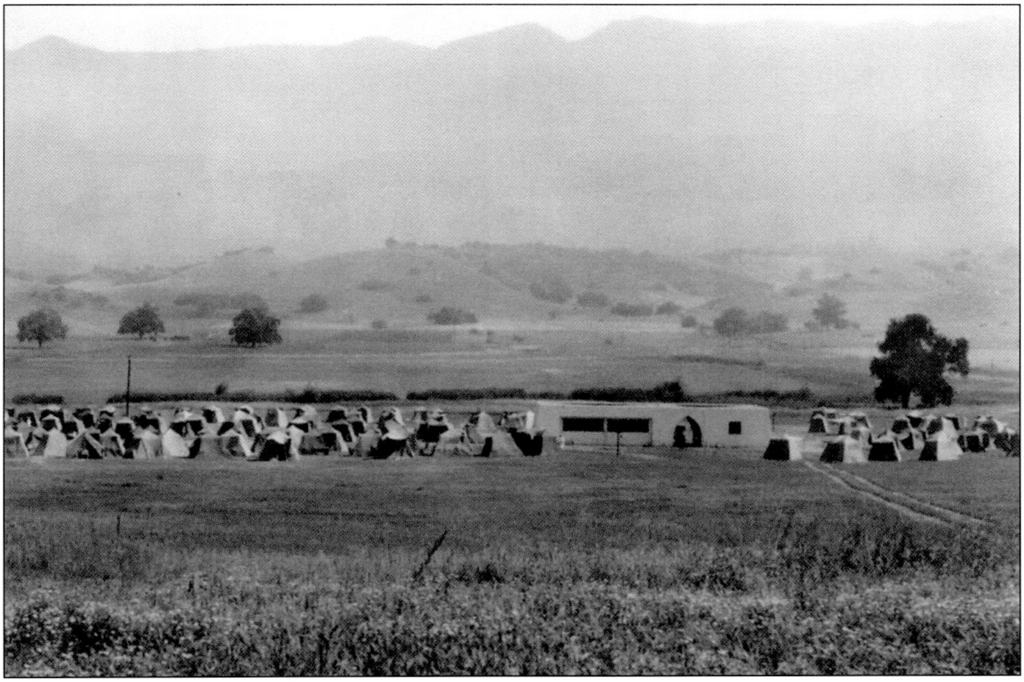

KRISHNAMURTI'S STAR CAMPS. In the late 1920s, while head of the Order of the Star, Krishnamurti organized several Star Camps in Ojai. His followers camped in the field next to the Oak Grove to hear Krishnamurti speak on themes that grew out of his association with Theosophy. In 1929, however, Krishnamurti rejected his role as the "World Teacher" and dissolved the Order of the Star. From that time forward, he spoke on themes that came from his own insights. "Truth is a pathless land," he proclaimed. He believed that anyone who would see the truth must reject all spiritual authority, including that of priests, gurus, churches, and religious organizations. Krishnamurti died at the age of 91 in his home at Arya Vihara. Today Arya Vihara serves as the Krishnamurti Education Center, operated by the Krishnamurti Foundation of America. (Above, Patty Lunetta collection; below, David Mason collection.)

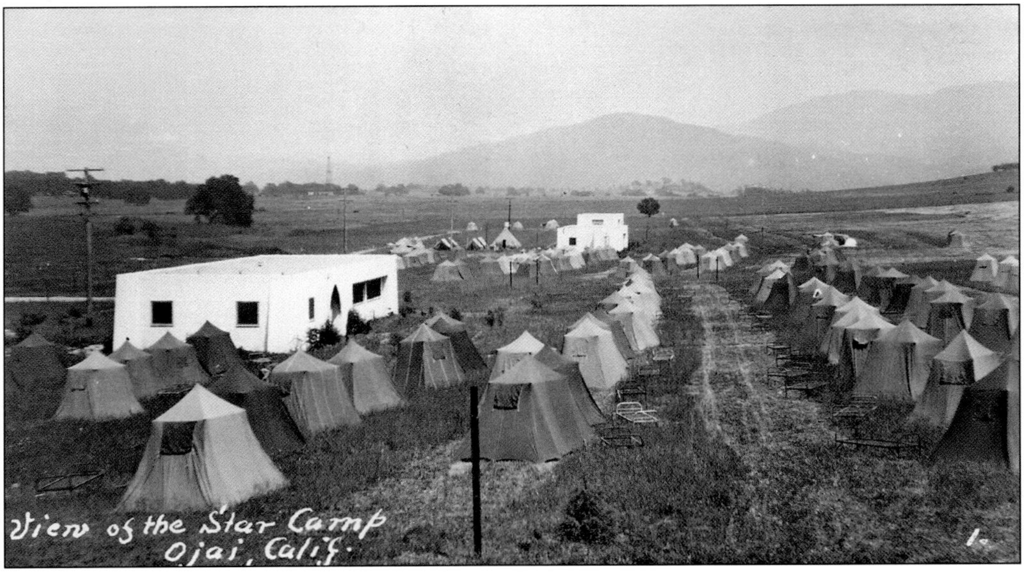

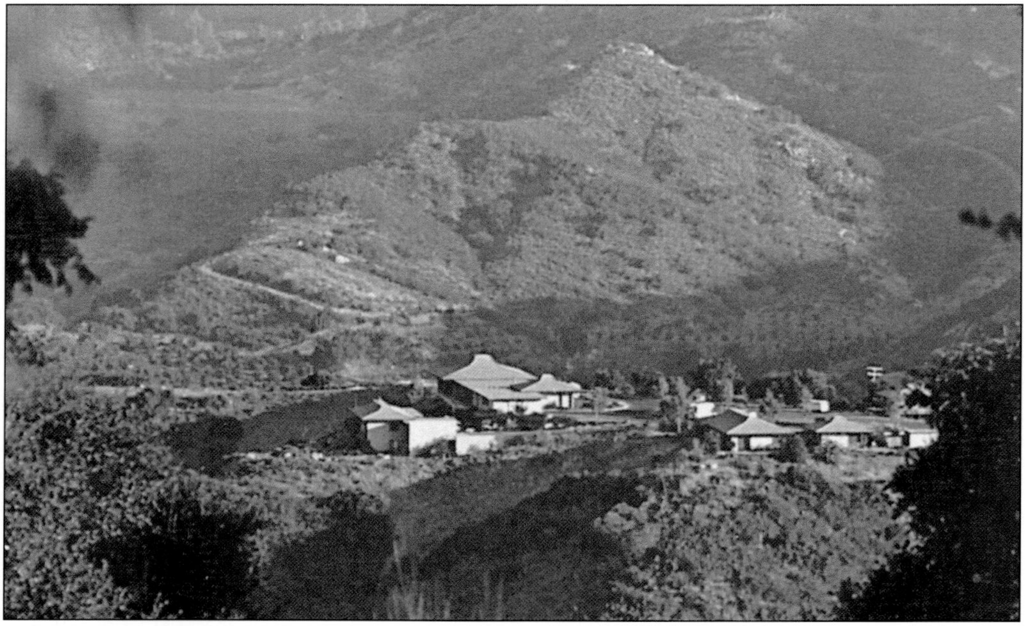

MEDITATION MOUNT. Meditation Mount is the home of Meditation Groups, Inc. Located on a high knoll at the east end of the Ojai Valley, Meditation Mount affords spectacular views of the valley. The facility was completed in 1971 under the direction of Ojai architect Zelma Wilson. Meditation Mount holds regular full-moon meditations and educational programs that are open to the public. (OVM Collection.)

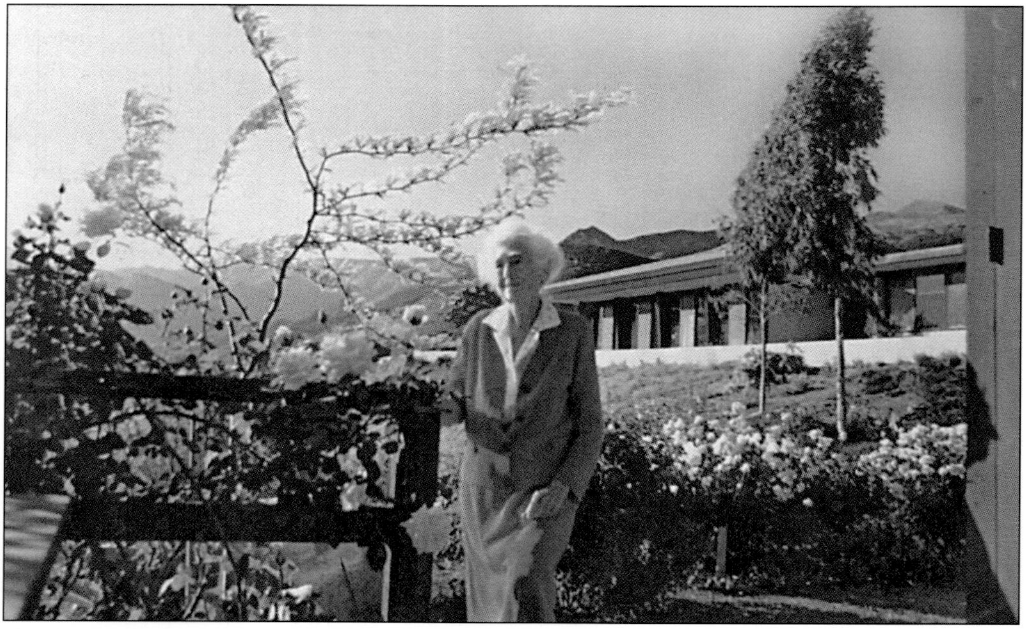

FLORENCE GARRIGUE AT MEDITATION MOUNT. Florence Garrigue came to Ojai in 1968 from New York to establish Meditation Mount. She was part of the Group for Creative Meditation, an international organization founded by Italian psychologist Robert Assagioli, who believed that "the power of focused meditation is an essential element in birthing a world that works for all." (OVM Collection.)

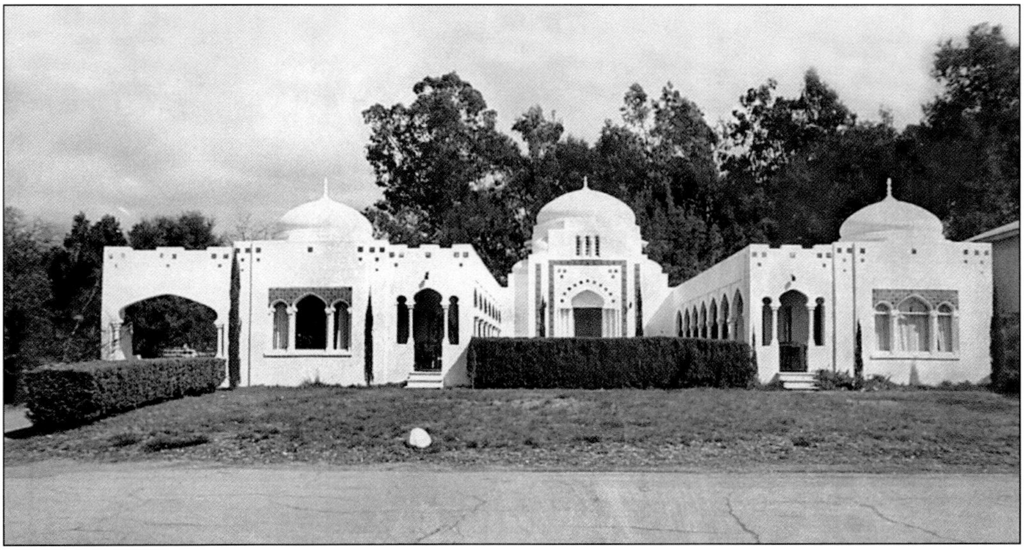

THE PLEIADES. Known locally as the "Taj Mahal," the Pleiades was created in 1930 by Edward Martin, a priest at Ojai's Liberal Catholic Church. Martin dedicated it to Krishnamurti, who he hoped would form a bond with him over the building. Krishnamurti never responded, although he is purported to have once driven by to view it under a full moon. John Roine designed the building, and Martin's wife named it the Pleiades. (David Mason collection.)

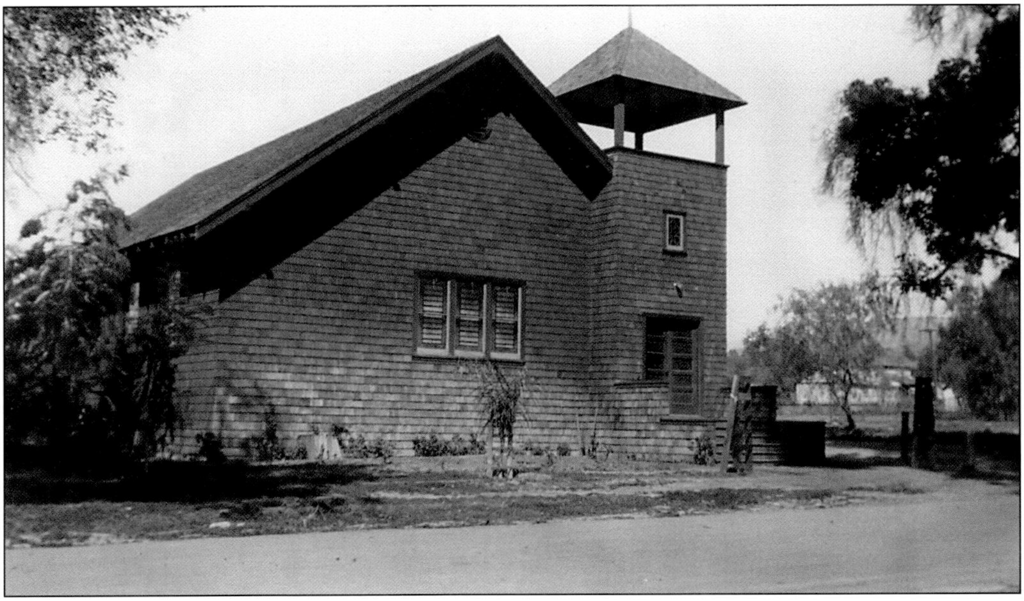

FIRST BAPTIST CHURCH. The First Baptist Church was established in 1909 at the southwest corner of Matilija and Ventura Streets. The original building, purchased from the Christian church, was destroyed by the great fire of 1917. The new church, shown above, was completed in 1918. When the congregation moved to Grand Avenue in 1964, the sanctuary (above) was removed. (David Mason collection.)

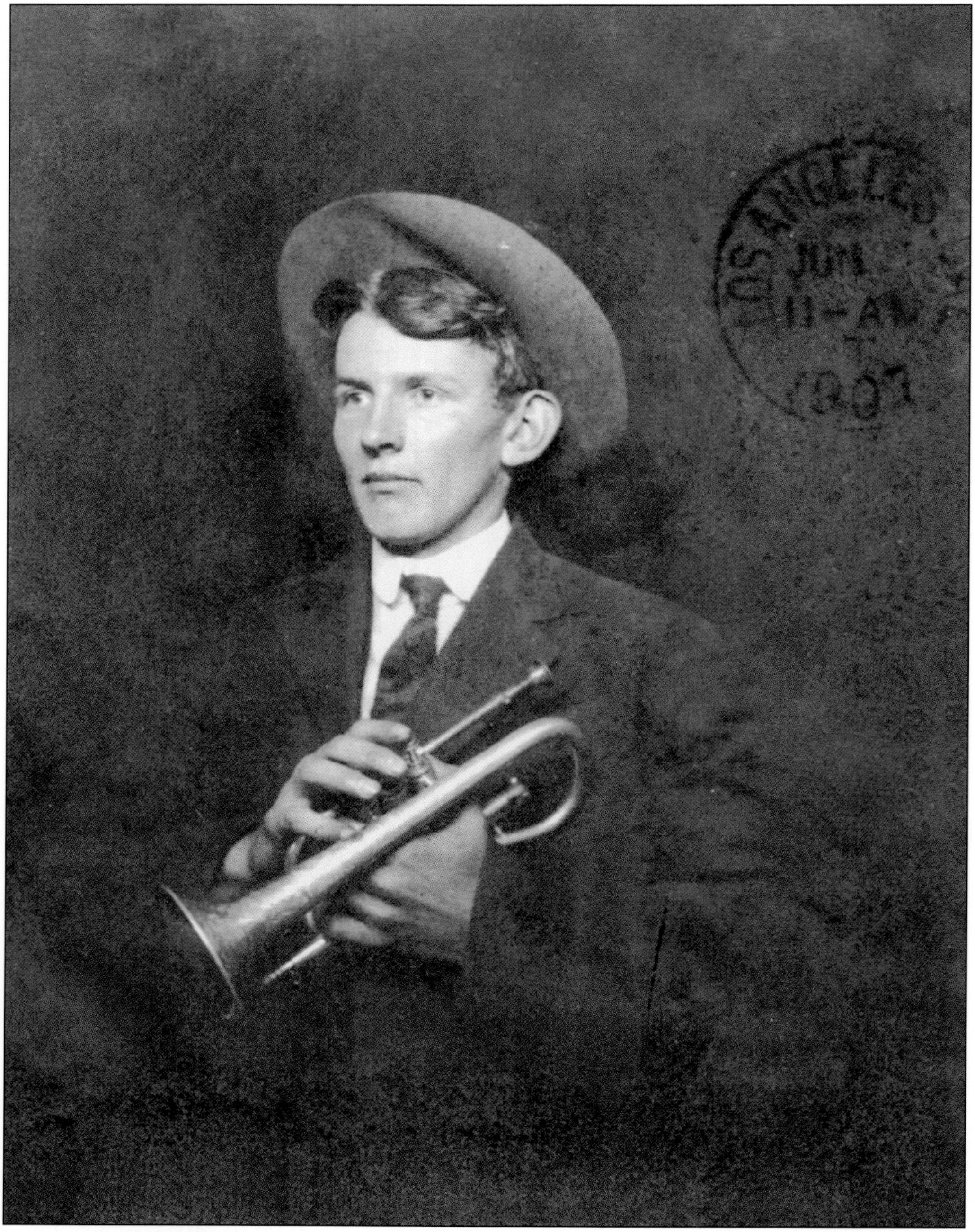

OJAI MUSICIAN ROY SMITH. Ojai has always had its own talented musicians to entertain the community. The Ojai Band was first organized in 1894 by the Ojai Club. Since then, it has reappeared in different forms, including a modern Ojai Band organized in 1991 by Sarah Beeby. The Ojai Music Festival, founded by Ojai resident John Bauer in 1947, has brought world-class music to Ojai for over 60 years. (OVM Collection.)

Nine

Cultural Life in Ojai

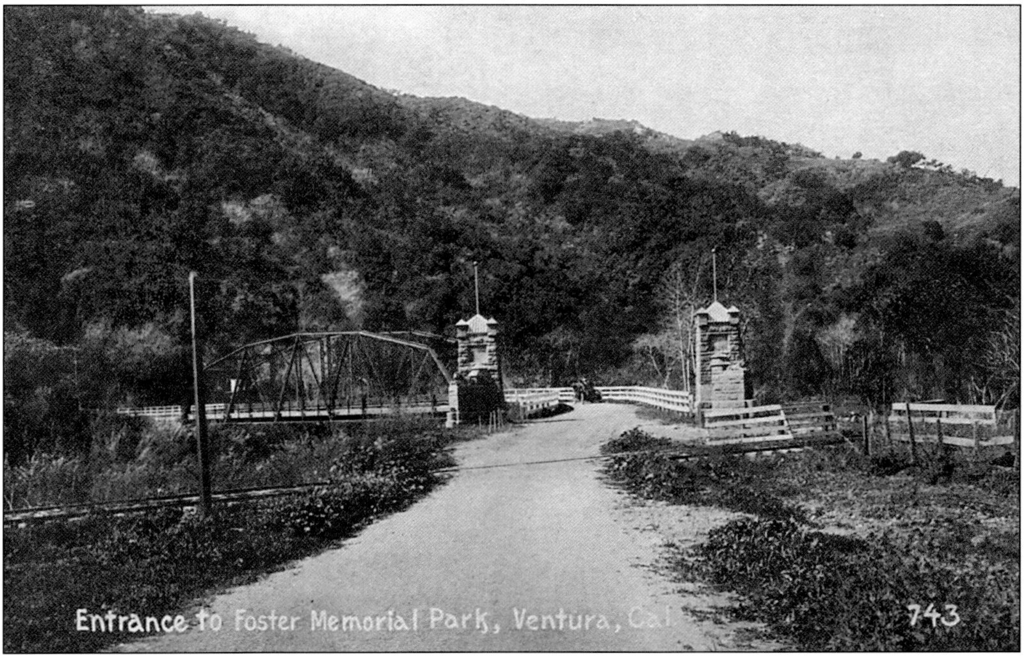

Entrance to Foster Park. The climate of the Ojai Valley has encouraged residents and visitors alike to gather outdoors, and Ojai has many parks and recreation areas to accommodate them. Shown above are the gates to Foster Park, located at the southwest entrance to the valley. Other popular Ojai Valley parks are Dennison Park, Soule Park, Camp Comfort, Sarzotti Park, Libbey Park, Oak View Park, and the Ojai Valley Bicycle Trail. (Brian and Connie Aikens collection.)

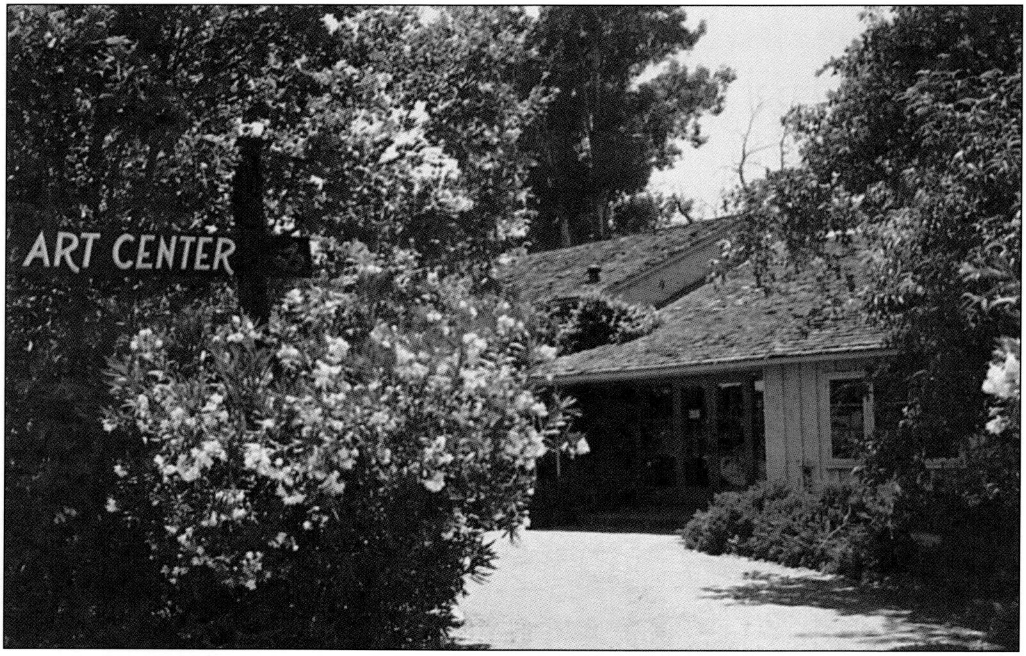

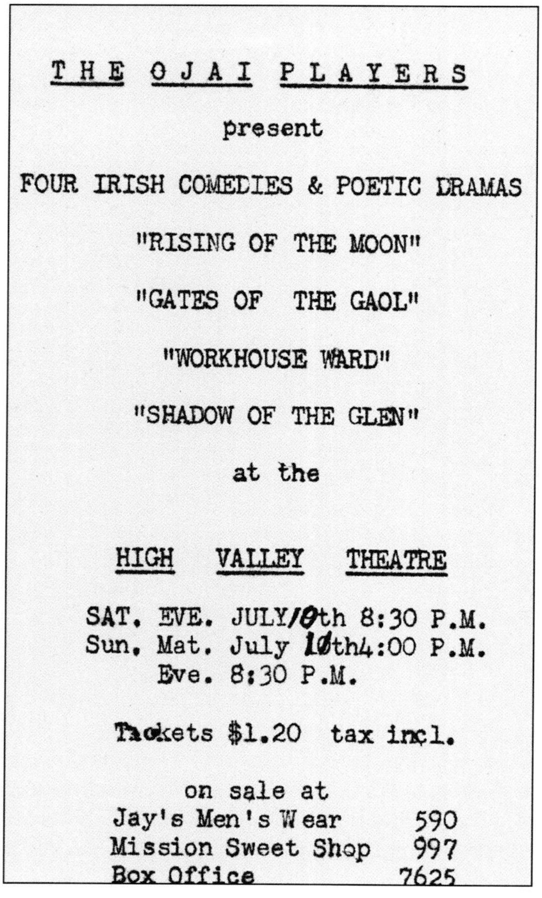
THE OJAI PLAYERS

present

FOUR IRISH COMEDIES & POETIC DRAMAS

"RISING OF THE MOON"

"GATES OF THE GAOL"

"WORKHOUSE WARD"

"SHADOW OF THE GLEN"

at the

HIGH VALLEY THEATRE

SAT. EVE. JULY/0th 8:30 P.M.
Sun. Mat. July 10th4:00 P.M.
Eve. 8:30 P.M.

Tickets $1.20 tax incl.

on sale at

Jay's Men's Wear	590
Mission Sweet Shop	997
Box Office	7625

THE OJAI CENTER FOR THE ARTS. In 1936, Dr. Charles Butler envisioned a community center where artists of all varieties—painters, poets, actors, dancers, singers—could practice their craft. He spearheaded the campaign to raise the funds and served as its first director. Local architect Austen Pierpont designed the building. The Ojai Center for the Arts opened in 1939, and it has been an important community center ever since. (George Finn collection.)

THE OJAI PLAYERS. Sometimes known as the Chekhov Players, the Ojai Players were Ventura County's first professional acting troupe. Among them were director Alan Harkness and actors Iris Tree, Daphne Moore, Ford Rainey, and Sidney Chaplin. When the art center decided to host only amateur theater productions, the group formed the High Valley Theater in Upper Ojai. They also trained actors in the acting techniques of Michael Chekhov. (OVM Collection.)

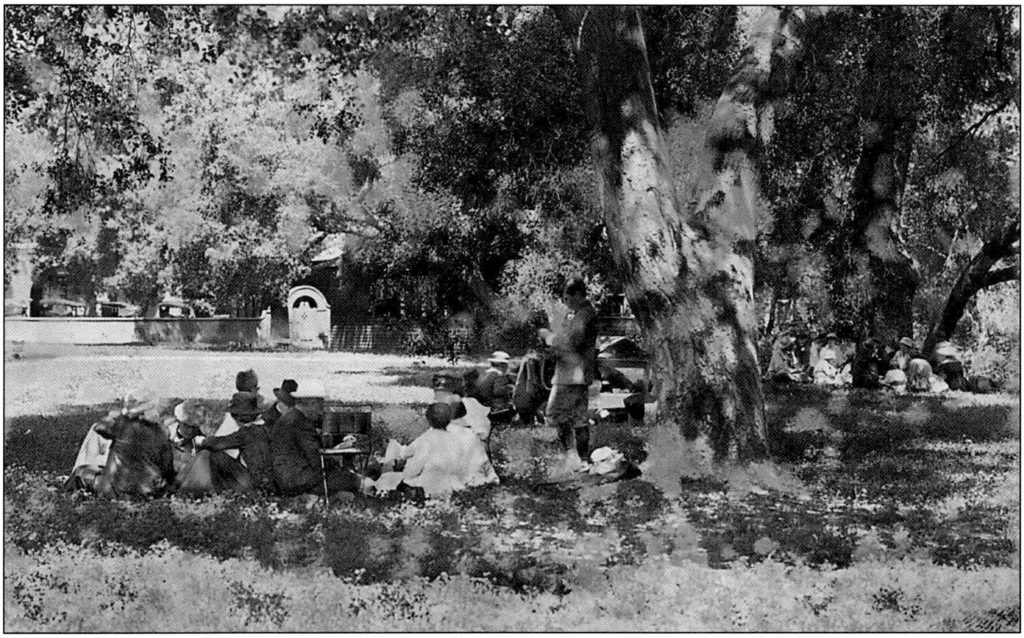

The First Ojai Day, 1917. One of Ojai's earliest community events was Ojai Day, which celebrated Edward Libbey's transformation of the downtown. The event featured a community picnic with music and speeches. It was celebrated each year until 1928. In 1991, Ojai Day was revived by Craig Walker to celebrate the renovation of the arcade. It continues as one of Ojai's most popular annual events. (David Mason collection.)

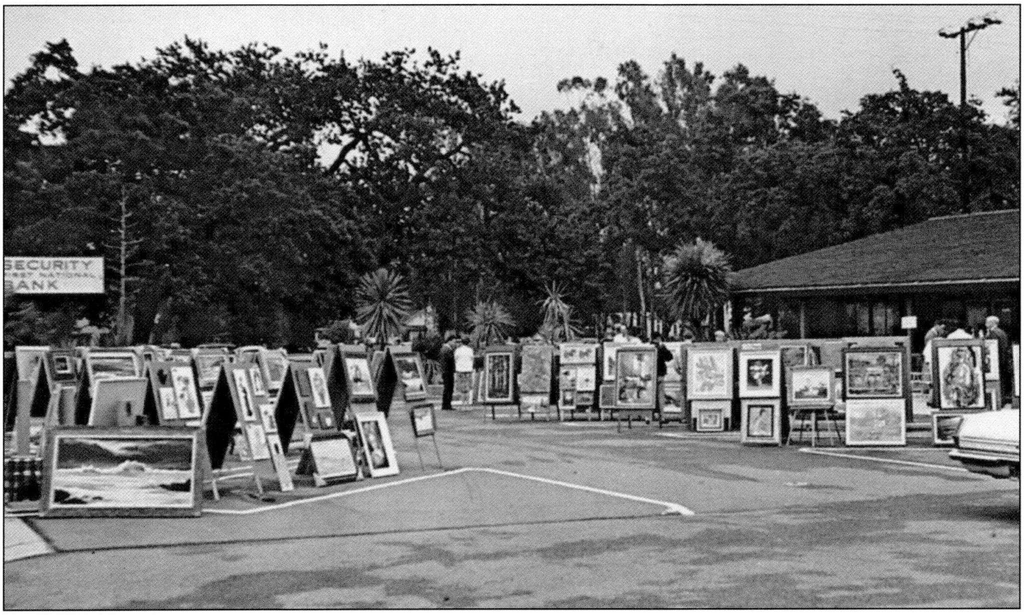

Art Sunday Parking Lot Display. In the early 1970s, a group of local artists called the Ojai Artists began displaying and selling their paintings every Sunday in the parking lot of the Security First National Bank (now the Bank of America). On any given Sunday, 12 to 15 artists would display their work. Among them were such established local artists as Doris Gilbert, Lois Powers, Harry Lauter, and David Borgen. (Brian and Connie Aikens collection.)

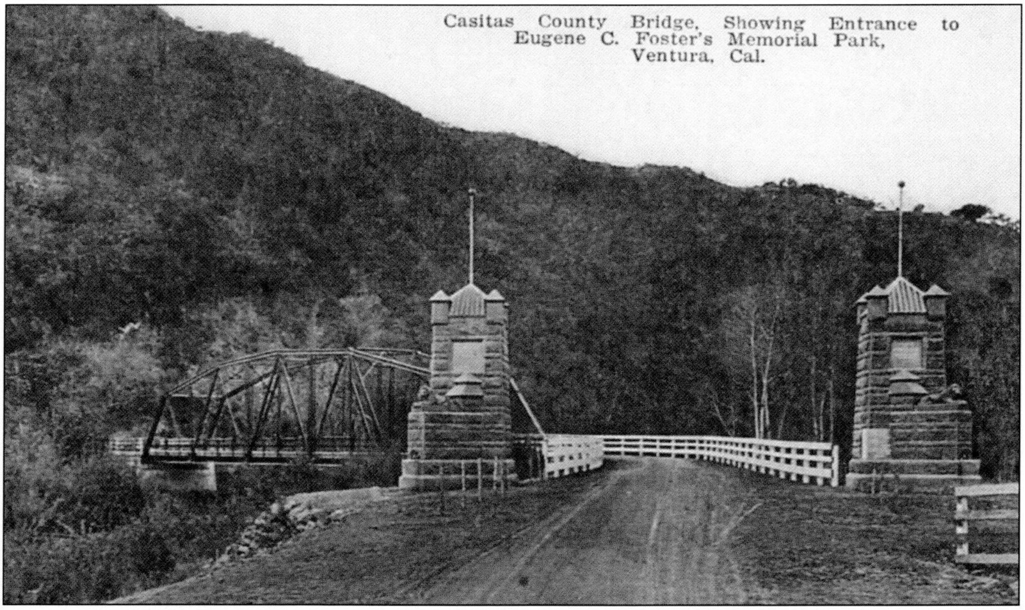

ENTRANCE TO FOSTER MEMORIAL PARK. Ventura County historian Edwin M. Sheridan wrote of Eugene Preston Foster: "His hobby was thinking in terms of benefits for posterity." Foster, a Ventura County pioneer and philanthropist, initiated the idea of a Ventura County Parks system in 1904. Three of the parks he personally created are located in the Ojai Valley —Foster Park, Camp Comfort, and Dennison Park. The 205-acre Foster Park was established in 1908 on land donated by the Fosters in memory of their son. An amphitheater, designed by Roy Wilson, was dedicated in 1928. Although the amphitheater has fallen into disrepair, the park has seen new life as a resting spot on the new Ojai-Ventura Trail. E. P. Foster was also responsible for the Ventura County Fairgrounds, the E. P. Foster Library, Community Memorial Hospital, and the Rincon Road. (Above, OVM Collection; below, John Fritsche collection.)

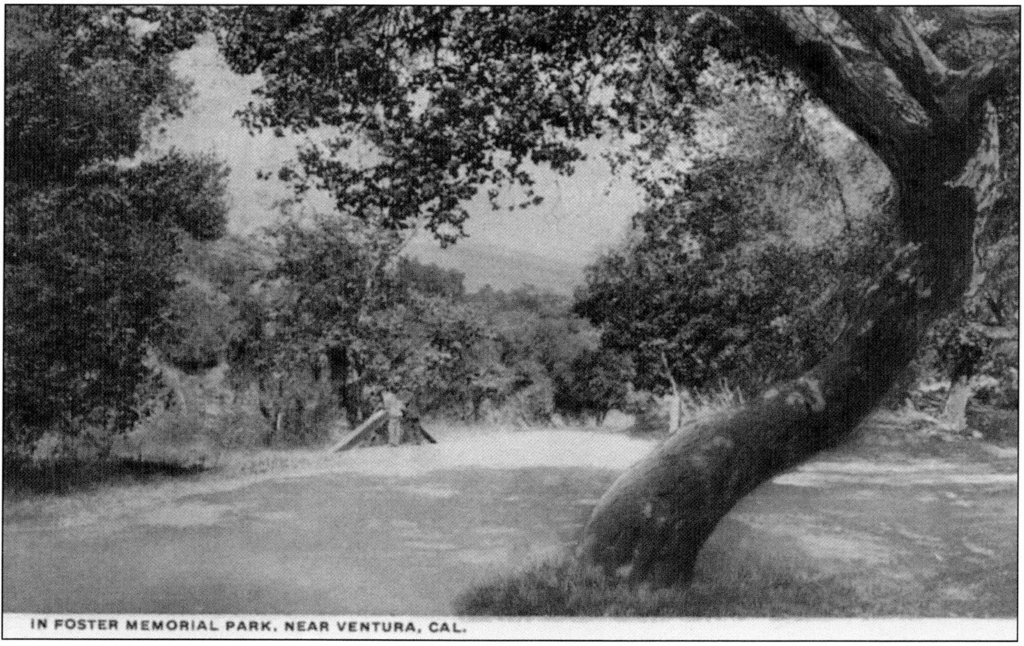

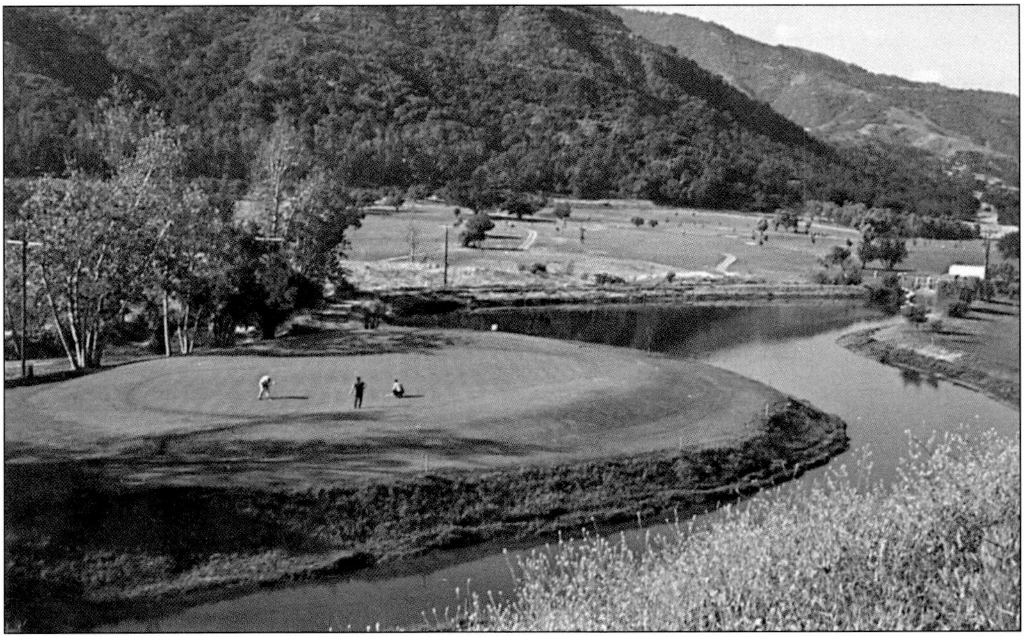

Soule Park Golf Course. The Soule family settled on this property in 1873, farming wheat, alfalfa, and barley. In 1957, daughter Zaidee Soule, who served as Ojai's librarian for 30 years, donated the ranch to the County of Ventura. In 1961, the county opened a beautiful 223-acre park on the land, with an 18-hole golf course, tennis courts, softball diamond, equestrian arenas, and horseshoe pits. (George Finn collection.)

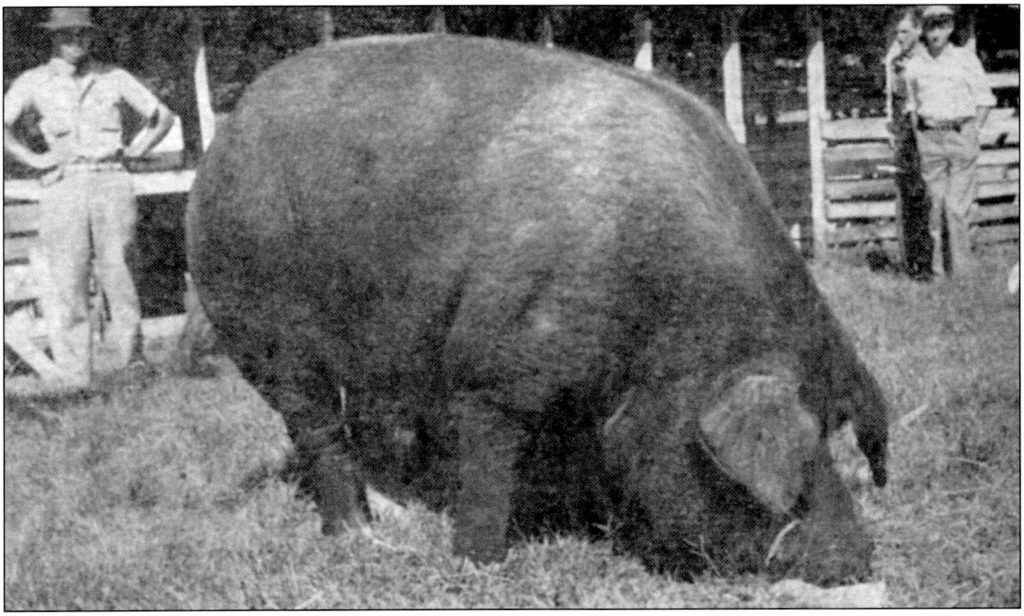

World's Largest Hog. Numerous traveling shows have passed through Ojai over the years, including revival meetings, carnivals, healers, and this "World's Largest Hog" attraction in 1946. In addition to the oversized Duroc, the card also advertises "a troupe of African monkeys headed by the one and only Grandma Wrinklenose. The pranks and antics of the cute little simians always delight the children." (George Finn collection.)

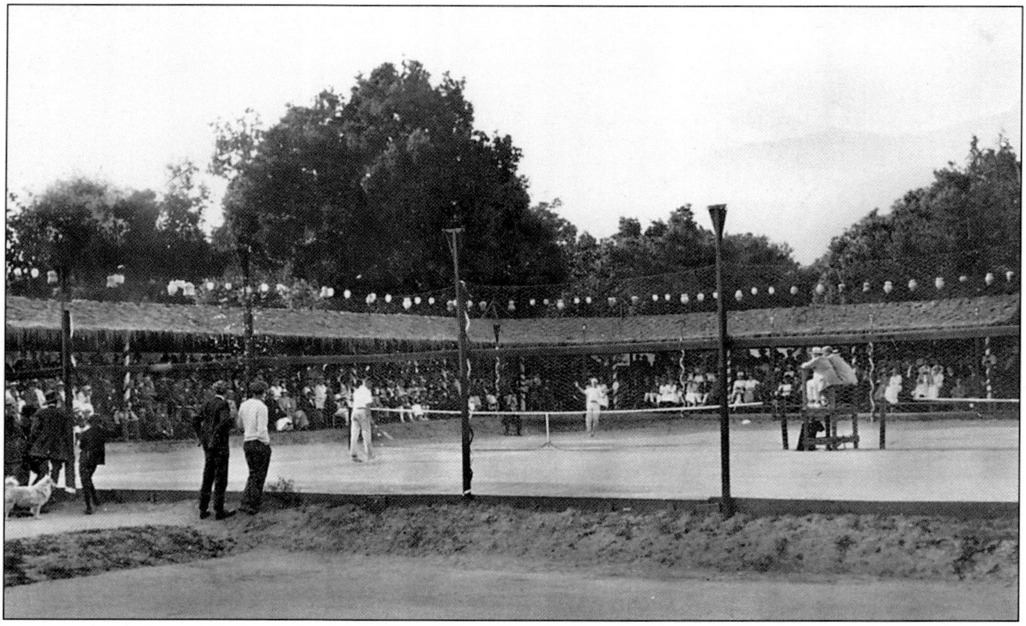

The Ojai Tennis Tournament. The Ojai is one of the oldest amateur tennis tournaments in the United States. William Larned Thacher, a former U.S. Intercollegiate Doubles Champion, started the tournament in 1896. That first year, the Ojai champs played the Ventura champs—and Ojai won. The main foundation of the tournament was laid in 1899, when the Boy's Interscholastic Championships, both singles and doubles, were added to the men's singles. Women's events were added in 1900. With the exception of five years when the Ojai tournament was cancelled due to war or disease, it has been held every year since 1896. Many young participants at the Ojai have gone on to dominate the game as professionals, including Arthur Ashe, Jimmy Connors, Pete Sampras, Billie Jean King, Tracy Austin, and Lindsey Davenport. (Above, Carol Cohen collection; below, OVM Collection.)

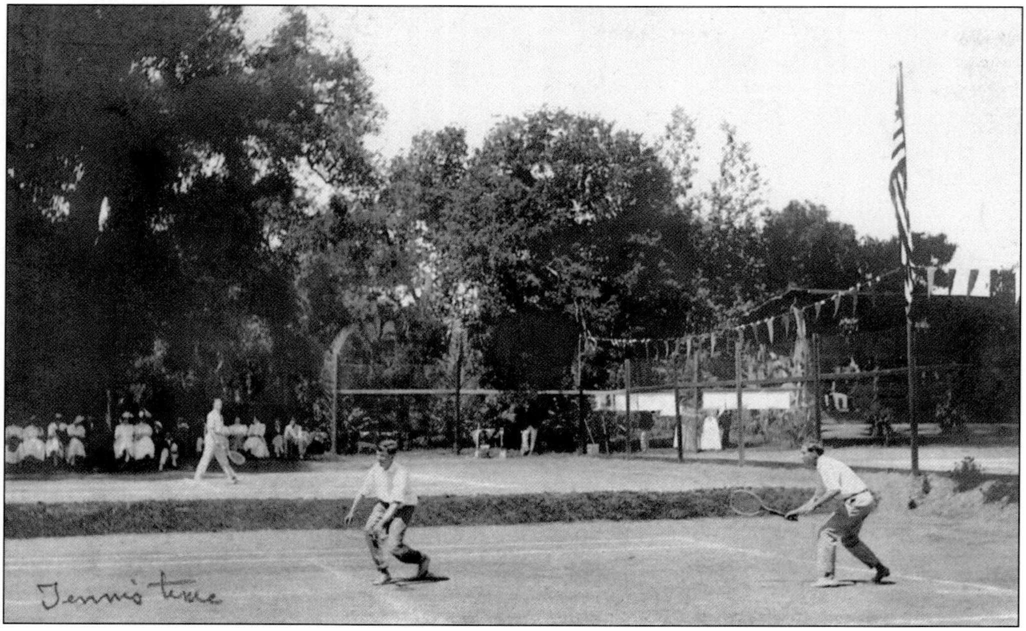

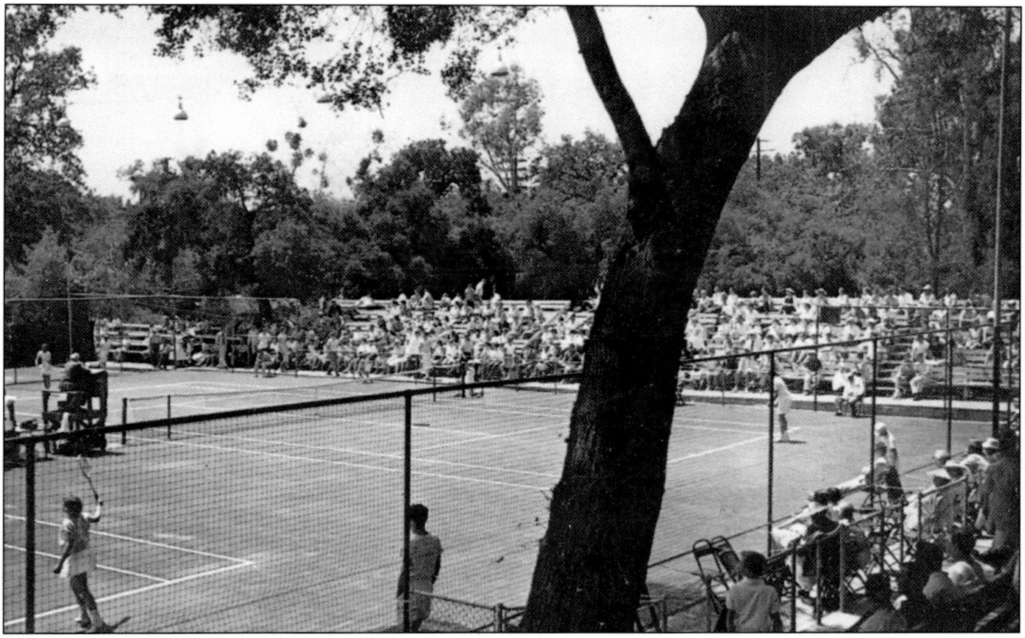

An Ojai Tradition. Since its beginning in 1896, the Ojai has brought the entire community together in a spirit of fun and tradition. In 1904, the tradition began of serving afternoon tea for players and spectators. It is still an honor today to serve as tea pourer at the Ojai. Ojai residents not only fill the stands (above), but tennis has become a popular Ojai sport, with over 64 tennis courts in the valley. The Weil Tennis Academy, which has trained many successful college and professional players, opened in Ojai in 1997. In 2009, Ojai was named runner-up in the USTA's first "Best Tennis Town in the United States" competition. The event is coordinated and run by volunteers (below), residents open their homes to accommodate the players, and an annual tennis dance welcomes both players and Ojai's young people. (Both, OVM Collection.)

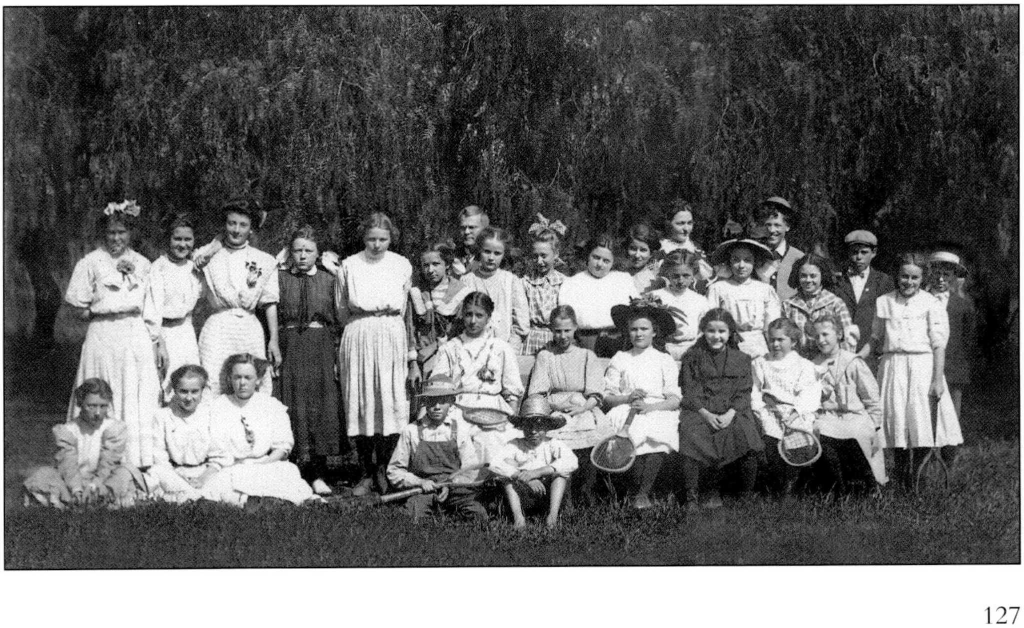